In View of the Great Want of Labor

A Legislative History of African American Conscription in the Confederacy

Compiled by
E. Renée Ingam

Willow Bend Books
Westminster, Maryland
2002

Willow Bend Books

65 East Main Street
Westminster, Maryland 21157-5026
1-800-876-6103

WB7378

Source books, early maps, CDs -- Worldwide

For our listing of thousands of titles offered by hundreds of publishers, see our website at:
www.WillowBendBooks.com

Visit our retail store

Author's other publications, acknowledgements and contributions:

Stanton Family Cemetery
Virginia Landmarks of Black History: Sites on the Virginia Landmarks Register and the National Register of Historic Places, ed. Calder Loth, Charlottesville: University of Virginia Press, 1995.

Ingram, E. Renée. Preserving Our African American Cemeteries: The Stanton Family Heritage
Heritage: A Song of Soul, A Sanction of Self, ed. Lemuel Berry, Jr. Ph.D.
Paper of research completed and presented in a public forum at the Second Annual Conference of the National Association of African-American Studies, Petersburg, Virginia. February 15-19, 1994. Ann Arbor, Michigan: UMI Press, part 1, 1994.

Stanton Family Cemetery, *National Register of Historic Places: African American Historic Places*, ed. Beth L. Savage, Washington, D.C.: U.S. Department of the Interior, National Park Service, 1994.

American Society of Landscape Architects (ASLA) Awards, Research: Special Mentions, The Stanton Family Cemetery National Register Nomination, *Landscape Architecture*, November 1994.

Ingram, E. Renée. "Stanton Family Cemetery," *African-American Archaeology Newsletter of the African-American Archaeology Network*, 12, Winter 1994.

©1999 E. Renée Ingram
Reprinted 2001 by Willow Bend Books

International Standard Book Number: 1-58549-018-0

Printed in the United States of America

In memory
of
my loving father, James Gilmore Ingram
and
my friend and mentor, James Dent Walker

To my family in appreciation for their support
in my historic preservation endeavors.

Table of Contents

Acknowledgements

I would like to personally thank the following individuals for their assistance and support with the content and format on this important subject matter: *Ervin L. Jordan, Jr.,* Associate Curator of Technical Services, Special Collections Department, University of Virginia Library; *Michael P. Musick,* Archivist, Military Reference Branch, National Archives and Record Administration; and, *Ambassador Ronald D. Palmer,* Professor, Elliott School of International Affairs, George Washington University, Washington, D.C.

In addition, the following individuals have provided valuable information and sources in conducting this research: *Barbara Batson,* Library of Virginia, Richmond, Virginia; *Arthur Bergeron, Jr.,* Historian, Pamplin Park Civil War Site, Petersburg, Virginia; *Charles Brewer,* Genealogist and Historian, Washington, D.C.; *Norman Chase,* Reference Technician, Newspaper and Current Periodical Division, Library of Congress; *John Coski,* The Museum of the Confederacy, Richmond, Virginia; *Lucious Edwards, Jr.,* University Archivist, Virginia State University; *Elizabeth Gushee,* Library of Virginia, Richmond, Virginia; *Gregg Kimball,* Library of Virginia, Richmond, Virginia; *Peter Lysy,* Archivist, University of Notre Dame, Indiana; *L. Eileen Parris,* Associate Archivist, Division of Manuscripts and Archives, Virginia Historical Society, Richmond, Virginia; *Kym S. Rice,* Interim Director, Museum Studies Program, The George Washington University, Washington, D.C.; *Teresa Roane,* Supervisor of Reference Services, Valentine Museum, Richmond; *E. Lee Shepard,* Assistant Director and Senior Archivist, Division of Manuscripts and Archives, Virginia Historical Society, Richmond, Virginia; *Janet Sims-Wood,* Assistant Chief Librarian, Reference and Reader Services Department, Moorland-Spingarn Research Center, Howard University, Washington, D.C.; and, *Charles W. White,* Author and Historian, Buckingham, Virginia.

Preface

Prior to the Civil War, the total slave population in the United States was approximately 3.9 million. Virginia had a total slave population of more than 491,000 or 13 percent of the total slaves in the Confederacy. The total free African American population in the United States was slightly more than 488,000; of whom 251,000; resided in the South. Such persons in Virginia totaled 58,000; or 23 percent of all free African Americans in the South.[1]

Throughout the war, the Confederacy attempted almost continuously to cope with the problems of how to use and manage this massive manpower. Neither the Confederate nor the United States governments seriously contemplated the use of African Americans, free or slave, for combat service until 1863. Before that time, the North had authorized African American employment in various auxiliary services as teamsters and other military laborers and servants. In the South, the use of African American manpower was always conditioned on the need to keep African Americans in a subordinate or servile position in the society consistent with the property status of slaves and the ambiguous but clearly subordinate status of "free" African Americans.

The Virginia experience illustrates this dilemma. Initially, Virginia sought to use free African Americans as civilian war workers to release whites for combat duty. This strategy was continued throughout the war. Eventually African Americans, both free and slave, were subject to impressment and conscription but always as noncombatants. They played important roles as noncombatants and were used in essential sectors where their labor was critical, particularly in the iron works industry, railroads and agriculture.

From February 1862 until February 1864, five impressment laws constituted the most significant acts dealing with the mobilization of Virginia's African American population for noncombatant purposes. The General Assembly of the State passed three of the five laws, while the Confederate Congress enacted the other two. The first state law subjected the free African American to the draft as a laborer, the second law placed a ceiling on the number of slaves that could be impressed, and the third law exempted the slaves from counties where impressment would materially effect agricultural production. The two wartime regulations passed by the Confederate Congress not only made provision for tapping Virginia's African American reservoir but also were designed to minimize conflicts between Confederate and state authorities over the impressment of slaves and to correct glaring defects of state impressment laws.[2]

After authorizing the impressment of free African Americans for military service, Virginia lawmakers next considered the slave. In 1862 and 1863, the state's legislature enacted these two laws to put a portion of its large African American labor market in readiness for effective war service. By the late summer of 1862, it was apparent that ample slave labor could not be obtained with specific legislative action, thus on October 3, 1862, the legislature passed an act providing for the public defense of the state. The act required that a census be taken of all male slaves

---

[1] James H. Brewer, *The Confederate Negro: Virginia's Craftsmen and Military Laborers, 1861-1865* (Durham, N.C., 1969), 3.

[2] Brewer, *The Confederate Negro*, 6-7.

between the ages of eighteen and forty-five. Upon requisition from the President of the Confederate States, the Governor of Virginia would impress slaves to work on entrenchments and to do other labor necessary for the defense of the state.[3]

In March of 1863, the General Assembly passed a third act that exempted agricultural counties where slave impressment would materially effect production. The act of 1863 also extended to fifty-five, the age limit for the impressment of slaves. Any owner who refused to send a slave was subject to a maximum fine of $10 for each day of noncompliance. Failure on the part of the sheriff to deliver a drafted bondsman carried a fine from $50 to $200.

As the Civil War entered its twenty-third month, the Confederate Congress was forced to take more drastic steps to procure African American labor. On March 26, 1863, it passed its first significant act to tap the Confederacy's African American military labor force. President Jefferson Davis replaced the state governor as the chief enforcing agent in procuring African American labor. The act of March of 1863, designed to correct the defects of state impressment laws, specifically legalized slave impressment by Confederate authorities "according to the rules and regulations provided in the laws of the state wherein they are impressed."[4]

Throughout 1863 demands to impress or conscript free African Americans as military laborers intensified. On November 11, 1863, Major Samuel W. M. Melton, the Assistant Adjutant General, suggested to War Department Secretary Seddon that conscription might be extended to free African Americans. Major Melton insisted that their services were "as clearly due as those of any other class in the Confederacy."[5]

Consequently, the 1863 law was supplemented by amendatory act of February 17, 1864, which authorized a levy of 20,000 slaves throughout the Confederate States between the ages of eighteen and fifty, when conditions should require. Slaves were to be impressed, however, only if the supply of free African Americans failed to meet the needs of the War Department. This act was also designed to make all free African American males between the ages of eighteen and fifty liable "to service in war manufactories, in erecting defensive works, and in military hospitals." The act moreover, required that free African American males be taken in preference to the 20,000 slaves ineligible to be impressed, and that such free African Americans should receive the same pay and subsistence as soldiers. The 1864 conscription act allowed the creation of the Bureau of Conscription to administer the drafting persons. A bureaucracy of officers, medical examiners, and other agents was authorized to handle the task of enrolling or exempting white males between the ages of seventeen and fifty. The Bureau was also entrusted with the task of procuring African Americans, free and slave. In the spring of 1864, War Secretary Seddon, instructed Brigadier General John S. Preston, Chief of the Bureau of Conscription, to bring into service the free African Americans authorized by the act of Congress.

---

[3] Tinsley Lee Spraggins, *"Mobilization of Negro Labor for the Department of Virginia and North Carolina, 1861-1865"* North Carolina Historical Review, XXIV, No. 2 (April 1947): 173.

[4] *Journal of the Congress of the Confederate States of America, 1861-1865*

[5] U.S. War Department. *The War of the Rebellion: A Compilation of the Official Records of the Union and Confederate Armies.* Ser.1-4, 128 vols. Washington, D.C.: GPO, 1880-1901, Ser. 4, 2:947.

Among the approximately 28,000 free African American males in Virginia, there were approximately 5,000 who were between the ages of eighteen and forty-five, and thus liable for military service. However, more than 50 percent were already usefully employed in transportation, mining, and industrial pursuits as well as in government shops, depots, and yards. In addition, free African Americans were working in arsenals, armories, salt works, niter works, and military hospitals. In part, this explains the reason why the Assistant Adjutant General was informed by the Bureau of Conscription that the orders for the enrollment and assignment of free African Americans had been carried out as effectively as possible under the circumstances. Many officers from the Quartermaster Department and the Engineer Bureau received assistance, however, were demanding more support. All of these demands were of the utmost importance and the numbers required by these officers exceeded the number of free African Americans within the prescribed age range for military service. Moreover, there were a number of free African Americans who either deserted or successfully managed to evade the enrolling officers.

The entire story of the conscription of free African Americans and their war experiences can never be told in its entirety because of the lack of documentation. However, this reference book which contains the names of more than 1,800 conscripted free African Americans from Virginia, is a companion piece to the scholarly works previously written. The original document referenced, *Chapter 1, Volume 241, Bureau of Conscription, VA, The Register of Free Negroes Enrolled and Detailed. May 1864-January 1865,* is located at the National Archives and Records Administration in Washington, D.C. A microfilm copy was offered to the National Archives and Records Administration. Microfilm copies have been donated to Moorland-Spingarn Research Center at Howard University, The Library of Virginia, The Virginia Historical Society and Virginia State University. The advertisements, excerpts from the Journal of the Confederate States of America, and rare letters and photographs that are included in this book provide the reader insight on the significance and the extensive involvement of Virginia's African Americans. This book is intended to intrigue the reader to pursue and delve into this subject further.

Foreword

Historians have studied the use of black slaves as military, industrial and agricultural laborers by the Confederate South but have largely ignored free blacks. Two pioneering scholars, Luther Porter Jackson (*Free Negro Labor and Property Holding in Virginia, 1830-1860*, 1942) and James H. Brewer (*The Confederate Negro: Virginia's Craftsmen and Military Laborers, 1861-1865*, 1969), characterized free blacks as "casualties of history...forgotten and unknown in lonely unmarked graves." Yet according to the 1860 census, nearly 250,000 free blacks lived in the antebellum South. Although barely two percent of the region's population, they were its most urbanized African-Americans. Neither slave nor citizen, legal and racial circumstances compelled them to behave as loyal citizens though whites usually treated them like slaves without masters or as potential enemies of the state. Virginia required them to register their residency periodically; an 1856 law authorized free blacks to renounce their freedom and become slaves voluntarily. Arkansas was the only antebellum slave state to enact and enforce a law requiring free blacks to leave or suffer reenslavement. If the Confederacy had won the American Civil War, slavery would have continued and free blacks would have lost their freedom.

One of the most discriminatory aspects of free black noncitizenship was their coerced patriotism and service as military laborers. Of the two antagonists, the South was first to seize the initiative in putting blacks to work as hewers of wood, drawers of water, and builders of fortifications. Other than running away or going into hiding they had few alternatives because outright refusal would have meant brutal repercussions. Many black Southerners pragmatically sought wary neutrality as the fortunes of war shifted across the South's killing fields. Some free blacks renounced their race by seeking to recast themselves as Afro-Confederates. Free blacks believed they had to act more Confederates than white Southerners because they were under suspicion by a volatile and heavily armed racist white population. Free blacks considered it expedient to support what they believed was the winning side; fear was a powerful motivator for their loyalty and cautiousness. Black folk did not forget the fate of antebellum blacks that nervous whites suspected of rebelliousness--taut nooses and bulging-eyed corpses slowly twisting beneath trees.

The first casualty of war is truth, and the duty of historians is to report it without bias or favoritism. E. Renée Ingram's *Register of Free Negroes Enrolled, 1864-1865, Chapter 1, Volume 241*, as far as I know, is the first time this remarkable document has been published it its entirety. She brings this and other overlooked documentary sources to the public's attention including legislation concerning slave and free black impressment, contemporary newspaper advertisements, letters and rare photographs. Her book joins a small but growing number of free black studies (most of which examine those who were antebellum slaveholders or consist of free black registers), but much of the black experience remains undocumented or unacknowledged in the history books. In this book the author is content to be a nonpartisan scholar. Her style is unpretentious, and she has presented the facts as they are, believing they can and should speak for themselves.

The implications of the documents reproduced in this book are profound. First, the register shows that the complexions and eye colors of many mulattoes meant miscegenation was more widespread in the South than has been admitted (by 1860, 55 percent of black Virginians were mulattoes). Second, that numerous free black male adults held skilled occupations of value to the economic well-being of antebellum and wartime communities. Third, the eighteen hundred free blacks enrolled at Camp Lee during 1864-65 represented a potential nucleus for Afro-Confederate military regiments. Believing the South might soon need black men as soldiers (but hoping to deflect criticism by whites vehemently opposed to the arming of slaves as a racially risky infringement of property right), General Robert E. Lee, commander of the Army of Northern Virginia, laid plans in 1864 for Confederate Negro Labor Battalions as regiments and battalions, with muster rolls, regular inspections and Confederate officers as their commanders. When the Confederacy belatedly enlisted black troops in the spring of 1865, this camp served as their primary induction center--a reality which did not go unnoticed by worried Northern black leaders such as Frederick Douglass. Thomas Morris Chester, the *Philadelphia Press's* only black reporter, worriedly claimed 20,000 blacks were receiving military training at Camp Lee in March 1865. He exaggerated their numbers but the potential existed nonetheless.

During the last thirty years African American history has become a means for the recognition and affirmation of the achievements of a people often overlooked. Our knowledge is expanding and improving as scholars from a variety of backgrounds increasingly research previously ignored or forgotten records. This book represents an overdue beginning in redefining African-Americans as participants of Civil War history. It is a wonderful example of the recovery of our national and cultural memories.

Professor Ervin L. Jordan, Jr.
University of Virginia
August 1998

JOURNAL
of the
CONGRESS OF THE CONFEDERATE STATES OF AMERICA,
1861-1865

From 1861 to 1865 there were three Congresses that convened as the legislative bodies for the Confederacy. The first, known as the Provisional Congress, was a unicameral body consisting of delegates chosen by state legislatures to organize a government for the Confederate States of America. It held five sessions between 4 February 1861 and 17 February 1862 and drafted both the provisional and permanent Confederate constitutions. The first Congress met for two years beginning in February 1862. The second Congress held two sessions before adjourning on 18 March 1865, just weeks before the collapse of the Confederacy.[1]

These excerpts from the Journal are a chronology of discussions regarding the employment of free negroes and slaves during the Civil War.

---

[1] Donald C. Bacon, *The Encyclopedia of the United States Congress,* (New York: Simon & Schuster, 1995), 520-521.

SIXTY-SEVENTH DAY - TUESDAY, February 11, 1862

Secret Session

Mr. Chilton *[Alabama]* introduced

A resolution instructing the Committee on Military Affairs to inquire into the propriety of employing slaves as cooks and nurses, etc.; which was read and agreed to...

Journal of the Senate [Mar. 8, 1862] p. 45

SATURDAY, March 8, 1862

Open Session.

Mr. Phelan *[Mississippi]* submitted the following resolution; which was considered and agreed to:

Resolved, That the Committee on Military Affairs be instructed to inquire in to the expediency of providing for the employment and payment of negro musicians in the Army of the Confederate States.

Adjutant and Inspector General's Office

Richmond March 19, 1862

It is necessary for the War Department to impress slaves and free negroes, preferably the latter, for service as teamsters and carpenters, in the Quartermaster's Department of the Confederate Army. The bearer hereof Mr. J. A. Clayton, is hereby directed to call upon the Citizens of Madison, Green and Albemarle Counties in Virginia for male slaves of free negroes, between the ages of 16 and 50 for the above purpose to the number of 240. The negroes will be paid for at the rate of $30 for mechanics - $20 for teamsters, and $15 for laborers per month each, and receive an ample supply of provisions, the money to be paid by the Quartermaster's Department to their Masters, promptly at the places where they may work.

Payment will be made personally to the free negroes, or to such agents as may be legally authorized by them. The cost of transportation to be paid by the Government, the agent will collect the negroes, and a fair compensation will be paid him for the trouble, by the Quartermaster's Department.

The agent Mr. J. A. Clayton is authorized to give receipts for the negroes, and from the dates of said receipts, the Government of the Confederate States will be responsible for the slaves according to the laws of Virginia, with the additional responsibility for their value should they escape to or be injured by the Enemy.

These negroes will be sent to the nearest wharves or railroad depots, in accordance to instructions to be given by the agent, cost of transportation will be paid upon the production of evidence signed by the agent, that it has been furnished.

By order of the Secretary of War
Signed S. Cooper
A & I General

Journal of the House of Representatives [Mar. 25, 1862] p. 142

THIRTY-FIRST DAY - TUESDAY, March 25, 1862

Open Session.

Mr. Perkins *[Louisiana]* offered

...Also, a bill to provide for the employment of negroes on Government works; which was read the first and second times and referred to the Committee on Military Affairs...

Journal of the House of Representatives [Mar. 28, 1862] p. 158

THIRTY-FOURTH DAY - FRIDAY, March 28, 1862

Open Session.

Mr. Miles *[South Carolina]*, from the same committee [Military Affairs], to whom was referred A bill to provide for the employment of negroes on Government work, reported the same back with recommendation that it pass.

The rules were suspended;
The bill was taken up, and having been read as follows, to wit:

With a view to secure against loss the owners of negroes in portions of the Confederacy exposed to invasion by the enemy, and to enable the Government to make available for purposes of defense the labor of such negroes: Therefore,

Be it enacted by the Congress of the Confederate States of America, That the President be, and he is hereby, authorized to employ for the service of the Confederate States, during the continuance of the war, such able-bodied negro men from the age of sixteen to fifty as may tendered by their owners, to be employed in Government works, in Government foundries, in the fabrication of saltpeter, the construction of military roads, the erection of fortifications, or in such other labor as their services may be found valuable, on condition of their being clothed and fed by the Government and returned to their owners at the end of the war or their value paid.

Sec. 2. *Be it further enacted,* That it shall be the duty of the President to have the value of such negroes fixed at the time of their employment and to provide suitable regulations and officers for their proper care and control,

Mr. Smith of North Carolina moved to amend the same by striking out the words "either in kind or value" and inserting in lieu thereof the words " or their value paid."

The amendment was agreed to.

Mr. Hilton *[Florida]* moved to amend by adding after the words "continuance of the war" the words "at not more than one-half of the current rate of hire in the locality where employed."

On motion of Mr. McLean *[North Carolina],* the bill and amendments were placed on the Calendar and ordered to be printed.

Journal of the Senate [Apr. 1, 1862] p. 113

TUESDAY, April 1, 1862

Open Session.

Mr. Phelan *[Mississippi]* submitted the following resolution; which was considered and agreed to:

Resolved, That the Committee on Military Affairs be instructed to inquire into the expediency of employing negroes as teamsters in the Army of Confederate States.

Journal of the Senate [Apr. 2, 1862] p. 118

WEDNESDAY, April 2, 1862

Open Session.

Mr. Wigfall *[Texas],* from the Committee on Military Affairs, to whom was referred

A resolution inquiring into the expediency of employing negro teamsters in the Army of the Confederate States, submitted an adverse report in relation thereto.

Journal of the Senate [Apr. 11, 1862] p. 152

FRIDAY, April 11, 1862

Open Session.

Mr. Phelan *[Mississippi]* submitted the following resolution; which was considered and agreed to:

Resolved, That the Committee on Military Affairs be instructed to inquire in the expediency of enlisting a certain number of cooks for each company in the Army, or of making some other provision by which the soldiers may be relieved from the preparation of their own food, and said service performed by person specially employed for that purpose. Also, that the committee inquire into the expediency of obtaining the services of slaves for that purpose.

Journal of the Senate [Apr. 16, 1862] p. 174

WEDNESDAY, April 16, 1862

Open Session.

On motion by Mr. Sparrow *[Louisiana],*

Resolution inquiring into the expediency of enlisting cooks for the Army and obtaining the services of slaves for that purpose.

Journal of the House of Representatives [Apr. 19, 1862] p. 277

FIFTY-THIRD DAY - SATURDAY, April 19, 1862

Open Session.

Mr. Miles *[South Carolina]* moved that the House take up from the Calendar a bill for the employment of negroes on Government work.

The motion was lost.

EIGHTH DAY- TUESDAY, August 26, 1862

Open Session.

Mr. Foster *[Alabama]* offered

...Also, a resolution instructing the Military Committee to inquire and report to this House, at a day as early as practicable, as to the expediency and policy of authorizing the President to call out and place in the service of the Confederate States, during the war, all the male negroes who are resident or owned in the Confederate States between the ages of 20 and 30 years at the time the said call shall be made, for the purposes of hereinafter mentioned -- that is to say, as teamsters, cooks, nurses in the various hospitals, and laborers or mechanics in the arsenals, on railroads, in workshops, forges, foundries, furnaces, and manufactories of the Confederate States, or which may hereafter be under their control, engaged in the production of salt, saltpeter, lead, iron, leather, and such other articles necessary and proper for the efficient and successful conduct of military operations against the public enemy, under such legal limitations and restrictions as shall secure the owner of the property a just and reasonable compensation for the labor of said negroes on the one hand, and the Confederate States their services on the other, during this momentous crisis; which was read and agreed to.

No. 11
A Bill further to provide for the publick defence
[August 28, 1862]

Sec. 1. *Be it enacted,* That the President be and he is hereby authorized to hire and take into his possession all able bodied male slaves between the ages of twenty and thirty years or as many of them as may be necessary for the purposes herein after mentioned and employ them in all the public factories and employ in procuring materials for manufacture, to attend hospitals, to work in all railroads, the government may undertake to repair or build and to work in all forts and other publick defences - and to do all public work necessary to the publick defence not however to be employed as soldiery in the army of the Confederate States.

Sec. 2. *Be it further enacted,* That the owners of such slaves so hired and taken shall receive hire for each of them so taken at the rate of one hundred and fifty dollars per annum, payable monthly at the rate of twelve dollars 60/100 per month and if any of such slave so taken and employed be lost or destroyed by reason of such employment, the owner shall receive reasonable compensation.

Therefore

Sec. 3. *Be it further enacted,* That the owners of such slaves are hereby required to yield us such slaves to the President or to such person or persons as may be appointed by him to receive them. Hereby the owner of such slave have no other male slave between the ages of 18 and fifty and but one between the ages 20 and 30. In such case the owner may refuse to hire his slave, between the ages of twenty and thirty.

Sec. 4. *Be it further enacted,* That the owners of such slaves as may be taken into the publick service for the purposes aforesaid shall receive a receipt for his slave or slaves containing the age name and description of such slave and during the time such slave shall be in the publick service the government shall clothe and feed such slaves and provide them with proper medicine and medical attention.

Resolved, That the President be requested to inform this House whether the Governor of Va. has communicated to him certain Acts of the General Assembly of Va., passed October 3d, 1862, and March 13th, and March 30th, 1863, concerning the draft or impressment of slaves into the service of the Confederate States at the request of the President, made to the said Governor; whether the said Acts provide that the Confederate States shall pay for such slaves, or for injury done them in certain cases, and that any request for slaves made by the President or the Governor shall be regarded assent to and acceptance of the provisions of the said Acts, whether any slaves have been called for and accepted under the authority of said Acts, and if so, whether the Government has paid, or holds itself ready to pay for loss of such slaves.

THIRTY-FIFTH DAY - SATURDAY, September 27, 1862

Open Session.

Mr. Hilton *[Florida]*, from the same committee [Military Affairs], to whom was referred

A resolution in relation to employing male slaves, reported the same back, asked to be discharged from its further consideration, and that it lie upon the table; which was agreed to.

AN ACT

To amend an Act entitled "An Act to organize and supply negro labor for coast defense in compliance with requisitions of the Government of the Confederate States;" and to authorize and direct the Governor to proceed to furnish negro labor under said Act.

SECTION 1. Be it enacted by the Senate and House of Representatives, now met and sitting in General Assembly, and by the authority of the same, That an Act entitled "an Act to organize and supply negro labor for coast defense, in compliance with requisitions of the Government of the Confederate States," passed on the 18th day of December, anno Domini, eighteen hundred and sixty two, be, and the same is hereby, amended, and that the State agent appointed under the fourth section of said Act, shall have the power, and is hereby authorized to appoint, with the approval of the Governor, such number of assistant agents as in his judgment may be necessary to enable him to execute the provisions of the sixth section of said Act, and as a compensation for their services while so employed, they shall be entitled to receive two dollars per diem.

SECTION 2. That the eleventh section of said Act be so amended that instead of the fines and penalties, therein imposed upon such owners of slaves as shall neglect or refuse to send their slaves, according to the requirements of said Act, such defaulters shall be liable to a fine of 1 1/2 dollars per diem for each slave, for the time they shall be liable to send such slaves, to be imposed and collected by the Commissioner of Roads in the district where such default has been made, in the manner now provided by law for default in the performance of said duty.

SECTION 3. That the Governor be, and is hereby, authorized and directed to proceed to furnish negro labor to the Confederate Government under said Act, notwithstanding said Government has not, through the proper officer, authorized, thereto, assented and agreed to the provision contained in said Act, declaiming said Government liable to the owner for any loss or damage of or to the slave or slaves during his or their service; Provided, however, that the State does not by this Act waive the right to insist upon such liability, as well as all the provisions of said Act, and the amendments thereto, and he is hereby directed to take such proceedings as he may deem necessary and proper to bring said provisions to the notice of the Congress of the Confederate States, and procure their assent to all its terms and conditions.

In the Senate House the sixth day of February in the year of our Lord one thousand eight hundred and sixty three and in the eighty seventh year of the sovereignty and independence of the State of South Carolina.

[Signed] W. D. Porter Pres[iden]t of Senate
[Signed] A. P. Aldrich Speaker House of Rep[resentative]s

I certify that the foregoing is a correct copy of the Act now on file in the Secretary of States Office.

[Signed] B. F. Arthur

JOINT RESOLUTION
In relation to the increase of the Army of the Confederate States.

WHEREAS, The Confederate Government demands the services of all persons subject to conscription to fill up the ranks of our regiments now in the field, and our State taxed to its utmost to furnish troops for State defense; and whereas there are large numbers of able-bodied men connected with the army of the Confederate States on service as clerks, agents, &c., of post or direct quartermasters or commissary, or are otherwise employed than in active military service; and whereas our army has been greatly reduced on account of the numberless details of soldiers to labor in government workshops and other places, and upon railroads, performing such work as can be and has usually been rendered by slaves,

1. *Be it resolved by the Senate and House of Representatives of the State of Alabama in General Assembly convened,* That in the opinion of this general assembly public sentiment and the exigencies of the country require that all able-bodied men in the service of the Confederate States as clerks, or employed in any other capacity in any of the quartermaster or commissary departments of the government, should be put into active military service without delay, and that their places should be filled with soldiers or citizens who are unfit for active military service.

2. *Be it further resolved,* That this general assembly are of the opinion that the details of soldiers from the army to labor in workshops, foundries, and other places, and upon railroads, have been entirely too numerous, and in many instances useless, and that in the opinion of this body slaves should be required by the Confederate States to take the places of all those soldiers who are detailed to labor in the places herein mentioned, when it can be done without prejudice to the service, and that prompt and efficient measures should at once be adopted to effect these purposes.

3. *Be it further resolved,* That this general assembly earnestly calls the attention of the President and Secretary of War of the Confederate States to this subject as requiring immediate and energetic action on the part of the government.

4. *Be it further resolved,* That this general assembly recommend to Congress such a modification of the exemption law as will correct the evils herein named, and thereby increase the strength of our military force.

5. *Be it further resolved,* That in view of the fact that the government of the United States has determined to put in the field negro soldiers, and are enlisting and drafting slaves of the people of the South, this general assembly submits for the consideration of Congress the propriety and policy of using some effective a certain per centage of the male slave population of the Confederate States, and to perform such service as Congress may by law direct.

6. *Be it further resolved,* That the Governor transmit a copy of these resolutions to the President of the Confederate States, the Secretary of War, and a copy to each of our Senators and Representatives from this State in the Confederate Congress.

Approved August 29, 1863.

Hon
Wm. P. Miles [*William Porcher Miles, South Carolina,*
Chairman of Military Affairs]

Dear Sir, In the discharge of the duties of my office, the past two years, embracing a wide & extended jurisdiction over the slaves & free persons of color within this District, my attention has been repeatedly called to an anomalous state of things that exists among us, throughout the whole Confederacy. I ask leave to bring it to your notice, that if you should deem the matter worthy of consideration, you may submit it before the Committee of which you are the Chairman. It is this - that whilst our entire white male population between the ages of 18 and 45, are in the service of the Confederacy, & those of other ages occasionally are liable to military duty, & whilst our slaves are busily engaged in the pursuits of agriculture & in working upon the fortifications, there is yet a class among us, which enjoys singular privileges & immunities, & is with limited exceptions not held liable to public duty to wit; the free colored population. Not only does this class pursue its usual avocations, but with a greatly enlarged sphere for the employment of its industry, in consequence of the withdrawal from many occupations of the white men of our country. The freeman of color thus enjoys the increased profits of his business & makes money, whilst the white man does the hard work of the day at the risk of health & life, with a very poor monied compensation, & away from home & family. The more I reflect upon this subject the more glaring does its inequality & injustice appear to me and I have thought that it would prove an convincebly wise & wholesome policy to place the free persons of color, say between the ages of 16 & 50, to do the menial & much of the mechanical service of the army, for the war & at a moderate rate of wages. They might be employed as Teamsters - Ostlers - Musicians - Hospital Stewards - Attendants & Nurses - Caterers & Cooks - Shoemakers & Cobblers - & generally as assistant artisans. As matters now are, large numbers of men are detailed from the ranks to fill these offices, the duties as pertaining to which might bear well & faithfully discharged by the class alluded to, thus gaining to the ranks many thousands of able-bodied soldiers. The ties of home, of family & of property will serve a sufficient guaranty for the usefulness & fidelity of this class, if thus employed.

Having bestowed much time & thought upon the subject, I submit with much deference, the issues above expressed.

I am, Dear Sir
Very respectfully
Yours
Francis T. Parker
Provost Marshal
of Georgetown District
So. Ca.

Open Session.

The following message was received from the President of the Confederate States, by
Mr. B. N. Harrison, his Private Secretary:

To the Senate and House of Representatives of the Confederate States.

THE ARMY

To the report of the Secretary of War you are referred for details relative to the condition of the Army
and the measures of legislation required for maintaining its efficiency, recruiting its numbers, and
furnishing the supplies necessary for its support…

"… In view of the large conscription recently ordered by the enemy, and their subsequent call for
volunteers, to be followed, if ineffectual, by a still further draft, we are admonished that no effort must
be spared to add largely to our effective force as promptly as possible. The sources of supply are to be
found by restoring to the Army all who are improperly absent, putting an end to substitution, modifying
the exemption law, restricting details, and placing in the ranks such of the able-bodied men now
employed as wagoners, nurses, cooks, and other employees as are doing service for which the negroes
may be found competent…"

If to the above measures be added a law to enlarge the policy of the act of the 21st April, 1862, so as to
enable the Department to replace not only enlisted cooks, but wagoners and other employees in the
Army by negroes, it is hoped that the ranks of the Army will be so strengthened for the ensuing
campaign as to put at defiance the utmost efforts of the enemy…"

Open Session.

The following message was received from the President of the Confederate States, by Mr. B. N. Harrison, his Private Secretary:

To the Senate and House of Representatives of the Confederate States.

THE ARMY

To the report of the Secretary of War you are referred for details relative to the condition of the Army and the measures of legislation required for maintaining its efficiency, recruiting its numbers, and furnishing the supplies necessary for its support...

"... In view of the large conscription recently ordered by the enemy, and their subsequent call for volunteers, to be followed, if ineffectual, by a still further draft, we are admonished that no effort must be spared to add largely to our effective force as promptly as possible. The sources of supply are to be found by restoring to the Army all who are improperly absent, putting an end to substitution, modifying the exemption law, restricting details, and placing in the ranks such of the able-bodied men now employed as wagoners, nurses, cooks, and other employees as are doing service for which the negroes may be found competent..."

If to the above measures be added a law to enlarge the policy of the act of the 21st April, 1862, so as to enable the Department to replace not only enlisted cooks, but wagoners and other employees in the Army by negroes, it is hoped that the ranks of the Army will be so strengthened for the ensuing campaign as to put at defiance the utmost efforts of the enemy..."

Conscription of Free Negroes
Dec 10th 1863
Military Office
January 5, 1864
[passed February 17, 1864]

A BILL

To be entitled An Act to increase the efficiency of the Army by the employment of free negroes and slaves in certain capacities.

Whereas the efficiency of the Army is greatly diminished by the withdrawal from the ranks of able-bodied soldiers to act as teamsters and in various other capacities in which free negroes and slaves might be advantageously employed _ Therefore

Sec. 1. The Congress of the Confederate States do enact that all male free negroes resident in the Confederate States between the ages of 18 and 50 years shall be held liable to perform such duties with the army or in conjunction with the military defenses of the country in the way of work upon fortifications or in government works for the production or preparation of materials of War or in Military Hospitals as the Secretary of War may from time to time prescribe and while engaged in the performance of such duties shall receive rations and clothing and compensation at the rate of Eleven dollars a month under such rules & regulations as the said Secretary may establish - Provided that the Secretary of War with the approval of the President may exempt from the operation of this Act such free negroes as the interests of the country may require should be exempted or such as he may think proper to exempt on grounds of justice, equity or necessity.

Sec. 2. Be it further enacted That this Secretary of War is hereby authorized to employ for similar duties to those indicated in the preceding section of this Act as many male negro slaves, not to exceed as in his judgment the wants of the service may require, furnishing them while so employed with proper rations and clothing under rules and regulations to be established by him and paying to the owners of said slaves wages at the rate of Eleven dollars per month for their use and service and in the event of the loss of slaves, while so employed, by the act of the enemy or by escape to the enemy or by death inflicted by the enemy or by disease incurred in consequence of the discharge of any service required of said slaves then the owners of the same shall be entitled to receive the full value of such slaves to be paid under such rules and regulations as the Secretary of War may establish.

Sec. 3. Be it further enacted That when the Secretary of War shall be unable to procure the services of slaves in any military Department in sufficient numbers for the necessity of the Department upon the terms and conditions set forth in the preceding section then he is hereby authorized command of such Dept. to impress the services of as many male slaves as may required from time to time to discharge the duties indicated in the first section of this Act under such rules and regulations as the said Secretary may establish - Provided that slaves so impressed shall while employed received the same rations and clothing in kind and quantity as slaves regularly hired from their owners and in the event of their loss shall be paid for in the same manner and under the same rules and regulations as those who may been hired.

14

FOURTH DAY - FRIDAY, December 11, 1863

Open Session.

Mr. Miles *[South Carolina]* offered the following resolution; which was adopted, viz:

Resolved, That the Committee on Military Affairs be instructed to inquire into the expediency of conscribing all able-bodied male free negroes in the Confederate States, for the purpose of employing them on Government work and for the discharge of the duties of teamsters, cooks, etc. in the Army.

Journal of the House of Representatives [Dec. 11, 1863] p. 526

FOURTH DAY - FRIDAY, December 11, 1863

Open Session.

Mr. Welsh *[Mississippi]*, by unanimous consent, offered the following resolution; which was adopted:

Resolved, That the Committee on Military Affairs be requested to inquire into the expediency of conscribing one hundred thousand male slaves, between the ages of eighteen and forty-five years, to be placed in the service of the Confederate States in the capacity of teamsters, cooks for our soldiers, waiters in hospitals, laborers on fortifications, and in such other capacity as they can be profitably employed.

Journal of the House of Representatives [Dec. 28, 1863] **p. 567**

SEVENTEENTH DAY - MONDAY, December 28, 1863

Open Session.

Mr. Clopton *[Alabama]* introduced

A bill to increase the efficiency of the Army by the employment of slaves; **which** was read a first and second time and referred to the Committee on Military Affairs.

Journal of the Senate [Dec. 30, 1863] p. 496

WEDNESDAY, December 30, 1863

Open Session.

Mr. Phelan *[Mississippi]*, presented the following resolutions of the legislature of the State of Mississippi; which were severally read, viz:

…A resolution in relation to the practicability of using negro men in the **armies of** the Confederate States as teamsters, nurses, and pioneer corps.

Ordered, That they be referred to the Committee on Military Affairs and **printed.**

Journal of the House of Representatives [Jan. 4, 1864] p. 589

TWENTY-FOURTH DAY - TUESDAY, January 4, 1864

Open Session.

Mr. Miles *[South Carolina]*, from the Committee on Military Affairs, reported

A bill to increase the efficiency of the Army, by the employment of free negroes and slaves in certain capacities; which was read a first and second time, postponed, placed upon the Calendar, and ordered to be printed.

Journal of the Senate [Jan.12, 1864] p. 553

TUESDAY, January 12, 1864

Open Session.

Mr. Clay *[Alabama]* presented a communication from V. Sheliha, chief engineer of the Department of the Gulf, in relation to the organization of a sufficient number of negroes into a corps of engineer laborers, to serve during the war; which was referred to the Committee on Military Affairs.

Journal of the Senate [Jan. 18, 1864] p. 584

MONDAY, January 18, 1864

Open Session.

Mr. Orr *[South Carolina]* submitted the following resolution; which was considered and agreed to:

Resolved, That the Committee on Military Affairs be instructed to inquire into the expediency of placing in the military service of the Confederate States all male free persons of color, between the ages of eighteen and fifty years, to be employed as cooks, teamsters, and laborers.

FORTIETH DAY - SATURDAY, January 23, 1864

Open Session.

Mr. Miles *[South Carolina]* moved that the rules be suspended to take up for consideration the bill from the Calendar to increase the efficiency of the Army by the employment of free negroes and slaves in certain cases.

The motion was agreed to.

Mr. Baldwin *[Virginia]* moved to amend the first section of the bill by adding at the end thereof the following:

And no free negro engaged in the production of food or forage shall be taken under this act.

Pending which,

The House, on motion of Mr. Jones *[Tennessee],* resolved itself into secret session; and having spent some time therein, again resolved itself into Open Session.

Journal of the Senate [Jan. 30, 1864] p. 633

SATURDAY, January 30, 1864

Open Session.

Mr. Orr *[South Carolina]* (by leave) introduced

A bill (S. 211) to place free persons of color in the military service of the Confederate States; which was read the first and second times and referred to the Committee on Military Affairs.

S. 211

A bill to place free persons of color in the military service of the Confederate States.

SENATE, January 30, 1864.--Read first and second times.

[By Mr. Orr *[South Carolina]*, by leave, from the Committee on Military Affairs]

February 5, 1864 Committee discharged.

A bill to be entitled "an act to place free persons of color in the military service of the Confederate States."

The Congress of the Confederate States of America do enact, That all male free persons of color between the ages of eighteen and fifty years are hereby declared to be in the military service of the Confederate States for the war and shall be employed as laborers, nurses and in such other employments as the Secretary of War by regulation may prescribe.

FORTY-SEVENTH DAY - MONDAY, February 1, 1864

Open Session.

The House then took up the bill to increase the efficiency of the Army by the employment of free negroes and slaves in certain capacities.

The question being on the amendment of Mr. Baldwin *[Virginia]*,

Mr. Atkins *[Tennessee]* called the question; which was ordered, and the amendment of Mr. Baldwin *[Virginia]* was lost.

Mr. Smith of Alabama moved to amend the bill by striking out the first section; which is as follows, viz:

That all male free negroes resident in the Confederate States, between the ages of eighteen and fifty-five years, shall be held liable to perform such duties with the Army, or in connection with the military defenses of the country, in the way of work upon fortifications, or in Government works for the production or preparation of material of war, or in military hospitals, as the Secretary of War may from time to time prescribe; and while engaged in the performance of such duties shall receive rations and clothing and compensation at the rate of eleven dollars a month, under such rules and regulations as the said Secretary may establish: *Provided,* That the Secretary of War, with the approval of the President, may exempt from the operations of this act such free negroes as the interests of the country may require should be exempted, or such as he may think proper to exempt on grounds of justice, equity, or necessity.

Mr. Clark *[Missouri]* called the question; which was ordered, and the amendment of Mr. Smith of Alabama was lost.

Mr. Machen *[Kentucky]* moved to amend section 2 by striking out, in line 4, the words, "not to exceed."

The amendment was lost.

Mr. Miles *[South Carolina]* moved to amend the filling the blank with the words "twenty thousand."

Mr. Dargan *[Alabama]* moved to amend the amendment by striking out "twenty thousand and inserting "forty thousand."

Mr. Goode *[Virginia]* called the question; which was ordered, and the amendment of Mr. Dargan was lost, and the amendment of Mr. Miles was agreed to.

Mr. Miles *[South Carolina]* submitted the following amendment:

20

In section 2, line 12, strike out the words "incurred in consequence of the discharge of" and insert in lies thereof the words "contracted while in."

The amendment was agreed to.

Mr. Ralls *[Alabama]* moved to amend by striking out the words "or by disease contracted while in any service required of said slaves, then the owners of the same shall be entitled to receive the full value of such slaves."

Mr. Foster *[Alabama]* called the question; which was ordered, and the amendment of Mr. Ralls *[Alabama]* was lost.

Mr. Gray *[Texas]* moved to amend section 2 by inserting, in line 14, after the word "slaves," the words "to be ascertained by agreement, or by appraisement under the laws regulating impressments, and."

Mr. Foster *[Alabama]* called the question; which was ordered, and the amendment of Mr. Gray *[Texas]* was agreed to.

Mr. Hilton *[Florida]* moved to amend the third section of the bill by [inserting], in line 6, after the word "slaves," the words "not to exceed twenty thousand;" which was agreed to.

Mr. Baldwin *[Virginia]* move to amend the third section by striking out, in lines 8 and 9, the words, under such rules and regulations as the said Secretary may establish" and inserting the words "according to the laws regulating impressments of slaves in other cases."

The amendment was agreed to.

Mr. Baldwin *[Virginia]* also submitted the following amendment:

In section 3, lines 13 and 14, strike out the words "and regulations as those who may have been hired and insert the words "established by the said impressment laws;" which was agreed to.

Mr. Dargan *[Alabama]* submitted the following amendment:

Add at end of third section the following: "*Provided,* That if the owner have but one male slave within the ages of eighteen and fifty he shall not be impressed against the will of the owner;" which was agreed to.

Mr. Barksdale *[Mississippi]* submitted the following amendment as an independent section:

Sec. 4. Impressment of slaves shall, as far as practicable, be made in counties or districts the productions of which are least available for use of the Army, or remote from facilities for transportation, and shall be apportioned as nearly as practicable among the owners, according to numbers of laboring hands.

Mr. Dupré *[Louisiana]* moved to amend the amendment of Mr. Barksdale *[Mississippi]* by adding at the end thereof the following:

Provided, That no slave laboring on a farm or plantation exclusively devoted to the production of grain and provisions, and not exceeding ten hands to each farm, shall be impressed without the consent of the owner.

Mr. Hilton *[Florida]* called the question; which was ordered, and the amendment of Mr. Dupré was agreed to.

Mr. Ashe *[North Carolina]* submitted the following amendment to the amendment of Mr. Barksdale (as a substitute therefor):

That the slaves required to be impressed shall be apportioned pro rata among several States and the several owners each State as far as practicable.

Mr. Foster *[Alabama]* called the question; which was ordered, and the amendment of Mr. Ashe was lost.

Mr. Goode *[Virginia]* moved to amend the bill by striking out the third section as amended; which reads as follows, viz.

That when the Secretary of War shall be unable to procure the services of slaves in any military Department in sufficient numbers for the necessities of the department upon the terms and conditions set forth in the preceding section then he is hereby authorized to impress the services of as many male slaves, not to exceed twenty thousand, as may be required from time to time to discharge the duties indicated in the first section of this act, according to laws regulating impressments of slaves in other cases: *Provided,* That slaves so impressed shall while employed, receive the same rations and clothing in kind and quantity as slaves regularly hired from their owners, and in the event of their loss, shall be paid for in the same manner and under the same rules established by the said impressment laws.

Mr. Foster *[Alabama]* called the question; which was ordered, and the amendment of Mr. Goode *[Virginia]* was lost.

Mr. Welsh *[Mississippi]* moved to amend the amendment of Mr. Barksdale *[Mississippi]* as follows, viz:

Strike out all of said amendment and insert in lieu thereof the following, viz:

"*Provided further,* That in making the impressments, not more than one of every five male slaves between the ages of eighteen and forty-five shall be taken from any owner."

The amendment was agreed to.

Mr. Conrad *[Louisiana]* moved to reconsider the vote just taken, by which the amendment of Mr. Welsh *[Mississippi]* was agreed to, and demanded the yeas and nays thereon;

Which was ordered,

And recorded as follows, viz: {   Yeas.......35
                                                         Nays......34

Yeas: Arrington *[North Carolina]*, Baldwin *[Virginia]*, Barksdale *[Mississippi]*, Bell *[Missouri]*, Boteler *[Virginia]*, Boyce *[South Carolina]*, Bridgers *[North Carolina]*, Horatio W. Bruce *[Kentucky]*, Chilton *[Alabama]*, Clopton *[Alabama]*, Conrad *[Louisiana]*, Dargan *[Alabama]*, Dupré *[Louisiana]*, Ewing *[Kentucky]*, Farrow *[South Carolina]*, Foster *[Alabama]*, Gartrell *[Georgia]*, Goode *[Virginia]*, Heiskell *[Tennessee]*, Holcombe *[Virginia]*, Ingram *[Georgia]*, Johnston *[Virginia]*, Jones *[Tennessee]*, Lewis *[Georgia]*, Lyon *[Alabama]*, Machen *[Kentucky]*, Menees *[Tennessee]*, Miles *[South Carolina]*, Preston *[Virginia]*, Pugh *[Alabama]*, Russell *[Virginia]*, Singleton *[Mississippi]*, Staples *[Virginia]*, Strickland *[Georgia]*, and Villeré *[Louisiana]*.

Nays: Ashe *[North Carolina]*, Atkins *[Tennessee]*, Clapp *[Mississippi]*, Clark *[Missouri]*, Davidson *[North Carolina]*, Foote *[Tennessee]*, Funsten *[Virginia]*, Gaither *[North Carolina]*, Gardenshire *[Tennessee]*, Garland *[Arkansas]*, Graham *[Texas]*, Gray *[Texas]*, Hartridge *[Georgia]*, Hilton *[Florida]*, Lander *[North Carolina]*, Martin *[Florida]*, McLean *[North Carolina]*, McQueen *[South Carolina]*, McRae *[Mississippi]*, Miller *[Virginia]*, Munnerlyn *[Georgia]*, Perkins *[Louisiana]*, Ralls *[Alabama]*, Sexton *[Texas]*, Simpson *[South Carolina]*, Smith *[Alabama]*, Swan *[Tennessee]*, Tibbs *[Tennessee]*, Trippe *[Georgia]*, Welsh *[Mississippi]*, Wilcox *[Texas]*, Wright *[Georgia]*, Wright *[Texas]*, and
Mr. Speaker.

So the motion to reconsider prevailed.

Mr. Miles *[South Carolina]* moved to reconsider the vote by which the amendment of Mr. Dupré *[Louisiana]* was agreed to.

Mr. Foote *[Tennessee]* called the question; which was ordered, and the motion to reconsider prevailed, and the amendment of Mr. Dupré *[Louisiana]* was lost.

Mr. Welsh *[Mississippi]* moved to amend the amendment of Mr. Barksdale *[Mississippi]* by adding the following, viz:

Provide further, That in making the impressments, not more than one of every five male slaves between the ages of eighteen and forty-five shall be taken from any owner.

The amendment was agreed to, and the amendment of Mr. Barksdale *[Mississippi]*, as amended, was agreed to.

Mr. Hilton *[Florida]* moved to amend the fourth section by adding at the end thereof the following:

Provided, That no slaves shall be impressed in one State to labor on fortifications in another.

Mr. Foster *[Virginia]* called the question; which was ordered, and the amendment of Mr. Hilton *[Florida]* was lost.

Mr. Gardenshire *[Tennessee]* submitted the following amendment:

Add at the end of last section the following: "*Provided further,* That free negroes shall be first impressed, and if there should be a deficiency it shall be supplied by the impressment of slaves according to the foregoing provisions;"

which was agreed to.

Mr. Foster *[Alabama]* moved to amend the fourth section by adding the following:

Provided, That the slaves of the First and Third Congressional districts of Alabama be exempted from the provisions of this act.

Mr. Wilcox *[Texas]* moved to amend the amendment of Mr. Foster *[Alabama]* by adding the following:

Provided, That they be exempted from taxation and representation during the war.

Mr. Gray *[Texas]* moved to lay the amendment of Mr. Foster and the amendment to the amendment on the table; which motion was agreed to.....

Mr. Miles *[South Carolina]* moved to amend the first section of the bill by inserting after the word "negroes" the words "and other free persons of color."

Mr. Dargan *[Alabama]* moved to amend the amendment of Mr. Miles *[South Carolina]* by adding thereto the words "not including those who are free under the treaty of Paris of eighteen hundred and three, or under the treaty with Spain of eighteen hundred and nineteen."

The amendment of Mr. Dargan *[Alabama]* was agreed to.

The amendment of Mr. Miles *[South Carolina],* as amended, was also agreed to.

The bill was then engrossed and read a third time.

The question recurring on the passage of the bill,

Mr. Foster *[Alabama]* demanded the yeas and nays; which were not ordered, and the bill was passed.

The title of the bill was agreed to.

Mr. Miles *[South Carolina]* moved to reconsider the vote by which the bill was passed.

The motion was lost.

Journal of the Senate [Feb. 2, 1864] p. 655

TUESDAY, February 2, 1864

Open Session.

A message from the House of Representatives, by Mr. Dalton *[Assistant Clerk of House of Representatives]*:

Mr. President: The Speaker of the House of Representatives having signed sundry enrolled bills and an enrolled joint resolution, I am directed to bring them to the Senate for the signature of their President.

The House of Representatives have passed joint resolutions of the Senate of the following titles:

H.R. 107. An act to increase the efficiency of the Army by the employment of free negroes and slaves in certain cases [capacities].

The bills [H.R. 107] last mentioned were severally read the first and second times and referred to the Committee on Military Affairs.

Journal of the Senate [Feb. 5, 1864] p. 677

FRIDAY, February 5, 1864

Open Session.

Mr. Sparrow *[Louisiana]*, from the Committee on Military Affairs, to whom was referred the bill [H.R. 107] to increase the efficiency of the Army by the employment of free negroes and slaves in certain capacities, reported it without amendment.

On motion by Mr. Sparrow *[Louisiana]*,

Ordered, That the Committee on Military Affairs be discharged from the further consideration of the bill [S. 211] to place free persons of color in the military service of the Confederate States.

Journal of the Senate [Feb. 12, 1864] p. 719

FRIDAY, February 12, 1864

Open Session.

The Senate proceeded, as in Committee of the Whole, to the consideration of the bill [H.R. 107] to increase the efficiency of the Army by the employment of free negroes and slaves in certain capacities.

The Senate proceeded, as in Committee of the Whole, to the consideration of the bill [H.R. 107] to increase the efficiency of the Army by the employment of free negroes and slaves in certain capacities. On motion by Mr. Johnson of Arkansas, that it be transferred to the Secret Legislative Calendar

It was determined in the negative,　　{　　Yeas....................7
　　　　　　　　　　　　　　　　　　　　Nays ...…….........7

On motion by Mr. Johnson of Arkansas,

The yeas and nays being desired by one-fifth of the Senators present,

Those who voted in the affirmative are,

Messrs. Burnett [Kentucky], Caperton [Virginia], Hunter [Virginia], Johnson of Arkansas, Maxwell [Florida], Mitchel [Arkansas], and Orr [South Carolina]

Those who voted in the negative are,

Messrs. Haynes [Tennessee], Hill [Georgia], Johnson of Georgia, Oldham [Texas], Read [Kentucky], Sparrow [Louisiana], and Wigfall [Texas].

On motion by Mr. Orr.

Ordered, That there be a call of the Senate.

The roll having been called, the following-named Senators failed to answer their names:

James M. Baker [Florida], Robert W. Barnwell [South Carolina], A. G. Brown [Mississippi], Clement C. Clay [Alabama], William T. Dortch [North Carolina], Gustavus A. Henry [Tennessee], Robert Jemison, jr., [Alabama], Waldo P. Johnson [Missouri], James Phelan [Mississippi], T. J. Semmes [Louisiana], and William E. Simms [Kentucky].

Mr. Barnwell [South Carolina], Mr. Brown [Mississippi], Mr. Clay [Alabama], Mr. Johnson of Missouri, and Mr. Semmes [Louisiana], were then, on motion, severally excused for nonattendance.

On motion by Mr. Maxwell [Florida], that Mr. Baker [Florida] be excused,

It was determined in the negative.

On motion by Mr. Wigfall [Texas], that all the other absentees be excused,

It was determined in the negative.

Other Senators then appearing,

On motion by Mr. Clark [Missouri],

Whereupon,

The Senate resumed, as in Committee of the Whole, the consideration of the bill [H.R. 107] last mentioned; and on motion by Mr. Johnson of Arkansas,

Ordered, That the further consideration thereof be postponed to and made the special order for to-morrow at half past 11 o'clock, and that it be printed.

On motion by Mr. Oldham *[Texas],*

The Senate resolved into executive session.

Journal of the Senate [Feb. 13, 1864] p. 730

SATURDAY, February 13, 1864

Open Session.

The Senate resumed, as in Committee of the Whole, the consideration of the bill [H.R. 107] to increase the efficiency of the Army by the employment of free negroes and slaves in certain capacities; and

On motion by Mr. Johnson of Arkansas,

Ordered, That it be transferred to the Secret Legislative Calendar.

Journal of the Senate [Feb. 13, 1864] p. 740-741

SATURDAY, February 13, 1864

Secret Session

The Senate resumed, as in Committee of the Whole, the consideration of the bill (H.R. 107) to increase the efficiency of the Army by the employment of free negroes and slaves in certain capacities.

On motion by Mr. Mitchel *[Arkansas],* to amend the bill by inserting after "War," section 1 line 12, "or the commanding general of the Trans-Mississippi Department,"

It was determined in the affirmative.

On motion by Mr. Mitchel *[Arkansas],* to amend the bill by inserting after "War," section 1 line 18, "or the commanding general of the Trans-Mississippi Department,"

It was determined in the affirmative.

On motion by Mr. Jemison *[Alabama]*, to amend the bill by striking out the words," such wages as may be agreed upon with said owners for their use and service, " section 2, lines 8, 9, and 10, and inserting "eleven dollars per month each,"

It was determined in the negative.

On motion by Mr. Hunter *[Virginia]*, to amend the bill by striking out the third section thereof,

It was determined in the negative.

On motion by Mr. Mitchel *[Arkansas]*, to amend the bill by inserting at the end of the third section the words

Care being taken to allow in each case a credit for all slaves who have been already impressed and who are still in service, or have died or been lost while in service,

Mr. Maxwell *[Florida]*, demanded the question; which was seconded, and

The question being then put on agreeing to the amendment proposed by Mr. Mitchel *[Arkansas]*,

It was determined in the affirmative.

On motion by Mr. Hill *[Georgia]*, to reconsider the vote on agreeing to the amendment proposed by Mr. Mitchel *[Arkansas]*,

Mr. Maxwell *[Florida]* demanded the question; which was seconded, and
The question being then put on agreeing to the motion to reconsider,

It was determined in the affirmative.

The amendment proposed by Mr. Mitchel *[Arkansas]* being again under consideration,

On motion by Mr. Phelan *[Mississippi]*, to amend the same by inserting after "slaves who" the word "may" and by inserting after "impressed" the words "under this act,"

Mr. Maxwell *[Florida]* demanded the question; which was seconded, and

The question being put on agreeing to the amendment proposed by Mr. Phelan to the amendment proposed by Mr. Mitchel *[Arkansas]*,

It was determined in the affirmative.

On the question to agree to the amendment proposed by Mr. Mitchel *[Arkansas]*, as amended,

It was determined in the affirmative.

On motion by Mr. Jamison *[Alabama]*, to amend the bill by inserting at the end of the third section:

And all impressments under this act shall be taken in equal ratio from all owners in the same locality, city, county, or district.

It was determined in the affirmative.

No further amendment being proposed, the bill was reported to the Senate and the amendments were concurred in.

Ordered, That the amendments be engrossed and the bill read third time.

The said bill as amended was read a third time.

Resolved, That it pass with amendments.

Ordered, That the Secretary request the concurrence of the House of Representatives in the amendments.

Journal of the House of Representatives [Feb. 13, 1864] p. 815-816

FIFTY-EIGHTH DAY - SATURDAY, February 13, 1864

Open Session.

A message was received from the Senate, by Mr. Nash *[South Carolina]*, their Secretary, as follows, to wit:

Mr. Speaker: the Senate have passed, with amendments, a bill of this House [H.R. 107] to increase the efficiency of the Army by the employment of free negroes and slaves in certain capacities; in which amendments I am directed to request the concurrence of this House.

Mr. Miles *[South Carolina]* moved to postpone the unfinished business for the purpose of taking up for consideration the bill just returned from the Senate; which motion prevailed.

Mr. Hilton *[Florida]* moved that the rules be suspended for that purpose; which motion also prevailed, and the amendments of the Senate were read and concurred in as follows, viz:

1. In section 1, line 12, after the words "Secretary of War," insert "or the commanding general of the Trans-Mississippi Department.'

2. In section 1, line 18, after the words "Secretary of War," insert "or the commanding general of the Trans-Mississippi Department."

3. At the end of the third section add "Care being taken to allow in each case a credit for all slaves who have been already impressed under this act and who are still in service, or have died or been lost while in service, and all impressments under this act shall be taken in equal ratio from all owners in the same locality, city, county, or district."

The House then, on motion of Mr. Hilton *[Florida]*, resolved itself into secret session...

Journal of the House of Representatives [Feb. 16, 1864] p. 835

SIXTIETH DAY - TUESDAY, February 16, 1864

Open Session.

Mr. Elliott *[Kentucky]*, from the Committee on Enrolled Bills, reported as correctly enrolled bills of the following titles:

H.R. 107. An act to increase the efficiency of the Army by the employment of free negroes and slaves in certain capacities;...

Journal of the Senate [Feb. 16, 1864] p. 769

TUESDAY, February 16, 1864

Secret Session

A message from the House of Representatives by Mr. Dalton *[Assistant Clerk of House of Representatives]*:

Mr. President: The House of Representatives have agreed to the amendments of the Senate to the bill [H.R. 107] to increase the efficiency of the Army by the employment of free negroes and slaves in certain capacities.

The Speaker of the House of Representatives having signed an enrolled bill, I am directed to bring to the Senate for the signature of their President.

Mr. Caperton *[Virginia]* from the committee [Military Affairs], reported that they had examined and found truly enrolled

A bill [H.R. 107] to increase the efficiency of the Army by the employment of free negroes and slaves in certain capacities.

The President pro tempore having signed the enrolled bill last reported to have been examined, it was delivered to the Secretary of the Senate and by him forthwith presented to the President of the Confederate States for his approval.

Journal of the House of Representatives [Feb. 17, 1864] p. 863

SIXTY-FIRST DAY - WEDNESDAY, February 17, 1864

Open Session.

The following messages were received from the President, by Mr. Burton N. Harrison, his Private Secretary:

Mr. Speaker: The President has this day signed the following joint resolutions:

H.R. 107 An act to increase the efficiency of the Army by the employment of free negroes and slaves in certain capacities;...

Very respectfully, your obedient servant,

BURTON N. HARRISON,
Private Secretary

Journal of the Senate [Feb. 17, 1864] p. 793-794

WEDNESDAY, February 17, 1864

Open Session.

A message from the House of Representatives by Mr. Dalton *[Assistant Clerk of House of Representatives]:*

The President of the Confederate States has notified the House of Representatives that on the 13th instant he approved and signed the following acts:

H.R. 107 An act to increase the efficiency of the Army by the employment of free negroes and slaves in certain capacities;

HR 49

A Bill to be entitled an Act to amend an Act entitled "an Act to increase the efficiency of the Army by the employment of free negroes and slaves in certain capacities approved February 17, 1864," & to repeal an Act entitled "an Act for the enlistment of cooks in the Army," approved April 21st, 1862.

Section 1. <u>The Congress of the Confederate States of America do enact</u>, that the act to increase the efficiency of the Army, by the employment of free negroes and slaves in certain capacities, approved February 17th, 1864, to be amended that it shall be the duty of the Secretary of War where employed one hundred thousand slaves, as provided in said act, as so many should be necessary, to work upon fortifications, or in Government works, for the production or preparation of materials of War, or in military hospitals, or as teamsters, drivers, laborers in the Commissary and Quartermaster's Departments, and as cooks. While engaged in the performances of such duties said slaves shall receive rations and clothing, and their owners be entitled to compensation at the rate of six dollars per month for each slave so employed.

Sec. 2. That the cooks to be employed under the first section of this Act shall not exceed one for every ten privates, musicians, and now commissioned officers on duty and said slaves shall be required to perform all the duties incident to cooks, under such rules and regulations as may be prescribed by the Secretary of War.

Sec. 3. That an Act for the enlistment of cooks in the Army, approved April 21st, 1862, be and the same, is here by, repealed.

The Bill was postponed on June 14, 1864 and placed upon the Calendar.

FIFTH DAY - FRIDAY, May 6, 1864

Open Session.

Mr. Bell *[Georgia]* introduced

A bill "to compensate the owners of slaves in certain cases therein mentioned;" which was read a first and second time and referred to the Committee on Claims...

Mr. Orr *[Mississippi]* introduced

A bill "to amend an act entitled 'An act to increase the efficiency of the Army by employment of free negroes and slaves in certain capacities,' approved February seventeenth, eighteen hundred and sixty-four, and to repeal an act for the enlistment of cooks in the Army, approved April twenty-first, eighteen hundred and sixty-two;" which was read a first and second time, referred to the Committee on Military Affairs, and ordered to be printed.

Journal of the House of Representatives [June 14, 1864] p. 241

THIRTY-EIGHTH DAY - TUESDAY, June 14, 1864

Open Session.

Mr. Chambers *[Mississippi]*, from the same committee [Military Affairs], to whom had been referred

A bill [H.R. 49] " to amend an act entitled 'An act to increase the efficiency of the Army by employment of free negroes and slaves in certain capacities,' approved February seventeenth, eighteen hundred and sixty-four, and to repeal an act for the enlistment of cooks in the Army, approved April twenty-first, eighteen hundred and sixty-two," reported back the same with the recommendation that it do not pass.

The bill was postponed and placed upon the Calendar.

Conscript Office
Richmond, September 19, 1864
Capt. C. B. Duffield,
Assistant Adjutant – Gen[eral], Bureau of Conscription

Capt[ain]: the orders for the enrollment and assignment of free negroes have been carried out as effectually as could be done under the circumstances. Many deserted and otherwise evaded the officers. This class, like absconding men from the Army and those liable to conscription, required to be forced into service by an active and efficient guard. General Orders, No. 26, current series, has withdrawn all the assistance which could be relied on, and not one in twenty "light-duty" men can be made efficient as a guard. These remarks are made preliminary to a report which I desire to submit upon several communications referred to this office recently, but which will be returned with report and explanations for the information of the several military bureaus.

For the want of efficient and informed officers and the required number of clerks, report and consolidate returns cannot be made as promptly as desired, and for that reason it will be some time before a complete return of the enrollment and assignment of free negroes is made; but Bureau is assured that no time will be spared in forwarding promptly all returns due from the office. Upon a general examination of the returns of the enrolling officers it is manifest that all the labor of this which could well be has been withdrawn from the agricultural districts.

The Niter and Mining Bureau desires every one that can be found. Col[onel] Corley, chief quartermasters Army of Northern Virginia, calls for 500, and the Engineer Bureau makes a requisition for a large force on the line of the Richmond and Danville and South Side Railroad roads. Gen[eral] Walker, commanding the defenses on the Richmond and Danville Railroad, also call for assistance from this class. The officers of the Quartermaster's Department collecting forage in the Valley have received assistance, but are demanding more. Maj[or] J. G. Paxton, in charge of extensive operations for the Quartermaster's Department at Lynchburg and in the Piedmont counties, is asking for aid. All the demands are pressing and of the most vital importance, and the number required by the officers making the requisition for them approximates, if it does not exceed, the whole number of free negroes within the military lines of the prescribed ages. I have deem it advisable to submit these facts, in order that the Bureau may be informed of the impossibility of supplying the existing demands, and I would further respectfully suggest, if it meets the approbation of the superintendent, that the statements herein contained may be submitted to the War Department or the bureaus requiring labor. I have already replied to Gen[eral] Walker and to the local quartermasters, but suppose the Engineer Bureau and the chief quartermaster of the Army of Northern Virginia are not informed.

Enrolling officers will be instructed to continued without any abatement of zeal or effort to forward every man of every class for duty, but I regret to say, for want of responsible guards, I am apprehensive many will elude their vigilance.

Attention is respectfully invited to the enclosed copy of circular issued from this office September 7, requiring full and accurate returns from enrolling officers of the disposition made of this class of person; also a copy of instructions to enrolling officers to meet, if possible, the requisitions of Gen[eral] Gilmer.

I am captain, very respectfully, your obedient servant,

J. C. Shields
Lieut[enant] Col[onel] Commanding

Conscript Office
Richmond, September 7, 1864

I. You will send in at once a full perfect list of all male free negroes who have been enrolled in your district up to the 1st of September by medical board, and when and where assigned; if unassigned; state reason. Receipts for these assignments must accompany this report unless already sent in. Many officers have failed to make any report whatever of this enrollment, or else have made it very imperfectly, and it will be impossible for an intelligible return to be sent up from this office unless district officers will give this order their special attention.

II. A separate report is likewise required of all negro slaves who have been impressed up to 1st September, with descriptive lists and receipts, owners name and residence.

By order of Lieut[enant] Col[onel] J. C. Shields, commandant:

Jas. H. Binford
Lieut[enant] and Adjutant

[To District Officers]

Quartermaster's Department
Gordonsville, September 12, 1864.
Col[onel] John C. Porter:
[through Maj[or] W. B. Richards.]

I have been informed that there are a number of free negroes now in Culpeper liable to conscription, and who are kept out merely by applications for detail, made by some of their friends in Culpeper. These applications of course are only intended to delay the execution of the law, and are not even expected to be granted. And being without anything like a competent force to carry on the work necessary to same the large amount of Government forage thrown on my hands, and unable to procure negroes other than by impressment, I respectfully request that you send me an order upon Lieut[enant] William C. Graves, enrolling officer for Culpeper, for the same.

I am, very respectfully, your obedient servant,

Eustace Gibson
Capt[ain] and Assistant Quartermaster

Quartermaster's Officer
Gordonsville, September 12, 1864.

Capt[ain] Gibson has charge of forage department here. His duties are very heavy. I am unable to supply him with labor in consequence of the desertion of free negroes recently supplies[d] to me.

W. B. Richards, Jr.,
Maj[or] and Post Quartermaster

Enrolling Office, Eight[h] District
Orange Court-House, September 14, 1864

Respectfully referred to the commandant to know if the free negroes of Culpeper, if there be any liable to duty, can be turned over to Capt[ain] Gibson.

J. C. Porter,
Col[onel] and Enrolling Officer Eight[h] District.

Conscript Office,
Richmond, September 20, 1864.

Respectfully referred to the Bureau of Conscription.

This application under instructions of the Bureau can be disposed of at this office.

The necessity of this labor in Culpeper and other counties recently coming again into our military lines to enable the Quartermaster's Department to collect forage presents reasons as urgent as the necessity made apparent in Col[onel] Corley's application to secure fuel for the same army for which the forage is intended. After securing the forage a transfer of the force to obtain fuel would be judicious, but it is believed that nearly all will desert if transferred from their own sections.

Unless otherwise instructed I will turn them over for a limited time to the Quartermaster's Department for the collection of forage in the section referred to.

J. C. Shields,
Lieut[enant]-Col[onel] Commanding

Conscript Office
Richmond, Va., September 19, 1864.
Lieut[enant] J. E. Heath,
Enrolling Officer Fourth Congressional District:

Lieut[enant]: The commandant directs that you furnish this office with an immediate report in compliance with Circular No. 60, current series, from this office, and that you report any free negroes in your district not yet assigned to Capt[ain] W. G. Bender, Engineer Corps, at High Brigade, South Side Railroad descriptive list and taking receipts, to be forwarded to this office.

I am, very respectfully, &c.,
M. B. Langhorne,
Lieut[enant] and Acting Adjutant

Conscript Office,
Richmond, Va., September 19, 1864.
Capt[ain] R. S. Henley,
Enrolling Officer Fifth Congressional District:

Capt[ain]: The commandant directs that you furnish this office with an immediate report in compliance with Circular No. 60, current series, from this office, and that you report any free negroes in your district you assigned to Lieut[enant] J. D. Hunter, Engineer Bureau, at Wolf Trap Station, Richmond and Danville Railroad, furnishing descriptive list and taking receipts, to be forwarded to this office.

I am, very respectfully,
M. B. Langhorne,
Lieut[enant] and Acting Adjutant

Confederate States of America, War Department, Engineer Bureau,
Richmond Va., September 14, 1864

Hon[orable] J. A. Seddon,
Secretary of War, Richmond:

Sir: I have the honor to make the following statement and recommendations thereof for your consideration and action:

Capt[ain] W. G. Bender, Engineers, in charge of the defenses of the Richmond and Danville and South Side Railroads, reports great deficiency of labor on the works now progressing at and near the various brigades on those roads, and particularly on the fortifications at the High Bridge over the Appomattox River, and the Banister River brigade. At the former there are only some thirty negroes, all free and with that force it would require four months to complete the works contemplated at that point. At the latter point there will be, after the 15th of the present month, only about twenty-five free negroes. This Bureau attaches much importance to the defensive works along that line of railroad, and would respectfully urge the necessity of pressing them forward to completion.

Capt[ain] Bender, the engineer in charge, is informed that there is a number of free negroes still in the counties adjoining the points to be fortified, and is very desirous of securing their services on the works. I therefore have the honor to request that the Bureau of Conscription be directed to conscribe for this purpose the free negroes liable to enrollment from nine counties named herein, and that they be assigned to labor as follows, to wit: Those from counties of Appomattox, Prince Edward, Amelia, Buckingham and Cumberland, to be ordered to report to Capt[ain] W. G. Bender, Engineers, or to T. M. Hewitt, assistant engineer at High Brigade. Those from Charlotte, Lunenburg, Mecklenburg, and Halifax to report to Lieut[enant] J. D. Hunter, Engineers, at Wolf Trap Station, Banister River. If the labor of the free negroes liable to conscription in those counties can be obtained at will, to a great extent, insure the speedy completion of the defenses at those points.

I would also respectfully request, should the foregoing meet your approval, that the enrolling officers who conscribe the free negroes be directed to furnish to each negro at the time of enrollment a descriptive list, filled out in the usual form; this is desired in order to obviate much difficulty which continually arises in determining the pay and allowances due to these negroes. It will enable the officer under whose charge they labor to give to each, when he is dismissed, a statement showing up to what time they have been paid and what allowances they have received, for the information of those under whom they may next serve; this to be deposited in the hands of the officer in charge, to be returned by him at the expiration of time of service, with payments made and clothing issued endorsed on each.

Very respectfully, your obedient servant,

J. F. Gilmer, Maj[or] - Gen[eral] and Chief Engineer Bureau.

September 14, 1864
Conscription Bureau

The recommendations of this letter are approved and will be carried out. To every negro enrolled a descriptive list should be given by the officer and he enjoined to keep as necessary to enable him to receive his pay.

J.A.S. [J. A. Seddon]

Bureau of Conscription
Richmond, September 16, 1864

Respectfully referred to Lieut[enant]-Col[onel] for attention in compliance with the e[i]ndorsement of the Secretary of War.

By order of Gen[eral] Preston:

Thomas Pinckney,
Acting Assistant Adjutant-Gen[eral]

Conscript Office,
Richmond, September 20, 1864

Respectfully returned to the Bureau of Conscription.

In a communication forwarded to the Bureau yesterday will be found all the information which can be given, and will enable Gen[eral] Gilmer to see that but a limited amount of labor can be procured from this class. The order of the Hon[orable] Secretary of War has been communicated to the proper officer, as will appear by enclosures in the communication referred to.

J. C. Shields,
Lieut[enant] -Col[onel] Commanding

FIRST DAY - MONDAY, November 7, 1864

Open Session.

...The employment of slaves for service with the army as teamsters or cooks, or in the way of work upon fortifications, or in the Government workshops, or in hospitals, and other similar duties, was authorized by the act of 17th February last, and provision was made for their impressment to a number not exceeding 20,000, if it should be found impracticable to obtain them by contract with the owners. The law contemplated the hiring only of the labor of these slaves and imposed on the Government the liability to pay for the value of such as might be lost to the owners from casualties resulting from their employment in the service.

This act has produced less result than was anticipated, and further provision is required to render it efficacious. But my present purpose is to invite your consideration to the propriety of a radical modification in the theory of the law.

Viewed merely as property, and therefore as the subject of impressment, the service or labor of the slave has been frequently claimed for short periods in the construction of defensive works. The slave, however, bears another relation to the State -- that of a person. The law of last February contemplates only the relation of the slave to the master and limits the impressment to a certain term of service. But for the purposes enumerated in the act, instruction in the manner of encamping, marching, and parking trains is needful, so even in this limited employment length of service adds greatly to the value of the negro's labor. Hazard is also encountered in all the positions to which negroes can be assigned for service with the Army, and the duties required of them demand loyalty and zeal. In this aspect the relation of person predominates so far as to render it doubtful whether the private right of property can consistently and beneficially be continued, and it would seem proper to acquire for the public service the entire property in the labor of the slave and to pay therefor due compensation, rather than to impress his labor for short terms; and this more especially as the effect of the present law would vest this entire property in all cases where the slave might be recaptured after compensation for his loss had been paid to the private owner. Whenever the entire property in the service of a slave is thus acquired by the Government, the question is presented by what tenure he should be held. Should he be retained in servitude, or should his emancipation be held out to him as a reward for faithful service, or should it be granted at once on the promise of such service, and if emancipated, what action should be taken to secure for the freedman the permission of the State from which he was drawn to reside within its limits after the close of his public service? The permission would doubtless be more readily accorded as a reward for past faithful service, and a double motive for zealous discharge of duty would thus be offered to those employed by the Government--their freedom and the gratification of the local attachment which is so marked a characteristic of the negro, and forms so powerful an incentive to his action. The policy of engaging to liberate the negro on his discharge after service faithfully rendered seems to me preferable to that of granting immediate manumission or that of retaining him in servitude. If this policy should recommend itself to the judgment of Congress, it is suggested that, in addition to the duties heretofore performed by the slave, he might be advantageously employed as pioneer and engineer laborer; and in that event that the number should be augmented to 40,000.

Beyond this limit and these employments it does not seem to me desirable, under existing circumstances, to go. A broad moral distinction exists between the use of slaves as soldiers in the defense of their homes and the incitement of the same persons to insurrection against their masters. The one is justifiable, if necessary, the other is iniquitous and unworthy of a civilized people; and such is the judgement of all writers on public law, as well as that expressed and insisted on by our enemies in all wars prior to that now waged against us. By none have the practices of which they are now guilty been denounced with greater severity than by themselves in the two wars with Great Britain in the last and in the present century; and in the Declaration of Independence of 1776, when enumeration was made of the wrongs which justified the revolt from Great Britain, the climax of atrocity was deemed to be reached only when the English monarch was denounced as having "excited domestic insurrections amongst us."

The subject is to be viewed by us, therefore, solely in the light of policy and our social economy. When so regarded, I must dissent from those who advise a general levy and arming of the slaves for the duty of soldiers. Until our white population shall prove insufficient for the armies we require and can afford to keep in the field, to employ as a soldier the negro, who has merely been trained to labor, and as a laborer the white man accustomed from his youth to the use of firearms would scarcely be deemed wise or advantageous by any, and this is the question now before us. But should the alternative ever be presented of subjugation or of the employment of the slave as a soldier, there seems no reason to doubt what should then be our decision. Whether our view embrace what would, in so extreme a case, be the sum of misery entailed by the dominion of the enemy, or be restricted solely to the effect upon the welfare and happiness of the negro population themselves, the result would be the same.

The appalling demoralization, suffering, disease, and death which have been caused by partially substituting the invaders' system of police for the kind relation previously subsisting between the master and slave have been a sufficient demonstration that external interference with our institution of domestic slavery is productive of evil only. If the subject involved no other consideration than the mere right of property, the sacrifices heretofore made by our people have been such as to permit no doubt of their readiness to surrender every possession in order to secure their independence. But the social and political question, which is exclusively under the control of the several States, has a far wider and more enduring importance than that of pecuniary interest. In its manifold phases it embraces the stability if our republican institutions, resting on the actual political equality of all its citizens, and includes the fulfillment of the task which has been so happily begun--that of improving the condition and Christianizing the Africans who have, by the will of Providence, been placed in our charge. Comparing the results of our own experience with those of the experiments of others who have borne similar relations to the African race, the people of the several States of the Confederacy have abundant reason to be satisfied with the past and to use the greatest circumspection in determining their course. These considerations, however, are rather applicable to the improbable contingency of our need of resorting to this element of resistance than to our present condition. If the recommendation above made for the training of 40,000 negroes for the service indicated should meet your approval, it is certain that even this limited number by their preparatory training in intermediate duties, would form a more valuable reserve force, in case of urgency, than threefold their number suddenly called from field labor, while a fresh levy could, to a certain extent, supply their places in the special service for which they are now employed.

The regular annual reports of the Attorney-General, the Secretary of the Navy, and the Postmaster-General are appended, and give ample information relative to the condition of the respective departments. They contain suggestions for legislative provisions required to remedy such defects in the existing laws as have been disclosed by experience, but none of so general or important a character as to require that I should do more than recommend them to your favorable consideration.

The disposition of this Government for a peaceful solution of the issues which the enemy has referred to the arbitrament of arms has been too often manifested and is too well known to need new assurances. But while it is true that individuals and parties in the United States have indicated a desire to substitute reason for force, and by negotiation to stop the further sacrifice of human life, and to arrest the calamities which now afflict both countries, the authorities who control the Government of our enemies have too often and too clearly expressed their resolution to make no peace except on terms of our unconditional submission and degradation, to leave us any hope of the cessation of hostilities until the delusion of their ability to conquer us is dispelled. Among those who are already disposed for peace, many are actuated by principle and by disapproval and abhorrence of the iniquitous warfare that their Government is waging, while others are moved by the conviction that is no longer to the interest of the United States to continue a struggle in which success is unattainable. Whenever this fast-growing conviction shall have taken firm root in the minds of a majority of the Northern-people, there will be produced that willingness to negotiate for peace which is now confined to our side. Peace is manifestly impossible unless desired by both parties to this war, and the disposition for it among our enemies will be best and most certainly evoked by the demonstration on our part of ability and unshaken determination to defend our rights and to hold no earthly price too dear for their purchase. Whenever there shall be on the part of our enemies a desire for peace there will be no difficulty in finding means by which negotiation can be opened; but it is obvious that no agency can be called into action until this desire shall be mutual. When that contingency shall happen, the Government to which is confided the treaty-making power can be at no loss for means adapted to accomplish so desirable an end.

In the hope that the day will soon be reached when, under Divine favor, these States may be allowed to enter on their former peaceful pursuits and to develop the abundant natural resources with which they are blessed, let us, then, resolutely continue to devote our untied and unimpaired energies to the defense of our homes, our lives, and our liberties. This is the true path to peace. Let us tread it with confidence in the assured result.

JEFFERSON DAVIS
RICHMOND, VA, *November 7, 1864.*

MONDAY, November 7, 1864

Open Session.

...The employment of slaves for service with the army as teamsters or cooks, or in the way of work upon fortifications, or in the Government workshops, or in hospitals, and other similar duties, was authorized by the act of 17th February last, and provision was made for their impressment to a number not exceeding 20,000, if it should be found impracticable to obtain them by contract with the owners. The law contemplated the hiring only of the labor of these slaves and imposed on the Government the liability to pay for the value of such as might be lost to the owners from casualties resulting from their employment in the service.

This act has produced less result than was anticipated, and further provision is required to render it efficacious. But my present purpose is to invite your consideration to the propriety of a radical modification in the theory of the law.

Viewed merely as property, and therefore as the subject of impressment, the service or labor of the slave has been frequently claimed for short periods in the construction of defensive works. The slave, however, bears another relation to the State -- that of a person. The law of last February contemplates only the relation of the slave to the master and limits the impressment to a certain term of service. But for the purposes enumerated in the act, instruction in the manner of encamping, marching, and parking trains is needful, so even in this limited employment length of service adds greatly to the value of the negro's labor. Hazard is also encountered in all the positions to which negroes can be assigned for service with the Army, and the duties required of them demand loyalty and zeal. In this aspect the relation of person predominates so far as to render it doubtful whether the private right of property can consistently and beneficially be continued, and it would seem proper to acquire for the public service the entire property in the labor of the slave and to pay therefor due compensation, rather than to impress his labor for short terms; and this more especially as the effect of the present law would vest this entire property in all cases where the slave might be recaptured after compensation for his loss had been paid to the private owner. Whenever the entire property in the service of a slave is thus acquired by the Government, the question is presented by what tenure he should be held. Should he be retained in servitude, or should his emancipation be held out to him as a reward for faithful service, or should it be granted at once on the promise of such service, and if emancipated, what action should be taken to secure for the freedman the permission of the State from which he was drawn to reside within its limits after the close of his public service? The permission would doubtless be more readily accorded as a reward for past faithful service, and a double motive for zealous discharge of duty would thus be offered to those employed by the Government--their freedom and the gratification of the local attachment which is so marked a characteristic of the negro, and forms so powerful an incentive to his action. The policy of engaging to liberate the negro on his discharge after service faithfully rendered seems to me preferable to that of granting immediate manumission or that of retaining him in servitude. If this policy should recommend itself to the judgment of Congress, it is suggested that, in addition to the duties heretofore performed by the slave, he might be advantageously employed as pioneer and engineer laborer; and in that event that the number should be augmented to 40,000.

Beyond this limit and these employments it does not seem to me desirable, under existing circumstances, to go. A broad moral distinction exists between the use of slaves as soldiers in the defense of their homes and the incitement of the same persons to insurrection against their masters. The one is justifiable, if necessary, the other is iniquitous and unworthy of a civilized people; and such is the judgement of all writers on public law, as well as that expressed and insisted on by our enemies in all wars prior to that now waged against us. By none have the practices of which they are now guilty been denounced with greater severity than by themselves in the two wars with Great Britain in the last and in the present century; and in the Declaration of Independence of 1776, when enumeration was made of the wrongs which justified the revolt from Great Britain, the climax of atrocity was deemed to be reached only when the English monarch was denounced as having "excited domestic insurrections amongst us."

The subject is to be viewed by us, therefore, solely in the light of policy and our social economy. When so regarded, I must dissent from those who advise a general levy and arming of the slaves for the duty of soldiers. Until our white population shall prove insufficient for the armies we require and can afford to keep in the field, to employ as a soldier the negro, who has merely been trained to labor, and as a laborer the white man accustomed from his youth to the use of firearms would scarcely be deemed wise or advantageous by any, and this is the question now before us. But should the alternative ever be presented of subjugation or of the employment of the slave as a soldier, there seems no reason to doubt what should then be our decision. Whether our view embrace what would, in so extreme a case, be the sum of misery entailed by the dominion of the enemy, or be restricted solely to the effect upon the welfare and happiness of the negro population themselves, the result would be the same.

The appalling demoralization, suffering, disease, and death which have been caused by partially substituting the invaders' system of police for the kind relation previously subsisting between the master and slave have been a sufficient demonstration that external interference with our institution of domestic slavery is productive of evil only. If the subject involved no other consideration than the mere right of property, the sacrifices heretofore made by our people have been such as to permit no doubt of their readiness to surrender every possession in order to secure their independence. But the social and political question, which is exclusively under the control of the several States, has a far wider and more enduring importance than that of pecuniary interest. In its manifold phases it embraces the stability if our republican institutions, resting on the actual political equality of all its citizens, and includes the fulfillment of the task which has been so happily begun--that of improving the condition and Christianizing the Africans who have, by the will of Providence, been placed in our charge. Comparing the results of our own experience with those of the experiments of others who have borne similar relations to the African race, the people of the several States of the Confederacy have abundant reason to be satisfied with the past and to use the greatest circumspection in determining their course. These considerations, however, are rather applicable to the improbable contingency of our need of resorting to this element of resistance than to our present condition. If the recommendation above made for the training of 40,000 negroes for the service indicated should meet your approval, it is certain that even this limited number by their preparatory training in intermediate duties, would form a more valuable reserve force, in case of urgency, than threefold their number suddenly called from field labor, while a fresh levy could, to a certain extent, supply their places in the special service for which they are now employed.

The regular annual reports of the Attorney-General, the Secretary of the Navy, and the Postmaster-General are appended, and give ample information relative to the condition of the respective departments. They contain suggestions for legislative provisions required to remedy such defects in the existing laws as have been disclosed by experience, but none of so general or important a character as to require that I should do more than recommend them to your favorable consideration.

The disposition of this Government for a peaceful solution of the issues which the enemy has referred to the arbitrament of arms has been too often manifested and is too well known to need new assurances. But while it is true that individuals and parties in the United States have indicated a desire to substitute reason for force, and by negotiation to stop the further sacrifice of human life, and to arrest the calamities which now afflict both countries, the authorities who control the Government of our enemies have too often and too clearly expressed their resolution to make no peace except on terms of our unconditional submission and degradation, to leave us any hope of the cessation of hostilities until the delusion of their ability to conquer us is dispelled. Among those who are already disposed for peace, many are actuated by principle and by disapproval and abhorrence of the iniquitous warfare that their Government is waging, while others are moved by the conviction that is no longer to the interest of the United States to continue a struggle in which success is unattainable. Whenever this fast-growing conviction shall have taken firm root in the minds of a majority of the Northern-people, there will be produced that willingness to negotiate for peace which is now confined to our side. Peace is manifestly impossible unless desired by both parties to this war, and the disposition for it among our enemies will be best and most certainly evoked by the demonstration on our part of ability and unshaken determination to defend our rights and to hold no earthly price too dear for their purchase. Whenever there shall be on the part of our enemies a desire for peace there will be no difficulty in finding means by which negotiation can be opened; but it is obvious that no agency can be called into action until this desire shall be mutual. When that contingency shall happen, the Government to which is confided the treaty-making power can be at no loss for means adapted to accomplish so desirable an end.

In the hope that the day will soon be reached when, under Divine favor, these States may be allowed to enter on their former peaceful pursuits and to develop the abundant natural resources with which they are blessed, let us, then, resolutely continue to devote our untied and unimpaired energies to the defense of our homes, our lives, and our liberties. This is the true path to peace. Let us tread it with confidence in the assured result.

JEFFERSON DAVIS
RICHMOND, VA, *November 7, 1864.*

The message was read.

On motion by **Mr. Orr** *[South Carolina],*

Ordered, That it be laid upon the table and printed.

On motion by **Mr. Orr** *[South Carolina],*

Ordered, That so much of the President's message as relates to foreign affairs be referred to the Committee on Naval Affairs; that so much as relates to the finances be referred to the Committee on Finance, and that so much as relates to military affairs be referred to the Committee on Military Affairs.

Journal of the House of Representatives [Nov. 9, 1864] p. 263-264

THIRD DAY - WEDNESDAY, November 9, 1864

Open Session.

Mr. Wickham *[Virginia]* introduced

A bill "to amend an act to increase the efficiency of the Army by the employment of free negroes and slaves in certain capacities,' approved February seventeenth, eighteen hundred and sixty-four;" which was read a first and second time and referred to the Committee on Military Affairs.

Journal of the House of Representatives [Nov. 9, 1864] p. 264-265

THIRD DAY - WEDNESDAY, November 9, 1864

Open Session.

Mr. Villeré *[Louisiana]* introduced

A bill "to amend an act entitled 'an Act to increase the efficiency of the Army by the employment of free negroes and slaves in certain capacities;' " which was read a first and second time and referred to the Committee on Military Affairs.

Journal of the House of Representatives [Nov. 9, 1864] p. 265

THIRD DAY - WEDNESDAY, November 9, 1864

Open Session.

Mr. Swan *[Tennessee]* offered the following resolution; which was adopted, viz:

Resolved, That the Committee on Military Affairs be instructed to inquire into the expediency of providing by law for the certain removal, to points within our military lines, of all able-bodied adult male negroes, as the necessities of the war may constrain the abandonment of territory to the enemy; and that the committee report by bill or otherwise.

Journal of the Senate [Nov. 18, 1864] p. 270

FRIDAY, November 18, 1864.

Open Session.

Mr. Brown *[Mississippi]* submitted the following resolution; which was considered and agreed to:

Resolved, That the Committee on Military Affairs be instructed to inquire whether military officers in command of departments have authority, under existing laws, to impress negroes, wagons, teams, etc., for the purpose of building or repairing railroads belong to private companies; and if not, what legislation is necessary to restrain such military officers within reasonable and proper limits in this regard.

Journal of the Senate [Nov. 22, 1864] p. 282

FRIDAY, November 22, 1864.

Open Session.

Mr. Henry *[Tennessee]* from the Committee on Military Affairs, reported

A bill [S. 109] to amend an act entitled "An Act to increase the efficiency of the Army by the employment of free negroes and slaves in certain capacities," approved February 17, 1864;

Which was read the first and second times and ordered to be placed upon the Calendar and printed.

[SENATE BILL, No. 109]

SENATE, November 22, 1864.--Read first and second times and ordered to be placed upon the calendar and printed.

[By Mr. Henry *[Tennessee]*, from the Committee on Military Affairs]

AN ACT

To amend An Act entitled, "An act to increase the efficiency of the army by employing free negroes and slaves in certain capacities," approved February 17, 1864.

SECTION 1. The Congress of the Confederate States of America do enact, That the first section of said act be so amended as to increase the compensation given to the free negroes and other free persons of color named in said section to eighteen dollars per month.

Sec. 2. That the second section of said act be so amended as to authorize the Secretary of War to employ, for all the purposes named in the first session of said act, forty thousand slaves, instead of twenty thousand, as therein provided.

Sec. 3. That the third section of said act be so amended as to authorize the Secretary of War to impress forty thousand slaves in case he shall be unable to procure their services or hire as therein provided.

Sec. 4. That the fourth section of said act be amended by adding thereto, that after free negroes are impressed, in making impressments of slaves, those not engaged in agriculture, manufacturing, and mechanical pursuits, shall be first impressed, and in case there shall be then by any deficiency, further impressments of slaves shall be made by taking them from those persons who have fifteen or more able-bodied field hands between sixteen and fifty years of age.

Journal of the Senate [Nov. 24, 1864] p. 288

THURSDAY, November 24, 1864.

Open Session.

The Senate proceeded, as in Committee of the Whole, to the consideration of the bill [S.109] to amend an act entitled "An act to increase the efficiency of the Army by the employment of free negroes and slaves in certain capacities," approved by February 17, 1864; and

On motion by Mr. Caperton *[Virginia]*,

Ordered, That the further consideration thereof be postponed until to-morrow.

Journal of the Senate [Nov. 25, 1864] p. 292

FRIDAY, November 25, 1864.

Open Session.

The Senate resumed, as in Committee of the Whole, the consideration of the bill [S. 109] to amend an act entitled, "An act to increase the efficiency of the Army by the employment of free negroes and slaves in certain capacities," approved February 17, 1864; and

On motion by Mr. Caperton *[Virginia]*,

Ordered, That the further consideration thereof be postponed until to-morrow.

Journal of the Senate [Nov. 28, 1864] p. 295

MONDAY, November 28, 1864.

Open Session.

The Senate resumed, as in Committee of the Whole, the consideration of the bill [S. 109] to amend an act entitled, "An act to increase the efficiency of the Army by the employment of free negroes and slaves in certain capacities," approved February 17, 1864; and

On motion by Mr. Caperton *[Virginia]*, to amend the bill by inserting at the end of the second section the following proviso:

Provided, That the slaves so impressed shall not be employed for any other than the purposes contemplated by this and previous laws,

It was determined in the affirmative.

On motion by Mr. Garland *[Arkansas]*, to amend the bill by inserting at the end of the second section the following additional proviso:

Provided further, That under no circumstances shall the Secretary of War be allowed to keep in service more than forty thousand slaves for the purposes indicated in this act,

It was determined in the negative.

On motion by Mr. Semmes *[Louisiana]*,

Ordered, That the further consideration of the bill be postponed until to-morrow.

On motion by Mr. Caperton *[Virginia]*,

The Senate resolved into secret legislative session.

The doors having been opened,

On motion by Mr. Graham *[North Carolina]*,

The Senate adjourned.

Journal of the Senate [Nov. 29, 1864] p. 297

TUESDAY, November 29, 1864.

Open Session.

The Senate resumed, as in Committee of the Whole, the consideration of the bill [S. 109] to amend an act entitled, "An act to increase the efficiency of the Army by the employment of free negroes and slaves in certain capacities," approved February 17, 1864; and

On motion by Mr. Sparrow *[Louisiana]*,

Ordered, That it be recommitted to the Committee on Military Affairs.

FRIDAY, December 2, 1864.

Open Session.

Mr. Garland *[Arkansas],* (by leave) introduced

A bill [S. 129] to amend an act entitled "An act to increase the efficiency of the Army by the employment of free negroes and slaves in certain capacities," approved February 17, 1864; Which was read the first and second times and referred to the Committee on Military Affairs.

AMENDMENT

To Senate Bill [S. 129] to provide for the employment of free negroes and slaves to work upon fortifications, and to perform other labor connected with the defenses of the country.

The Committee recommend the following amendments:

Strike out in the 5th, 6th and 7th lines, 2d Section, the words "not to exceed thirty thousand in the States east of the Mississippi river, and ten thousand in the States west of the Mississippi river."

Insert in the 10th line 2d Section, after "upon," the words "not to exceed eighteen dollars [$18] per month."

Strike out in the 7th, 8th, 9th and 10th lines, Section 3d, the words "not at any time to exceed thirty thousand in the States east of the Mississippi river, and ten thousand in the States west of the Mississippi river."

Strike out in the 4th Section, the words beginning with "but when the slaves," in the 13th line, and ending with "states," in 19th line, and insert,

"But no such slaves shall be taken from any owner or estate when one-half of the male slaves between the ages of eighteen and forty-five, belong to such owner or estate, shall have absconded to the enemy or been abducted by them."

Strike out the last proviso in the 4th Section, beginning with the 27th line, and insert:

"*Provided,* The Secretary of War shall be authorized to exempt from the operations of this Act, any county, parish or district, or parts thereof, in which he may be satisfied that the labor of the slaves therein is indispensable to the production of grain, and provisions for the support of soldiers' families and non-producers in such county, parish or district; and the Secretary of War may exempt from impressment, slaves necessarily employed on works of internal improvement of importance to the common defense. But nothing contained in this proviso to diminish the quota of slaves in any State authorized to be impressed under the provisions of this Act."

Insert after Section 4:

"Sec. 5. If any slave is now held for service who is not liable thereto under the provisions of this Act, such slave shall be forthwith returned to the owner on demand and proof of the fact."

Insert after the last Section:

"Sec. 8. No slaves shall be hereafter impressed except in pursuance of the provisions of this Act, and any officer who may violate the provisions thereof, shall be court martialed and on conviction cashiered."

TWENTY-THIRD DAY - MONDAY, December 5, 1864

Open Session.

Mr. H. W. Bruce *[Kentucky]* introduced the following resolution; which was adopted viz:

Resolved, That the Committee on Quartermaster's and Commissary Departments be instructed to inquire and report by bill or otherwise whether any additional legislation is necessary to have sufficiently and properly fed the negroes employed by the Government on public works as teamsters and otherwise.

No 96 Resolution of House of Representatives

CSA, Executive Office
Richmond, Va. December 5th, 1864

Hon Secretary of War:
Sir:

I have the honor by direction of the President, to forward for your attention and the proper action, a copy of a Resolution of the House of Representatives of the 2nd inst[ant] as follows:

RESOLUTION

Resolved, That the President be requested to inform this House whether, at this time, there are in the employment of the Confederate States, slaves impressed, exceeding one in five of the male slaves between the ages of eighteen and forty-five, of one owner, and whether any slaves have been impressed and are now in service, on a basis of calculation including female slaves between the ages of eighteen and forty-five, and such employment have been made, by what authority it has been done, and whether the credit directed to be allowed in the employment of slaves by the provisions of the Act of February 17th, 1864, has been allowed."

Very respectfully
Your obedient servant
Burton N. Harrison
Private Secretary
[Secretary to the President]

TUESDAY, December 6, 1864.

Open Session.

Mr. Sparrow *[Louisiana],* from the Committee on Military Affairs, reported

A bill [S. 129] to provide for the employment of free negroes and slaves to work upon fortifications and perform other labor connected with the defenses of the country;

which was read the first and second times and ordered to be placed upon the Calendar and printed.

[Senate Bill, No. 129.]

SENATE, December 6, 1864 -- Read first and second times and ordered to be placed upon the calendar and printed.

[By Mr. Sparrow *[Louisiana]*, from the Committee on Military Affairs]

A BILL

To provide for the employment of free negroes and slaves to work upon fortifications and perform other labor connected with the defen[c]ses of the country.

Whereas, The efficiency of the army is at times greatly diminished by the withdrawal from the ranks of soldiers to perform labor and duties which can as well be done by free negroes and slaves--

SECTION 1. The Congress of the Confederate States of America do enact, That all free male negroes between the ages of eighteen and fifty years shall be held liable to perform any labor, or discharge any duties with the army, or in connection with the military defen[c]ses of the country, such as working upon fortifications, producing and preparing materials of war, building and repairing roads and bridges, and doing other work usually done by engineer troops and pontoneirs, acting as cooks, teamsters, stewards and waiters in military hospitals, or other labor which may be required or prescribed by the Secretary of War or the General commanding the trans-Mississippi department, from time to time. And said free negroes, whilst thus engaged, shall receive rations and clothing, under such regulations as the Secretary of War may prescribe, and shall receive pay at the rate of eighteen dollars per month.

Sec. 2. That the Secretary of War and the General commanding the trans-Mississippi department, are each authorized to employ, for the duties like those named in the first section of this act, as many male negro slaves, between the ages of eighteen and forty-five years, not to exceed thirty thousand in the States east of the Mississippi river, and ten thousand in the States west of the Mississippi river, as the wants of the service may require. And the said slaves, whilst so employed, shall be furnished rations and clothing as provided in the preceding section, and the owners paid such hire for their services as may be agreed upon; and in the event of the loss of any slave whilst so employed, by the act of the enemy or by escape to the enemy, or by wounds or death inflicted by the enemy, or by disease contracted whilst in any service required of said slaves, and by reason of said service, then the owners thereof, respectively, shall be entitled to receive the full value of such slaves, to be ascertained and fixed by agreement at the time said slaves are so hired, under rules to be prescribed by the Secretary of War.

Sec. 3. That whenever the Secretary of War, or the General commanding the trans-Mississippi department, shall be unable to procure the services of slaves by hiring them, as above provided, in sufficient numbers, then it shall be lawful for the said secretary or general to order the impressment, and to impress as many male slaves, within the ages named in the second section of this act, and for the purposes and uses above stated, not at any time to exceed thirty thousand in the States east of the Mississippi river, and ten thousand in the States west of the Mississippi river, as may be necessary:

Provided, That slaves so impressed shall, whilst in the Government employment, receive the same clothing and rations allowed to slaves hired from their owners, and in the event of their loss or death in the manner, or from the causes, above stated, their value shall be estimated and fixed as provided by the law regulating impressments and paid as in the case of slaves hired from their owners, and the value of the hire of said slaves shall be fixed in like manner.

Sec. 4. That the Secretary of War and the General commanding the trans-Mississippi department shall, in ordering the impressment of slaves, regulate the same as far as practicable, so that slaves shall be taken from each State in proportion to the number liable to impressment therein under this act, but not more than one in every five male slaves within the said ages of eighteen and forty-five years, shall be taken from any one owner if said slaves are employed by said owner or his lessee uniformly in agriculture or in mechanical pursuits, nor where an owner has but one male slave within said ages shall said slave be impressed, and all impressments under this act shall, as far as practicable, be taken in equal ratio from all owners in the same locality, city, county, or district.

Sec. 5. Duplicate rolls shall be prepared of all the slaves hired or impressed under this act, which shall contain a description of the slaves, the names and residences of the owners; and a statement of the value and rate of hire of the slaves at the date they are hired or impressed, one of which rolls shall, in the States east of the Mississippi river be forwarded to the Secretary of War, and in those west of the Mississippi river to the headquarters of the General commanding that department and the other roll shall be sent to the General commanding the army where said slaves may be employed, and the officer having charge of said slaves, or of the work upon which they may be engaged shall have a copy of said roll and shall regularly enter thereon the nature of the labor or duties in which said slaves are engaged, and any changes which may be made therein, and of the absence, sickness, or death of any of said slaves and make monthly returns thereof to the General commanding the army where said slaves are employed, who shall transmit the same to the Secretary of War or to the commanding General in the trans-Mississippi department, as the case may be.

Sec. 6. That all laws or parts of laws providing for the hiring or impressment of slaves be, and the same are hereby, repealed, except so far as they may provide for regulating and fixing in case of impressment the value of said slaves or the value of their services.

Journal of the Senate [Dec. 8, 1864] p. 326

THURSDAY, December 8, 1864.

Open Session.

Mr. Sparrow *[Louisiana]*, from the Committee on Military Affairs, to whom was referred the bill [S. 109] to amend an act entitled "an act to increase the efficiency of the Army by the employment of free negroes and slaves in certain capacities," approved February 17, 1864, reported it with the recommendation that it ought not to pass.

Journal of the Senate [Dec. 9, 1864] p. 330-331

FRIDAY, December 9, 1864.

Open Session.

The Senate proceeded, as in Committee of the Whole, to the consideration of bill [S. 129] to provide for the employment of free negroes and slaves to work upon fortifications and perform other labor connected with the defenses of the country; and

On motion by Sparrow *[Louisiana]*,

Ordered, That the further consideration thereof be postponed to and made the special order for Monday next, at half past 12 o'clock.

Mr. Hunter *[Virginia]* (by leave) introduced

A bill [S. 133] to regulate the impressment of slaves in the State of Virginia;
which was read the first and second times and referred to the Committee on Military Affairs.

Ordered, That the bill be printed.

The Senate resumed, as in Committee of the Whole, the consideration of the bill [S.109] to amend an act entitled "An act to increase the efficiency of the Army by employment of free negroes and slaves in certain capacities," approved February 17, 1864; and

On motion by Mr. Sparrow *[Louisiana]*,

Ordered, That the further consideration thereof be postponed indefinitely.

On motion by Mr. Semmes *[Louisiana]*,

The Senate resolved into secret legislative session.
The doors having been opened,
On motion by Mr. Barnwell *[South Carolina]*,
The Senate adjourned.

SENATE, December 9, 1864 -- Read first and second times and referred to Committee on Military Affairs and ordered to be printed.

[By Mr. Hunter *[Virginia]*, by leave.]

A BILL

To regulate the impressment of slaves in the State of Virginia.

Whereas, by the act entitled "An act to increase the efficiency of the army by employment of free negroes and slaves in certain capacities," approved February 17, 1864, the Secretary of War is authorized to impress slaves "according to laws regulating impressment of slaves in other cases;" and whereas the general impressment law, approved March 26, 1863, enacted that "when slaves are impressed by the Confederate Government to labor on fortifications or other public works, the impressment shall be made by said Government according to the rules and regulations provided in the laws of the State wherein they are impressed;" and whereas, the State of Virginia, by a law in regard to the impressment of slaves "to labor on fortifications and other public works," passed March 13, 1863, enacted that the Governor might exempt the counties which had lost so a large portion of their slaves as materially to effect their agriculture products, and also such counties as he may deem it expedient to exempt, "on account of their geographical position, or contiguity to the public enemy," and provided for the exemption from such impressment of the slaves of persons who had "lost one-third part of their slaves liable to work on the public works;" and whereas, the wishes of the State of Virginia are thus expressed in regard to the impressment of slaves within her borders, and it is the declared policy of the Government of the Confederate States to respect the wishes of the several States in executing their laws for the impressment of slaves in those States; now therefore---

SECTION 1. *The Congress of the Confederate States of America do enact,* That, in the State of Virginia, where any county or corporation shall prove to the satisfaction of the Governor, that it has lost one-third of its male slaves between the ages of eighteen and fifty-five years, or, where any individual shall prove, to the satisfaction of the county or corporation court, in said county or corporation, that he or she, or the estates of minors or decedents under their management, have suffered such a loss as aforesaid, then the said counties or individuals shall be exempted from all impressment of their slaves.

Sec. 2. That no slaves shall be impressed in any county in the said State of Virginia, which the Governor may deem it expedient to exempt on account of their geographical position or contiguity to the public enemy.

Sec. 3. If slaves have already been impressed who would have been exempted under the operation of this act; had it then been in force, they shall be returned to their owners, if demanded by them.

MONDAY, December 12, 1864.

Open Session.

The Senate resumed, as in Committee of the Whole, the consideration of bill [S. 129] to provide for the employment of free negroes and slaves to work upon fortifications and perform other labor connected with the defenses of the country.

On motion by Mr. Hunter *[Virginia],* to amend the bill by inserting at the end of the fourth section the following:

But when the slaves in any locality, or of any person or persons, have been or shall be exempted by the laws or regulations of any State from impressment to labor on the fortifications or other public works of the Confederate States, then the said slaves shall not be impressed for any purpose whatever by the authorities of the Confederate States: *Provided, however,* That nothing herein contained shall be so construed as to exempt any State from furnishing its fair quota of slaves for the purposes herein specified, and according to the provisions of this act,

It was determined in the affirmative.

On motion by Mr. Sparrow *[Louisiana],* to amend the bill by inserting at the end of the fourth section the following proviso:

Provided further, That in each case care be taken to allow each owner a credit for all male slaves between the ages aforesaid heretofore impressed, or impressed under this act, or hired to the Government, who are still in service, or who may have died or been lost while in service,

It was determined in the affirmative.

On motion by Mr. Garland *[Arkansas],* to amend the bill by inserting after "district," section 4, line 23, the following:

And in case the laws of the States provide for contributions of slaves to the public service, the Secretary of War and the general commanding the Trans-Mississippi Department shall conform to the rules prescribed in those laws, as far as practicable, for the apportionment of the contribution among the owners of slaves; and if the governors of the States will undertake to fulfill the requisition to be made upon any State, the Secretary of War shall proceed to collect the quota by means of such requisition: *Provided, however,* That if from any cause the contribution be not supplied within the term of thirty days from the date of the same, the Secretary of War may proceed to collect the number unsupplied by impressments, to be made by such Confederate officers or agents as he may appoint for that purpose, having reference in such impressments to the principle of equality before specified, and to securing the industrial pursuits of the community from embarrassment,

It was determined in the negative.

On motion by Mr. Graham *[North Carolina]*, to amend the bill by inserting at the end of the fourth section the following proviso:

Provided further, That all slaves impressed as hereinbefore provided shall be held at labor and service as aforesaid for a term not more than twelve months at any one time, except with the consent of the owner,

It was determined in the affirmative.

No further amendment being made, the bill was reported to the Senate and the amendments were concurred in.

Ordered, That the bill be engrossed and read a third time.

The said bill was read the third time.

Resolved, That it pass, and that the title thereof be as aforesaid.

Ordered, That the Secretary request concurrence of the House of Representatives therein.

Journal of the Senate [Dec. 13, 1864] p. 341-342

TUESDAY, December 13, 1864.

Open Session.

On motion Mr. Walker *[Alabama]*, the vote on passing the bill [S. 129] to provide for the employment of free negroes and slaves to work upon fortifications and perform other labor connected with the defenses of the country was reconsidered.

On motion by Mr. Walker *[Alabama]*, the votes by which the bill was ordered to its engrossment and third reading was also reconsidered.

The Senate resumed, as in Committee of the Whole, the consideration of the said bill.

On motion by Mr. Walker *[Alabama]*, to reconsider the vote on agreeing to the following amendment proposed to the bill by Mr. Graham *[North Carolina]*, to wit:

At the end of the fourth section insert the following proviso:

Provided further, That all slaves impressed as hereinbefore provided shall be held at labor and service as aforesaid for a term not more than twelve months at any one time, except with the consent of the owner.

It was determined in the affirmative.

The Senate resumed the consideration of the said amendment; and

On the question to agree thereto,

It was determined in the negative.

On motion by Mr. Watson *[Mississippi]*, to amend the bill by inserting at the end of the fourth section the following proviso, viz:

Provided further, That if the governor of any State shall certify to the Secretary of War or the commanding general of the Trans-Mississippi Department, that slaves can not be impressed in any locality, county, district, parish or city in said State without great detriment to said locality, county, district, parish, or city, then the quota of such locality, county, district, parish, or city shall be impressed from other portions of such State,

It was determined in the affirmative.

The bill having been further amended on the motion of Mr. Sparrow *[Louisiana]*, it was reported to the Senate and the amendments were concurred in.

Ordered, That the bill be engrossed and read a third time.

Resolved, That it pass, and that the title thereof be as aforesaid.

Ordered, That the Secretary request the concurrence of the House of Representatives therein.

Journal of the House of Representatives [Dec. 14, 1864] p. 357

THIRTY -FIRST DAY - WEDNESDAY, December 14, 1864

Open Session.

A message was received from the Senate, by Mr. Nash, *[South Carolina]*, their Secretary; which is as follows, viz:

Mr. Speaker: The Senate have passed a bill and joint resolutions of the following titles, viz:

S. 129. An act to provide for the employment of free negroes and slaves to work upon fortifications and perform other labor connected with the defenses of the country;...

In which I am directed to ask the concurrence of this House.

THIRTY -SECOND DAY - THURSDAY, December 15, 1864

Open Session.

...Also, a Senate bill [S. 129] "to provide for the employment of free negroes and slaves to work upon fortifications and perform other labor connected with the defenses of the country;" which was read a first and second time.

Mr. Montague *[Virginia]* moved to suspend the rule requiring the bill to be referred to a committee.

Two-thirds not voting in favor of the suspension, the motion was lost.

Mr. Baldwin *[Virginia]* moved that the bill be referred to the Special Committee on Impressments.

Mr. Wickham *[Virginia]* moved to amend the motion of Mr. Baldwin *[Virginia]* by referring the bill to the Committee on Military Affairs.

The amendment was concurred in, and the motion as amended was agreed to.

So the bill was referred to the Committee on Military Affairs and ordered to be printed.

Journal of the Senate [Dec. 19, 1864] p. 378

MONDAY, December 19, 1864.

Open Session.

Mr. Sparrow *[Louisiana]* from the Committee on Military Affairs, to whom was referred the bill [S. 125] to amend an act entitled "An act to increase the efficiency of the Army by the employment of free negroes and slaves in certain capacities," approved February 17, 1864, reported it with the recommendation that it ought not to pass.

The Senate proceeded, as in Committee of the Whole, the consideration of the said bill; and

On motion by Mr. Sparrow *[Louisiana]*,

Ordered, That the further consideration thereof be postponed indefinitely.

FORTY-FIRST DAY - WEDNESDAY, December 28, 1864

Open Session.

Mr. Gholson *[Virginia]* offered the following resolution:

Resolved, That whilst this House has unshaken confidence in the integrity, patriotism, and capacity of our Chief Magistrate, yet it can not approve the recommendation contained in his last message to Congress, that the Government purchase such slaves as may be needed for "teamsters, cooks, to work upon fortifications, or in the Government workshops, or in hospitals, and other similar duties," and engage "to liberate them on their discharge after service faithfully rendered."

On motion of Mr. Clark *[Missouri],* the resolution was referred to the Committee on Military Affairs.

Journal of the House of Representatives [Jan. 13, 1865] p. 454

FIFTY-FIFTH DAY - FRIDAY, January 13, 1865

Open Session.

Mr. Miles *[South Carolina],* from the Committee on Military Affairs, reported back, with amendments, a Senate bill "in relation to the employment of slaves to work on fortification:" which was ordered to be printed, and made the special order after existing special orders are disposed of.

Journal of the House of Representatives [Jan. 20, 1865] p. 470

SIXTY-FIRST DAY - FRIDAY, January 20, 1865

Open Session.

Mr. Miller *[Virginia]* submitted the following resolution; which was adopted:

Resolved, That it be referred to the Committee on Ways and Means to inquire into the expediency of increasing the pay of free negroes impressed into the service of the Confederate States.

SIXTY-SEVENTH DAY - FRIDAY, January 27, 1865

Open Session.

Mr. Garland *[Arkansas]* moved that the rules be suspended, and that the Senate bill [S. 129] "to provide for the employment of free negroes and slaves to work upon fortifications and perform other labor connected with the defenses of the country" be taken from the Calendar and made the special order for the morning hour.

Mr. Moore *[Kentucky]* demanded the yeas and nays thereon;

Which were ordered,

And recorded as follows, viz: { Yeas..........56
                                                  Nays............5

Yeas: Anderson *[Georgia]*, Batson *[Arkansas]*, Baylor *[Texas]*, Bell *[Georgia]*, Blandford *[Georgia]*, Horatio W. Bruce *[Kentucky]*, Burnett *[Kentucky]*, Carroll *[Arkansas]*, Chambers *[Mississippi]*, Chilton *[Alabama]*, Chrisman *[Kentucky]*, Clopton *[Alabama]*, Cluskey *[Tennessee]*, Colyar *[Tennessee]*, Conrow *[Missouri]*, Cruikshank *[Alabama]*, Dickinson *[Alabama]*, Ewing *[Kentucky]*, Farrow *[South Carolina]*, Foster *[Alabama]*, Fuller *[North Carolina]*, Gaither *[North Carolina]*, Garland *[Arkansas]*, Gholson *[Virginia]*, Gilmer *[North Carolina]*, Gray *[Texas]*, Hanly *[Arkansas]*, Hartridge *[Georgia]*, Holder *[Mississippi]*, Keeble *[Tennessee]*, Lam[p]kin *[Mississippi]*, J. M. Leach *[North Carolina]*, J. T. Leach *[North Carolina]*, Lester *[Georgia]*, Logan *[North Carolina]*, Lyon *[Alabama]*, Machen *[Kentucky]*, McMullin *[Virginia]*, Miles *[South Carolina]*, Miller *[Virginia]*, Montague *[Virginia]*, Moore *[Kentucky]*, Norton *[Missouri]*, Orr *[Mississippi]*, Ramsay *[North Carolina]*, Russell *[Virginia]*, Shewmake *[Georgia]*, Simpson *[South Carolina]*, J. M. Smith *[Georgia]*, W. E. Smith *[Georgia]*, Staples *[Virginia]*, Triplett *[Kentucky]*, Villeré *[Louisiana]*, Wickham *[Virginia]*, Wilkes *[Missouri]*, and Witherspoon *[South Carolina]*.

Nays: Boyce *[South Carolina]*, Herbert *[Texas]*, Johnston *[Virginia]*, Perkins *[Louisiana]*, and Smith *[North Carolina]*.

Two-thirds voting in the affirmative, the rules were suspended.

On motion of Mr. Garland *[Arkansas]*, the bill which had been reported from the Committee on Military Affairs, with sundry amendments, was made the special order for the morning hour, and the House proceeded to its consideration.

Mr. Miles *[South Carolina]* called the question; which was ordered.

The question being on the first amendment of the committee, which is as follows, viz:

Strike out, in the fifth, sixth and seventh lines, second section, the words "not to exceed thirty thousand in the States east of the Mississippi River and ten thousand in the States west of the Mississippi River,"

Mr. J. T. Leach *[North Carolina],* demanded the yeas and nays;
Which were ordered,

And recorded as follows, viz: {   Yeas..........46
                                           Nays..........28 [27]

Yeas: Akin *[Georgia],* Anderson *[Georgia],* Atkins *[Tennessee],* Baylor *[Texas],* Horatio W. Bruce *[Kentucky],* Burnett *[Kentucky],* Carroll *[Arkansas],* Chambers *[Mississippi],* Clark *[Missouri],* Clopton *[Alabama],* Cluskey *[Tennessee],* Conrow *[Missouri],* Dickinson *[Alabama],* Elliott *[Kentucky],* Ewing *[Kentucky],* Farrow *[South Carolina],* Foster *[Alabama],* Gaither *[North Carolina],* Garland *[Arkansas],* Gholson *[Virginia],* Goode *[Virginia],* Gray *[Texas],* Hanly *[Arkansas],* Hartridge *[Georgia],* Hatcher *[Missouri],* Holder *[Mississippi],* Johnston *[Virginia],* Keeble *[Tennessee],* Lyon *[Alabama],* Marshall *[Kentucky],* Miles *[South Carolina],* Montague *[Virginia],* Moore *[Kentucky],* Norton *[Missouri],* Perkins *[Louisiana],* Pugh *[Alabama],* Read *[Kentucky],* Russell *[Virginia],* Shewmake *[Georgia],* Simpson *[South Carolina],* Snead *[Missouri],* Staples *[Virginia],* Triplett *[Kentucky],* Villeré *[Louisiana],* Wilkes *[Missouri],* and Witherspoon *[South Carolina].*

Nays: Baldwin *[Virginia],* Batson *[Arkansas],* Bell *[Georgia],* Blandford *[Georgia],* Boyce *[South Carolina],* Chilton *[Alabama],* Chrisman *[Kentucky],* Colyar *[Tennessee],* Cruikshank *[Alabama],* Darden *[Texas],* Fuller *[North Carolina],* Gilmer *[North Carolina],* Herbert *[Texas],* Lam[p]kin *[Mississippi],* J. M. Leach *[North Carolina],* J. T. Leach *[North Carolina],* Lester *[Georgia],* Logan *[North Carolina],* McMullin *[Virginia],* Orr *[Mississippi],* Ramsay *[North Carolina],* J. M. Smith *[Georgia],* W. E. Smith *[Georgia],* Smith *[North Carolina],* Turner *[North Carolina],* Wickham *[Virginia],* and Mr. Speaker.

So the amendment was agreed to.

Mr. Foster *[Alabama]* submitted to following amendment:

Strike out the word "forty-five," in the second section, and insert in lieu thereof the word "forty."

Mr. Atkins *[Tennessee],* demanded the yeas and nays thereon;
Which were ordered,

And recorded as follows, viz: {   Yeas..........37
                                           Nays..........36

Yeas: Akin *[Georgia],* Bell *[Georgia],* Cluskey *[Tennessee],* Colyar *[Tennessee],* Conrow *[Missouri],* Darden *[Texas],* Ewing *[Kentucky],* Foster *[Alabama],* Fuller *[North Carolina],* Garland *[Arkansas],* Gilmer *[North Carolina],* Gray *[Texas],* Herbert *[Texas],* Lam[p]kin *[Mississippi],* J. M. Leach *[North Carolina],* J. T. Leach *[North Carolina],* Lester *[Georgia],* Logan *[North Carolina],* Machen *[Kentucky],* Marshall *[Kentucky],* Montague *[Virginia],* Norton *[Missouri],* Orr *[Mississippi],* Perkins

[Louisiana], Pugh *[Alabama]*, Ramsay *[North Carolina]*, Russell *[Virginia]*, Simpson *[South Carolina]*, J. M. Smith *[Georgia]*, W. E. Smith *[Georgia]*, Smith *[North Carolina]*, Snead *[Missouri]*, Turner *[North Carolina]*, Villeré *[Louisiana]*, Wickham *[Virginia]*, Wilkes *[Missouri]*, and Mr. Speaker.

Nays: Anderson *[Georgia]*, Atkins *[Tennessee]*, Baldwin *[Virginia]*, Batson *[Arkansas]*, Baylor *[Texas]*, Boyce *[South Carolina]*, Branch *[Texas]*, Horatio W. Bruce *[Kentucky]*, Carroll *[Arkansas]*, Chambers *[Mississippi]*, Chilton *[Alabama]*, Chrisman *[Kentucky]*, Clark *[Missouri]*, Clopton *[Alabama]*, Cruikshank *[Alabama]*, Dickinson *[Alabama]*, Elliott *[Kentucky]*, Farrow *[South Carolina]*, Gaither *[North Carolina]*, Gholson *[Virginia]*, Goode *[Virginia]*, Hanly *[Arkansas]*, Hartridge *[Georgia]*, Hatcher *[Missouri]*, Holder *[Mississippi]*, Johnston *[Virginia]*, Lyon *[Alabama]*, McMullin *[Virginia]*, Miles *[South Carolina]*, Miller *[Virginia]*, Moore *[Kentucky]*, Read *[Kentucky]*, Shewmake *[Georgia]*, Staples *[Virginia]*, Triplett *[Kentucky]*, and Witherspoon *[South Carolina]*.

So the amendment was agreed to.

Mr. Marshall *[Kentucky]* moved to reconsider the vote just taken, and called the question; which was ordered.

The motion was lost.

The question recurring on the second amendment of the committee, which is as follows, viz:

Insert, in tenth line, second section, after the word "upon," the words "not to exceed eighteen dollars per month,"

It was decided in the affirmative,

Mr. Lester *[Georgia]* submitted the following amendment:

Add at end of section 2 the words "and if any of said slaves shall be physically injured whilst so employed, from any of the causes aforesaid, the owner shall receive full compensation for such injury;" which was not agreed to.

Mr. Burnett *[Kentucky]* moved to reconsider the vote by which the second amendment of the committee was agreed to.

The motion was lost.

The morning hour having expired,

On motion of Mr. Miles *[South Carolina]*, the Calendar was postponed, and the House proceeded with the consideration of the bill.

Mr. De Jarnette *[Virginia]* moved that the special order be postponed to enable him to present a memorial.

The motion was lost.

Mr. Conrow *[Missouri]*, called the question; which was ordered.

The question being on the third amendment of the committee, which is as follows, viz:

Strike out, in the seventh, eighth, ninth and tenth [lines], section 3, the words "not at any time to exceed thirty thousand in the States east of the Mississippi River and ten thousand in the States west of the Mississippi River,"

It was decided in the affirmative.

Mr. Miles *[South Carolina]* submitted the following amendment:

Strike out, in section 3, the words, "as may be necessary" and insert in lieu thereof the words "as the wants of the service may require;"

which was agreed to.

Mr. Goode *[Virginia]* submitted the following amendment:

insert after the amendment just adopted the following, viz: "*Provided*, That said impressment shall be made according to the rules and regulations provided in the laws of the State wherein they are impressed; and in the absence of such law, in accordance with which [such] rules and regulations not inconsistent with the provisions of this act as the Secretary of War shall from time to time prescribe."

Mr. Anderson *[Georgia]* called the question; which was ordered.

Mr. Marshall *[Kentucky]* demanded the yeas and nays thereon;

Which were ordered,

And recorded as follows, viz: {   Yeas............62
                                          Nays...........12

Yeas: Akin *[Georgia]*, Anderson *[Georgia]*, Atkins *[Tennessee]*, Baldwin *[Virginia]*, Barksdale *[Mississippi]*, Bell *[Georgia]*, Blandford *[Georgia]*, Boyce *[South Carolina]*, Branch *[Texas]*, Carroll *[Arkansas]*, Chrisman *[Kentucky]*, Clopton *[Alabama]*, Colyar *[Tennessee]*, Conrow *[Missouri]*, Cruikshank *[Alabama]*, Darden *[Texas]*, De Jarnette *[Virginia]*, Dickinson *[Alabama]*, Echols *[Georgia]*, Farrow *[South Carolina]*, Fuller *[North Carolina]*, Gaither *[North Carolina]*, Garland *[Arkansas]*, Gholson *[Virginia]*, Gilmer *[North Carolina]*, Goode *[Virginia]*, Gray *[Texas]*, Hanly *[Arkansas]*, Hatcher *[Missouri]*, Herbert *[Texas]*, Hilton *[Florida]*, Holder *[Mississippi]*, Johnston *[Virginia]*, Lam[p]kin *[Mississippi]*, J. M. Leach *[North Carolina]*, J. T. Leach *[North Carolina]*, Lester *[Georgia]*, Logan *[North Carolina]*, Machen *[Kentucky]*, Marshall *[Kentucky]*, McMullin *[Virginia]*, Menees *[Tennessee]*, Miller *[Virginia]*, Montague *[Virginia]*, Moore *[Kentucky]*, Norton

[Missouri], Orr *[Mississippi]*, Perkins *[Louisiana]*, Pugh *[Alabama]*, Ramsay *[North Carolina]*, Read *[Kentucky]*, Russell *[Virginia]*, Sexton *[Texas]*, Shewmake *[Georgia]*, Simpson *[South Carolina]*, J. M. Smith *[Georgia]*, Snead *[Missouri]*, Triplett *[Kentucky]*, Turner *[North Carolina]*, Wickham *[Virginia]*, Wilkes *[Missouri]*, and Witherspoon *[South Carolina]*.

Nays: Batson *[Arkansas]*, Baylor *[Texas]*, Horatio W. Bruce *[Kentucky]*, Burnett *[Kentucky]*, Dupré *[Louisiana]*, Elliott *[Kentucky]*, Ewing *[Kentucky]*, Hartridge *[Georgia]*, Keeble *[Tennessee]*, Lyon *[Alabama]*, Miles *[South Carolina]*, and W. E. Smith *[Georgia]*.

So the amendment was agreed to.

Mr. Atkins *[Tennessee]* moved to reconsider the vote just taken, and called the question; which was ordered.

The motion was lost.

Mr. Ramsay *[North Carolina]*, submitted the following amendment:

Insert after the amendment just adopted the following: "*Provided*, that said slaves shall not be armed or used as soldiers."

Pending which,

Mr. Chrisman *[Kentucky]* moved that the House resolve itself into secret session.

The motion was lost.

Mr. Marshall *[Kentucky]* moved that the further consideration of the amendment of Mr. Ramsay *[North Carolina]* be had in secret session.

Mr. Ramsay *[North Carolina]* demanded the yeas and the nays thereon;

Which were ordered,

And recorded as follows, viz: {   Yeas............35
                                          Nays...........39

Yeas: Atkins *[Tennessee]*, Barksdale *[Mississippi]*, Baylor *[Texas]*, Blandford *[Georgia]*, Boyce *[South Carolina]*, Bradley *[Kentucky]*, Burnett *[Kentucky]*, Carroll *[Arkansas]*, Chrisman *[Kentucky]*, Colyar *[Tennessee]*, Conrow *[Missouri]*, De Jarnette *[Virginia]*, Dickinson *[Alabama]*, Dupré *[Louisiana]*, Elliott *[Kentucky]*, Ewing *[Kentucky]*, Foster *[Alabama]*, Gray *[Texas]*, Hanly *[Arkansas]*, Hartridge *[Georgia]*, Hatcher *[Missouri]*, Keeble *[Tennessee]*, Lyon *[Alabama]*, Marshall *[Kentucky]*, Menees *[Tennessee]*, Moore *[Kentucky]*, Perkins *[Louisiana]*, Pugh *[Alabama]*, Read *[Kentucky]*, Sexton *[Texas]*, Shewmake *[Georgia]*, Snead *[Missouri]*, Triplett *[Kentucky]*, Villeré *[Louisiana]*, and Wilkes *[Missouri]*.

Nays: Akin *[Georgia]*, Anderson *[Georgia]*, Baldwin *[Virginia]*, Batson *[Arkansas]*, Bell *[Georgia]*, Eli M. Bruce *[Kentucky]*, Horatio W. Bruce *[Kentucky]*, Clark *[Missouri]*, Clopton *[Alabama]*, Cruikshank *[Alabama]*, Darden *[Texas]*, Echols *[Georgia]*, Farrow *[South Carolina]*, Fuller *[North Carolina]*, Gaither *[North Carolina]*, Garland *[Arkansas]*, Gholson *[Virginia]*, Gilmer *[North Carolina]*, Goode *[Virginia]*, Herbert *[Texas]*, Holder *[Mississippi]*, Lam[p]kin *[Mississippi]*, J. M. Leach *[North Carolina]*, J. T. Leach *[North Carolina]*, Lester *[Georgia]*, Logan *[North Carolina]*, Machen *[Kentucky]*, Miles *[South Carolina]*, Montague *[Virginia]*, Norton *[Missouri]*, Ramsay *[North Carolina]*, Russell *[Virginia]*, Simpson *[South Carolina]*, J. M. Smith [Georgia], W. E. Smith *[Georgia]*, Smith *[North Carolina]*, Wickham *[Virginia]*, Witherspoon *[South Carolina]*, and Mr. Speaker.

So the House refused to go into secret session.

After some time spent in debate,

Mr. E. M. Bruce *[Kentucky]* moved that the further consideration of the pending amendment be had in secret session.

Mr. Ramsay *[North Carolina]* demanded the yeas and nays thereon:

Which were ordered,

And recorded as follows, viz: {   Yeas............43
                                     Nays...........29

Yeas: Anderson *[Georgia]*, Atkins *[Tennessee]*, Barksdale *[Mississippi]*, Batson *[Arkansas]*, Baylor *[Texas]*, Blandford *[Georgia]*, Boyce *[South Carolina]*, Bradley *[Kentucky]*, Branch *[Texas]*, Eli M. Bruce *[Kentucky]*, Burnett *[Kentucky]*, Carroll *[Arkansas]*, Chrisman *[Kentucky]*, Colyar *[Tennessee]*, Conrow *[Missouri]*, De Jarnette *[Virginia]*, Dickinson *[Alabama]*, Dupré *[Louisiana]*, Elliott *[Kentucky]*, Ewing *[Kentucky]*, Foster *[Alabama]*, Garland *[Arkansas]*, Gray *[Texas]*, Hanly *[Arkansas]*, Hartridge *[Georgia]*, Hatcher *[Missouri]*, Hilton *[Florida]*, Keeble *[Tennessee]*, Lyon *[Alabama]*, Marshall *[Kentucky]*, Menees *[Tennessee]*, Moore *[Kentucky]*, Norton *[Missouri]*, Perkins *[Louisiana]*, Pugh *[Alabama]*, Read *[Kentucky]*, Sexton *[Texas]*, Shewmake *[Georgia]*, Snead *[Missouri]*, Triplett *[Kentucky]*, Villeré *[Louisiana]*, and Wilkes *[Missouri]*.

Nays: Baldwin *[Virginia]*, Bell *[Georgia]*, Chambers *[Mississippi]*, Clark *[Missouri]*, Clopton *[Alabama]*, Cruikshank *[Alabama]*, Darden *[Texas]*, Echols *[Georgia]*, Fuller *[North Carolina]*, Gholson *[Virginia]*, Gilmer *[North Carolina]*, Goode *[Virginia]*, Holder *[Mississippi]*, Johnston *[Virginia]*, Lam[p]kin *[Mississippi]*, J. M. Leach *[North Carolina]*, J. T. Leach *[North Carolina]*, Logan *[North Carolina]*, Machen *[Kentucky]*, McMullin *[Virginia]*, Miles *[South Carolina]*, Ramsay *[North Carolina]*, Russell *[Virginia]*, Simpson *[South Carolina]*, J. M. Smith *[Georgia]*, W. E. Smith *[Georgia]*, Smith *[North Carolina]*, Turner *[North Carolina]*, and Wickham *[Virginia]*.

So the House resolved itself into secret session; and having spent some time therein, resolved itself [into] open session.

Mr. J. M. Leach *[North Carolina]* submitted the following amendment:

Add the following proviso to the end of the third section: "*Provided further,* That in no event shall any portion of said slaves or free negroes so impressed have arms placed in their hands, or be mustered into the Confederate States service, or be used at any time as soldiers in said service."

Mr. J. M. Leach *[North Carolina]* called the question.

Mr. Marshall *[Kentucky]* demanded the yeas and nays thereon;

Which were ordered,

And recorded as follows, viz: {   Yeas............21
                                            Nays...........48

Yeas: Atkins *[Tennessee]*, Chambers *[Mississippi]*, Chrisman *[Kentucky]*, Clopton *[Alabama]*, Cruikshank *[Alabama]*, Echols *[Georgia]*, Fuller *[North Carolina]*, Garland *[Arkansas]*, Gholson *[Virginia]*, Gilmer *[North Carolina]*, Herbert *[Texas]*, Lam[p]kin *[Mississippi]*, J. M. Leach *[North Carolina]*, J. T. Leach *[North Carolina]*, Logan *[North Carolina]*, Miles *[South Carolina]*, Ramsay *[North Carolina]*, J. M. Smith *[Georgia]*, W. E. Smith *[Georgia]*, Turner *[North Carolina]*, and Wickham *[Virginia]*.

Nays: Akin *[Georgia]*, Baldwin *[Virginia]*, Barksdale *[Mississippi]*, Batson *[Arkansas]*, Baylor *[Texas]*, Bell *[Georgia]*, Blandford *[Georgia]*, Branch *[Texas]*, Horatio W. Bruce *[Kentucky]*, Burnett *[Kentucky]*, Carroll *[Arkansas]*, Chilton *[Alabama]*, Clark *[Missouri]*, Cluskey *[Tennessee]*, Colyar *[Tennessee]*, Conrow *[Missouri]*, Darden *[Texas]*, Dickinson *[Alabama]*, Dupré *[Louisiana]*, Elliott *[Kentucky]*, Ewing *[Kentucky]*, Farrow *[South Carolina]*, Gaither *[North Carolina]*, Goode *[Virginia]*, Gray *[Texas]*, Hatcher *[Missouri]*, Hilton *[Florida]*, Holder *[Mississippi]*, Johnston *[Virginia]*, Keeble *[Tennessee]*, Lester *[Georgia]*, Lyon *[Alabama]*, Machen *[Kentucky]*, Marshall *[Kentucky]*, McMullin *[Virginia]*, Menees *[Tennessee]*, Miller *[Virginia]*, Moore *[Kentucky]*, Orr *[Mississippi]*, Perkins *[Louisiana]*, Read *[Kentucky]*, Russell *[Virginia]*, Sexton *[Texas]*, Simpson *[South Carolina]*, Triplett *[Kentucky]*, Villeré *[Louisiana]*, Wilkes *[Missouri]*, and Witherspoon *[South Carolina]*.

So the question was not ordered.

Mr. Chilton *[Alabama]* moved to lay the amendment on the table.

Mr. Bell *[Georgia]* moved that the House do now adjourn.

The motion to adjourn was lost,

The question recurring on the motion to lay the amendment on the table,

Mr. J. M. Leach *[North Carolina]* demanded the yeas and nays;

Which were ordered,

And recorded as follows, viz: { Yeas............50
                                 Nays..........23

Yeas: Akin *[Georgia]*, Atkins *[Tennessee]*, Baldwin *[Virginia]*, Barksdale *[Mississippi]*, Batson *[Arkansas]*, Baylor *[Texas]*, Bell *[Georgia]*, Blandford *[Georgia]*, Branch *[Texas]*, Horatio W. Bruce *[Kentucky]*, Burnett *[Kentucky]*, Carroll *[Arkansas]*, Chilton *[Alabama]*, Clark *[Missouri]*, Clopton *[Alabama]*, Cluskey *[Tennessee]*, Colyar *[Tennessee]*, Conrow *[Missouri]*, Dickinson *[Alabama]*, Dupré *[Louisiana]*, Elliott *[Kentucky]*, Ewing *[Kentucky]*, Farrow *[South Carolina]*, Gaither *[North Carolina]*, Garland *[Arkansas]*, Gholson *[Virginia]*, Gray *[Texas]*, Hatcher *[Missouri]*, Hilton *[Florida]*, Holder *[Mississippi]*, Johnston *[Virginia]*, Keeble *[Tennessee]*, Lester *[Georgia]*, Lyon *[Alabama]*, Machen *[Kentucky]*, Marshall [*Kentucky]*, Menees *[Tennessee]*, Miller *[Virginia]*, Moore *[Kentucky]*, Norton *[Missouri]*, Read *[Kentucky]*, Russell *[Virginia]*, Sexton *[Texas]*, Shewmake *[Georgia]*, Simpson *[South Carolina]*, Snead *[Missouri]*, Triplett *[Kentucky]*, Villeré *[Louisiana]*, Wilkes *[Missouri]*, and Witherspoon *[South Carolina]*.

Nays: Anderson *[Georgia]*, Chambers *[Mississippi]*, Cruikshank *[Alabama]*, Darden *[Texas]*, Echols *[Georgia]*, Fuller *[North Carolina]*, Gilmer *[North Carolina]*, Goode *[Virginia]*, Herbert *[Texas]*, Lam[p]kin *[Mississippi]*, J. M. Leach *[North Carolina]*, J. T. Leach *[North Carolina]*, Logan *[North Carolina]*, McMullin *[Virginia]*, Miles *[South Carolina]*, Orr *[Mississippi]*, Ramsay *[North Carolina]*, J. M. Smith *[Georgia]*, W. E. Smith *[Georgia]*, Smith *[North Carolina]*, Turner *[North Carolina]*, Wickham *[Virginia]* and Mr. Speaker.

So the motion prevailed.

Mr. Akin *[Georgia]* moved to reconsider the vote just taken.

The motion was lost.

On motion of Mr. Blandford *[Georgia]*,

The House adjourned until 11 o'clock to-morrow.

SIXTY-SEVENTH DAY - FRIDAY, January 27, 1865

Secret Session.

The House being in secret session,

Proceeded to the consideration of the amendment of Mr. Ramsay *[North Carolina]* to the bill [S. 129] "to provide for the employment of free negroes and slaves to work upon fortifications and perform other labor connected with the defenses of the country."

The amendment having been read as follows, viz:

In section 3, after the amendment of Mr. Goode *[Virginia]* [which had been inserted after the word "necessary," in line 10], insert the following: *"Provided,* That said slaves shall not be armed or used as soldiers,"

Mr. Moore *[Kentucky]*, rose to a point of order, viz:

That the amendment of Mr. Ramsey *[North Carolina]* was not in order because it was a proposition different from that under consideration.

Mr. Baldwin *[Virginia]*, in the chair, overruled the point of order.

Mr. Foster *[Alabama]* appealed from the decision of the Chair.

The question was being put,

Shall the decision of the Chair stand as the judgment of the House?

It was decided in the affirmative.

Mr. Atkins *[Tennessee]*, moved to lay the amendment of Mr. Ramsay on the table.

Mr. McMullin *[Virginia]* demanded the yeas and nays thereon;

Which were ordered,

And recorded as follows, viz: {   Yeas............45
                                          Nays...........26

Yeas: Akin *[Georgia]*, Atkins *[Tennessee]*, Baldwin *[Virginia]*, Barksdale *[Mississippi]*, Batson *[Arkansas]*, Baylor *[Texas]*, Bell *[Georgia]*, Blandford *[Georgia]*, Boyce *[South Carolina]*, Bradley

[Kentucky], Branch *[Texas]*, Horatio W. Bruce *[Kentucky]*, Burnett *[Kentucky]*, Carroll *[Arkansas]*, Chambers *[Mississippi]*, Chilton *[Alabama]*, Clark *[Missouri]*, Clopton *[Alabama]*, Cluskey *[Tennessee]*, Conrow *[Missouri]*, Dickinson *[Alabama]*, Dupré *[Louisiana]*, Elliott *[Kentucky]*, Ewing *[Kentucky]*, Gaither *[North Carolina]*, Garland *[Arkansas]*, Gray *[Texas]*, Hatcher *[Missouri]*, Hilton *[Florida]*, Johnston *[Virginia]*, Keeble *[Tennessee]*, Lester *[Georgia]*, Lyon *[Alabama]*, Machen *[Kentucky]*, Marshall *[Kentucky]*, Menees *[Tennessee]*, Miller *[Virginia]*, Moore *[Kentucky]*, Orr *[Mississippi]*, Read *[Kentucky]*, Sexton *[Texas]*, Simpson *[South Carolina]*, Triplett *[Kentucky]*, Villeré *[Louisiana]*, Wilkes *[Missouri]*, and Witherspoon *[South Carolina]*.

Nays: Chrisman *[Kentucky]*, Colyar *[Tennessee]*, Cruikshank *[Alabama]*, Darden *[Texas]*, Farrow *[South Carolina]*, Fuller *[North Carolina]*, Gholson *[Virginia]*, Gilmer *[North Carolina]*, Goode *[Virginia]*, Herbert *[Texas]*, Holder *[Mississippi]*, Lam[p]kin *[Mississippi]*, J. M. Leach *[North Carolina]*, J. T. Leach *[North Carolina]*, Logan *[North Carolina]*, McMullin *[Virginia]*, Miles *[South Carolina]*, Perkins *[Louisiana]*, Ramsay *[North Carolina]*, Russell *[Virginia]*, J. M. Smith *[Georgia]*, W. E. Smith *[Georgia]*, Staples *[Virginia]*, Turner *[North Carolina]*, Wickham *[Virginia]*, and Mr. Speaker.

So the motion to lay on the table prevailed.

Mr. Garland *[Arkansas]*, moved to reconsider the vote just taken, and called the question, which was ordered.

The motion to reconsider was lost.

On motion of Mr. Read *[Kentucky]*,

The House resolved itself into open session.

SIXTY-EIGHTH DAY - SATURDAY, January 28, 1865

Open Session.

The House resumed the consideration of the special order, viz:

The bill [S. 129] "to provide for the employment of free negroes and slaves to work upon fortifications and perform other labor connected with the defenses of the country."

Mr. Shewmake *[Georgia]*, submitted the following amendment:

After the word "the," in line 15, section 3, strike out the words "law regulating impressments" and insert in lieu thereof the words "first section of an act to regulate impressments, passed on the twenty-sixth March, eighteen hundred and sixty-three."

Mr. Shewmake *[Georgia]*, demanded the yeas and nays thereon;
Which were ordered,

And recorded as follows, viz: {   Yeas............43
                                           Nays...........22

Yeas: Akin *[Georgia]*, Anderson *[Georgia]*, Barksdale *[Mississippi]*, Bell *[Georgia]*, Blandford *[Georgia]*, Boyce *[South Carolina]*, Horatio W. Bruce *[Kentucky]*, Carroll *[Arkansas]*, Clopton *[Alabama]*, Cluskey *[Tennessee]*, Colyar *[Tennessee]*, Cruikshank *[Alabama]*, Darden *[Texas]*, De Jarnette *[Virginia]*, Dickinson *[Alabama]*, Echols *[Georgia]*, Foster *[Alabama]*, Fuller *[North Carolina]*, Gaither *[North Carolina]*, Garland *[Arkansas]*, Gholson *[Virginia]*, Gilmer *[North Carolina]*, Goode *[Virginia]*, Hartridge *[Georgia]*, Heiskell *[Tennessee]*, Herbert *[Texas]*, Hilton *[Florida]*, Lam[p]kin *[Mississippi]*, J. M. Leach *[North Carolina]*, J. T. Leach *[North Carolina]*, Lester *[Georgia]*, Logan *[North Carolina]*, Miles *[South Carolina]*, Montague *[Virginia]*, Moore *[Kentucky]*, Ramsay *[North Carolina]*, Shewmake *[Georgia]*, Simpson *[South Carolina]*, J. M. Smith *[Georgia]*, W. E. Smith *[Georgia]*, Smith *[North Carolina]*, Wickham *[Virginia]*, and Witherspoon *[South Carolina]*.

Nays: Baylor *[Texas]*, Burnett *[Kentucky]*, Chilton *[Alabama]*, Chrisman *[Kentucky]*, Clark *[Missouri]*, Conrow *[Missouri]*, Elliott *[Kentucky]*, Ewing *[Kentucky]*, Hanly *[Arkansas]*, Hatcher *[Missouri]*, Johnston *[Virginia]*, Keeble *[Tennessee]*, Lyon *[Alabama]*, Machen *[Kentucky]*, McMullin *[Virginia]*, Norton *[Missouri]*, Perkins *[Louisiana]*, Pugh *[Alabama]*, Snead *[Missouri]*, Staples *[Virginia]*, Triplett *[Kentucky]*, and Turner *[North Carolina]*.

So the amendment was agreed to.

Mr. Anderson *[Georgia]* moved to reconsider the vote just taken, and called the question; which was ordered.

The motion to reconsider was lost.

Mr. Foster *[Alabama]* submitted the following amendment:

In section 4, line 7, strike out the word "forty-five" and insert "forty;"

which was agreed to.

Mr. Miles *[South Carolina]* submitted the following amendment:

In section 4, line 5, strike out the words "number liable to impressment therein" and insert in lieu thereof the words "whole number hired and impressed;"

which was agreed to.

Mr. Miles *[South Carolina]* submitted the following amendment:

In section 4, line 5, after the word "act," insert the words "whether owned by the citizens of the such State or not;"

which was agreed to.

Mr. Colyar *[Tennessee]* submitted the following amendment:

In section 4, lines 8 and 9, strike out the words "if said slaves are employed by said owner or his lessee uniformly in agriculture or in mechanical pursuits."

Mr. Lester *[Georgia]* called the question; which was ordered.

Mr. Foster *[Alabama]* demanded the yeas and nays thereon:

Which was ordered,

And recorded as follows, viz: {   Yeas............50
                                              Nays...........24

Yeas: Akin *[Georgia]*, Anderson *[Georgia]*, Baldwin *[Virginia]*, Barksdale *[Mississippi]*, Baylor *[Texas]*, Bell *[Georgia]*, Blandford *[Georgia]*, Boyce *[South Carolina]*, Bradley *[Kentucky]*, Branch *[Texas]*, Burnett *[Kentucky]*, Chrisman *[Kentucky]*, Clark *[Missouri]*, Cluskey *[Tennessee]*, Colyar *[Tennessee]*, Cruikshank *[Alabama]*, Darden *[Texas]*, Dupré *[Louisiana]*, Ewing *[Kentucky]*, Fuller *[North Carolina]*, Gilmer *[North Carolina]*, Goode *[Virginia]*, Gray *[Texas]*, Hanly *[Arkansas]*, Hatcher *[Missouri]*, Herbert *[Texas]*, Holder *[Mississippi]*, Keeble *[Tennessee]*, Lam[p]kin *[Mississippi]*, J. M. Leach *[North Carolina]*, J. T. Leach *[North Carolina]*, Lester *[Georgia]*, Logan *[North Carolina]*, Machen *[Kentucky]*, Menees *[Tennessee]*, Montague *[Virginia]*, Moore *[Kentucky]*, Murray *[Tennessee]*, Norton *[Missouri]*, Orr *[Mississippi]*, Ramsay *[North Carolina]*, Sexton *[Texas]*, Simpson *[South Carolina]*, Smith *[North Carolina]*, Snead *[Missouri]*, Triplett *[Kentucky]*, Turner *[North Carolina]*, Villeré *[Louisiana]*, Wickham *[Virginia]*, and Wilkes *[Missouri]*.

Nays: Batson *[Arkansas]*, Horatio W. Bruce *[Kentucky]*, Carroll *[Arkansas]*, Chambers *[Mississippi]*, Chilton *[Alabama]*, Clopton *[Alabama]*, Conrow *[Missouri]*, Dickinson *[Alabama]*, Echols *[Georgia]*, Farrow *[South Carolina]*, Foster *[Alabama]*, Gaither *[North Carolina]*, Garland *[Arkansas]*, Gholson *[Virginia]*, Hartridge *[Georgia]*, Johnston *[Virginia]*, Lyon *[Alabama]*, McMullin *[Virginia]*, Miles *[South Carolina]*, Pugh *[Alabama]*, Read *[Kentucky]*, Shewmake *[Georgia]*, J. M. Smith *[Georgia]*, and W. E. Smith *[Georgia]*.

So the amendment was agreed to.

Mr. Colyar *[Tennessee]* moved to reconsider the vote just taken, and called the question; which was ordered.

The motion was lost.

The morning hour having expired,

On motion of Mr. Miles *[South Carolina]*, the Calendar was postponed, and the House proceeded with the consideration of the bill.

Mr. Baldwin *[Virginia]* submitted the following amendment:

In section 4, line 10, strike out the words "but one male slave within said ages, shall said slave" and insert in lieu thereof the words "less than five male slaves within said ages, shall said slave."

Mr. Blandford *[Georgia]*, called the question; which was ordered, and the amendment was agreed to.

The fourth amendment of the committee was read as follows, viz:

In section 4, lines 13 to 19, strike out the words "but when the slaves in any locality or of any person or persons have been or shall be exempted by the laws or regulations of any State from impressment to labor on the fortifications or other public works of the Confederate States, then the said slaves shall not be impressed for any purpose whatever by the authorities of the Confederates States," and insert in lieu thereof the following: "but no such slaves shall be taken from any owner or estate when one-half of the male slaves between the ages of eighteen and forty-five belonging to such owner or estate shall have absconded to the enemy or been abducted by them."

Mr. Garland *[Arkansas]* submitted the following amendment to the amendment of the committee:

Strike out the word "forty-five" and insert "forty;"

which was agreed to.

The question recurring on the amendment of the committee, as amended,

Mr. Anderson *[Georgia]* called the question; which was ordered.

Mr. McMullin *[Virginia]* demanded the yeas and nays thereon;

Which were ordered,

And recorded as follows, viz: {   Yeas..............8
                                                Nays...........60 [61]

Yeas: Anderson *[Georgia]*, Baylor *[Texas]*, De Jarnette *[Virginia]*, Miles *[South Carolina]*, Miller *[Virginia]*, Montague *[Virginia]*, Smith *[North Carolina]*, and Villeré *[Louisiana]*.

Nays: Akin *[Georgia]*, Barksdale *[Mississippi]*, Batson *[Arkansas]*, Bell *[Georgia]*, Blandford *[Georgia]*, Boyce *[South Carolina]*, Bradley *[Kentucky]*, Branch *[Texas]*, Eli M. Bruce *[Kentucky]*, Horatio W. Bruce *[Kentucky]*, Carroll *[Arkansas]*, Chilton *[Alabama]*, Chrisman *[Kentucky]*, Clark *[Missouri]*, Cluskey *[Tennessee]*, Colyar *[Tennessee]*, Conrow *[Missouri]*, Cruikshank *[Alabama]*, Darden *[Texas]*, Dickinson *[Alabama]*, Dupré *[Louisiana]*, Echols *[Georgia]*, Ewing *[Kentucky]*, Farrow *[South Carolina]*, Fuller *[North Carolina]*, Gaither *[North Carolina]*, Garland *[Arkansas]*, Gholson *[Virginia]*, Gilmer *[North Carolina]*, Goode *[Virginia]*, Gray *[Texas]*, Hanly *[Arkansas]*, Hartridge *[Georgia]*, Hatcher *[Missouri]*, Herbert *[Texas]*, Holder *[Mississippi]*, Johnston *[Virginia]*, Keeble *[Tennessee]*, Lam[p]kin *[Mississippi]*, J. M. Leach *[North Carolina]*, J. T. Leach *[North Carolina]*, Logan *[North Carolina]*, Lyon *[Alabama]*, Machen *[Kentucky]*, McMullin *[Virginia]*, Murray *[Tennessee]*, Norton *[Missouri]*, Orr *[Mississippi]*, Perkins *[Louisiana]*, Pugh *[Alabama]*, Ramsay *[North Carolina]*, Read *[Kentucky]*, Shewmake *[Georgia]*, J. M. Smith *[Georgia]*, W. E. Smith *[Georgia]*, Snead *[Missouri]*, Staples *[Virginia]*, Triplett *[Kentucky]*, Turner *[North Carolina]*, Wickham *[Virginia]*, and Wilkes *[Missouri]*.

So the amendment of the committee was rejected.

Mr. Miles *[South Carolina]* submitted the following amendment:

Strike out the words proposed to be stricken out in the amendment just rejected.

Mr. Garland *[Arkansas]* called the question; which was ordered.

Mr. Garland *[Arkansas]* demanded the yeas and nays thereon;

Which was ordered,

And recorded as follows: {   Yeas...........35
                                                Nays...........29

Yeas: Akin *[Georgia]*, Anderson *[Georgia]*, Batson *[Arkansas]*, Blandford *[Georgia]*, Bradley *[Kentucky]*, Burnett *[Kentucky]*, Chilton *[Alabama]*, Clark *[Missouri]*, Clopton *[Alabama]*, Conrow *[Missouri]*, Dickinson *[Alabama]*, Dupré *[Louisiana]*, Elliott *[Kentucky]*, Ewing *[Kentucky]*, Farrow

[South Carolina], Foster [Alabama], Gaither [North Carolina], Gholson [Virginia], Goode [Virginia], Hanly [Arkansas], Johnston [Virginia], Keeble [Tennessee], Lam[p]kin [Mississippi], Machen [Kentucky], Miles [South Carolina], Moore [Kentucky], Orr [Mississippi], Perkins [Louisiana], Pugh [Alabama], Read [Kentucky], Simpson [South Carolina], Snead [Missouri], Triplett [Kentucky], Wilkes [Missouri], and Mr. Speaker.

Nays: Baldwin [Virginia], Boyce [South Carolina], Branch [Texas], Carroll [Arkansas], Colyar [Tennessee], Cruikshank [Alabama], Fuller [North Carolina], Garland [Arkansas], Gilmer [North Carolina], Hartridge [Georgia], Hatcher [Missouri], Herbert [Texas], Hilton [Florida], Holder [Mississippi], J. M. Leach [North Carolina], J. T. Leach [North Carolina], Logan [North Carolina], McMullin [Virginia], Menees [Tennessee], Montague [Virginia], Ramsay [North Carolina], Shewmake [Georgia], J. M. Smith [Georgia], W. E. Smith [Georgia], Smith [North Carolina], Staples [Virginia], Turner [North Carolina], Wickham [Virginia], and Witherspoon [South Carolina].

So the amendment was agreed to.

Mr. Goode [Virginia] submitted the following amendment:

Strike out, in section 4, lines 19, 20, 21, and 22, the following proviso: "Provided, however, That nothing herein contained shall be so construed as exempt any States from furnishing its fair quota of slaves for the purposes herein specified and according to the provisions of this act;"

which was agreed to.

Mr. Fuller [North Carolina] submitted the following amendment:

Insert, in section 4, in lieu of the proviso just stricken out, after word "States," in line 19, the following:

"Provided, That each State shall receive credit in the quota of slaves to be impressed to the full number of free negroes placed in the Army by this act."

Mr. Moore [Kentucky], called the question; which was ordered, and the amendment of Mr. Fuller [North Carolina] was rejected.

The fifth amendment of the committee was read as follows, viz:

Strike out the last proviso in section 4, which reads as follows, viz: "Provided further, That if the governor of any State shall certify to the Secretary of War or the commanding general of the Trans-Mississippi Department that slaves can not be impressed in any locality, county, district, parish, or city in such State without great detriment to such locality, county, district, parish, or city, then the quota of said locality, county, district, parish or city shall be impressed from other portions of said State," and insert in lieu thereof the following, viz: "Provided, The Secretary of War shall be authorized to exempt from the operations of this act any county, parish, or district or parts thereof, in which he may be satisfied that the labor of the slaves therein is indispensable to the production of grain and provisions for the support of soldiers' families and non-producers in such county, parish or district; and the Secretary of War may exempt from impressment slaves necessarily employed on works of internal improvement of importance to the common defense. But nothing contained in this proviso to diminish the quota of slaves in any State authorized to be impressed under the provisions of this act."

Mr. Foster *[Alabama]* called the question; which was ordered.

The amendment of the committee was rejected.

Mr. Perkins *[Louisiana]* submitted the following amendment:

In section 4, line 32, after the word "city," insert the words "can be impressed in another portion of the State without detriment;"

which was not agreed to.

Mr. Dupré *[Louisiana]* moved to reconsider the vote by which the fifth amendment of the committee was rejected, and moved to lay the motion on the table; which latter motion prevailed.

Mr. Gholson *[Virginia]* submitted the following amendment:

Strike out the last proviso in section 4;

which was not agreed to.

Mr. Logan *[North Carolina]* submitted the following amendment:

Add at the end of section 4 the following proviso: *"Provided further,* That impressments shall only be made for one year, and slaves impressed and serving out their time shall not be liable to another impressment until all other slaves liable to impressment shall have been impressed and served for one year.

Mr. Miles *[South Carolina]* called the question; which was ordered.

Mr. Logan *[North Carolina]* demanded the yeas and nays; which was not ordered, and the amendment was rejected.

Mr. Staples *[Virginia]* moved to reconsider the vote by which the amendment of Mr. Goode *[Virginia]*, striking out the first proviso in section 4, was agreed to.

The motion prevailed.

The question recurring on the amendment of Mr. Goode *[Virginia]*,

It was decided in the negative.

Mr. Staples *[Virginia]* submitted the following amendment:

Transfer the first proviso in section 4 to the end of the section:

which was agreed to.

The sixth amendment of the committee was read as follows, viz:

Insert after section 4 the following as an independent section;

"Sec. 5. If any slave is now held for service who is not liable thereto under the provisions of this act, such slave shall be forthwith returned to the owner on demand and proof of the fact."

Mr. Miles *[South Carolina]* called the question; which was ordered, and the amendment was agreed to.

Mr. Blandford *[Georgia]*, submitted the following amendment:

Insert after the section just inserted the following as an independent section:

"Sec. 6. In those States having no law regulating impressments, all impressments made under and by virtue of this act or any existing law shall be made under the direction of some proper and discreet person to be appointed by the President: and such person so appointed shall be over the age of forty-five years and shall reside in the Congressional district where such impressments are to be made, and shall have the rank and pay of a colonel of cavalry, to whom all orders for impressments shall be directed and who shall conduct the same according to law under such rules and regulations as shall be prescribed by the Secretary of War, or by the general commanding the Trans-Mississippi Department, as the case may be."

Mr. Anderson *[Georgia]* called the question; which was ordered.

Mr. Blandford *[Georgia]* demanded the yeas and nays; which were not ordered, and the amendment was lost.

Mr. Smith *[North Carolina]* moved to reconsider the vote just taken.

Mr. Hanly *[Arkansas]* moved that the House adjourn.

The motion was lost.

The question recurring on the motion to reconsider,

Mr. Colyar *[Tennessee]* demanded the yeas and nays;

Which were ordered,

And recorded as follows, viz: {   Yeas............31
Nays...........33

Yeas: Akin *[Georgia]*, Anderson *[Georgia]*, Barksdale *[Mississippi]*, Bell *[Georgia]*, Blandford *[Georgia]*, Cluskey *[Tennessee]*, Colyar *[Tennessee]*, Cruikshank *[Alabama]*, Dupré *[Louisiana]*, Echols *[Georgia]*, Fuller *[North Carolina]*, Gaither *[North Carolina]*, Gilmer *[North Carolina]*, Hatcher *[Mississippi]*, Holder *[Mississippi]*, Keeble *[Tennessee]*, Lam[p]kin *[Mississippi]*, J. M. Leach *[North Carolina]*, J. T. Leach *[North Carolina]*, Lester *[Georgia]*, Logan *[North Carolina]*, McMullin *[Virginia]*, Menees *[Tennessee]*, Miller *[Virginia]*, Murray *[Tennessee]*, Orr *[Mississippi]*, Ramsay *[North Carolina]*, Shewmake *[Georgia]*, Simpson *[South Carolina]*, J. M. Smith *[Georgia]*, W. E. Smith *[Georgia]*, and Smith *[North Carolina]*.

Nays: Batson *[Arkansas]*, Baylor *[Texas]*, Bradley *[Kentucky]*, Carroll *[Arkansas]*, Chambers *[Mississippi]*, Chilton *[Alabama]*, Clark *[Missouri]*, Clopton *[Alabama]*, Conrow *[Missouri]*, Dickinson *[Alabama]*, Ewing *[Kentucky]*, Farrow *[South Carolina]*, Garland *[Arkansas]*, Gholson *[Virginia]*, Goode *[Virginia]*, Gray *[Texas]*, Hanly *[Arkansas]*, Lyon *[Alabama]*, Machen *[Kentucky]*, Miles *[South Carolina]*, Moore *[Kentucky]*, Norton *[Missouri]*, Perkins *[Louisiana]*, Russell *[Virginia]*, Snead *[Missouri]*, Staples *[Virginia]*, Triplett *[Kentucky]*, Turner *[North Carolina]*, Villeré *[Louisiana]*, Wilkes *[Missouri]*, Witherspoon *[South Carolina]*, and Mr. Speaker.

So the motion to reconsider was lost.

Mr. Garland *[Arkansas]* moved the previous question; which was ordered.

The question being on the seventh amendment of the committee, which is as follows, viz:

After the last section insert the following as an independent section:

Sec. 8. No slaves shall be hereafter impressed except in pursuance of the provisions of this act, and any officer who may violate the provisions thereof shall be court-martialed and, on conviction, cashiered."

It was decided in the affirmative.

The question recurring on ordering the bill to be engrossed and read a third time.

It was decided in the affirmative.

The bill having been engrossed and read a third time,

Mr. Hanly *[Arkansas]* called the question; which was ordered.

The question being put,

Shall the bill pass?

It was decided in the affirmative.

Mr. Miles *[South Carolina]* moved to reconsider the vote by which the bill was passed, and called the question; which was ordered.

The motion to reconsider was lost.

On motion of Mr. Orr *[Mississippi]*,

The House adjourned until 11 o'clock to-morrow.

Journal of the Senate [Jan. 30, 1865] p. 506-507

MONDAY, January 30, 1865.

Open Session.

A message from the House of Representative, by Mr. Dalton   *[Assistant Clerk of House of Representatives]*:

Mr. President: The House of Representatives have passed the bill of the Senate [S. 129] to provide for the employment of free negroes and slaves to work upon fortifications and perform other labor connected with the defenses of the country with amendments; in which they request the concurrence of the Senate....

...The Senate proceeded to consider the amendments of the House of Representatives to the bill [S. 129] to provide for the employment of free negroes and slaves to work upon fortifications and perform other labor connected with the defenses of the country; and

Ordered, That they be referred to the Committee on Military Affairs.

Journal of the Senate [Feb. 1, 1865] p. 512

WEDNESDAY, February 1, 1865.

Open Session.

Mr. Burnett *[Kentucky]*, from the Committee on Military Affairs, to whom were referred the amendments of the House of Representatives to the bill [S. 129] to provide for the employment of free negroes and slaves to work upon fortifications and perform other labor connected with the defenses of the country, reported thereon.

Ordered, That the amendments be printed.

THURSDAY, February 2, 1865.

Open Session.

The Senate proceeded to consider the amendments of the House of Representatives to the bill [S. 129] to provide for the employment of free negroes and slaves to work upon fortifications and perform other labor connected with the defenses of the country; and

After debate,

On motion by Mr. Burnett *[Kentucky]*,

The Senate resolved into executive session.

The doors having been opened,

On motion by Mr. Maxwell *[Florida]*,

The Senate adjourned.

Journal of the Senate [Feb. 3, 1865] p. 519-520

FRIDAY, February 3, 1865.

Open Session.

The Senate resumed the consideration of the amendments of the House of Representatives to the bill [S. 129] to provide for the employment of free negroes and slaves to work upon fortifications and perform other labor connected with the defenses of the country.

The first amendment having been agreed to,

On the question to agree to the second amendment, viz: In section 2, line 5, strike out after the word "years," all down to and including the word "river," in line 8,

It was determined in the negative,   {   Yeas..........9
                                                              Nays.......10
On motion by Mr. Graham *[North Carolina]*,

The yeas and nays being desired by one-fifth of the Senators present,

Those who voted in the affirmative are,

Messrs. Brown *[Mississippi]*, Burnett *[Kentucky]*, Dortch *[North Carolina]*, Henry *[Tennessee]*, Johnson *[Missouri]*, Simms *[Kentucky]*, Sparrow *[Louisiana]*, Vest *[Missouri]*, and Watson *[Mississippi]*.

Those who voted in the negative are,

Messrs. Baker *[Florida]*, Caperton *[Virginia]*, Garland *[Arkansas]*, Graham *[North Carolina]*, Haynes *[Tennessee]*, Hill *[Georgia]*, Maxwell *[Florida]*, Orr *[South Carolina]*, Semmes *[Louisiana]*, and Wigfall *[Texas]*.

So the second amendment was disagreed to.

He fifth, seventh, eight, ninth, twelfth, thirteenth, fourteenth, and fifteenth amendments having been agreed to, the sixth amendment agreed to with an amendment, and the third, fourth, tenth, and eleventh amendment disagreed to,

On motion by Mr. Orr *[South Carolina]*, that the vote on disagreeing to the second amendment be reconsidered,

On motion by Mr. Caperton *[Virginia]*,

The Senate resolved into secret legislative session.

The doors having been opened,

On motion by Mr. Orr *[South Carolina]*,

The Senate adjourned.

Journal of the Senate [Feb. 4, 1865] p. 522

SATURDAY, February 4, 1865.

Open Session.

The Senate resumed the consideration of the amendments of the House of Representatives to the bill [S. 129] to provide for the employment of free negroes and slaves to work upon fortifications and perform other labor connected with the defenses of the country.

The question being on agreeing to the motion submitted on yesterday by Mr. Orr *[South Carolina]*, to reconsider the vote on disagreeing to the second amendment, to wit: In section 2, line 5, strike out after the word "years," all down to and including the word "river," in line 8; and

After debate,

On motion by Mr. Garland *[Arkansas]*,

Ordered, That the further consideration thereof be postponed until Monday next.

MONDAY, February 6, 1865.

Open Session.

The Senate resumed the consideration of the amendments of the House of Representatives to the bill [S. 129] to provide for the employment of free negroes and slaves to work upon fortifications and perform other labor connected with the defenses of the country.

On the question to agree to the motion submitted by Mr. Orr *[South Carolina]* on Friday last, to reconsider the vote on disagreeing to the second amendment, to wit: In section 2, line 5, strike out after the word "years," all down to and including the word "river," in line 8,

It was determined in the affirmative,   { Yeas.........12
                                          Nays..........8

On motion by Mr. Graham *[North Carolina]*,

The yeas and the nays being desired by one-fifth of the Senators present,

Those who voted in the affirmative are,

Messrs. Brown *[Mississippi]*, Burnett *[Kentucky]*, Dortch *[North Carolina]*, Henry *[Tennessee]*, Johnson of Missouri, Oldham *[Texas]*, Simms *[Kentucky]*, Sparrow *[Louisiana]*, Vest *[Missouri]*, Walker *[Alabama]*, Watson *[Mississippi]*, and Wigfall *[Texas]*.

Those who voted in the negative are,

Messrs. Baker *[Florida]*, Caperton *[Virginia]*, Graham *[North Carolina]*, Haynes *[Tennessee]*, Hunter *[Virginia]*, Maxwell *[Florida]*, Orr *[South Carolina]*, and Semmes *[Louisiana]*.

The Senate resumed the consideration of said amendment; and

On the question to agree thereto,

It was determined in the affirmative.

On motion by Mr. Sparrow *[Louisiana]*, to reconsider the vote on disagreeing to the fourth amendment, to wit: In line 8, section 3, after the word "stated," strike out all down to and including the word "necessary," in line 11, and insert in lieu thereof the words "as the wants of the service may require,"

It was determined in the affirmative.

The Senate resumed the consideration of the said amendment; and

On the question to agree thereto,

It was determined in the affirmative.

So it was.

Resolved, That the Senate agree to the first, second, fourth, fifth, seventh, eighth, ninth, twelfth, thirteenth, fourteenth, and fifteenth, and disagree to the third, tenth, and eleventh amendments of the House of Representatives to the said bill, and that they agree to the sixth amendment, with an amendment.

Ordered, That the Secretary inform the House of Representatives thereof.

Journal of the Senate [Feb. 7, 1865] p. 526-528

TUESDAY, February 7, 1865.

Open Session.

Mr. Brown *[Mississippi]* having submitted the following resolution for consideration:

Resolved, That the Committee on Military Affairs be instructed to report a bill with the least practicable delay, to take into the military service of the Confederate States a number of negro soldiers, not to exceed two hundred thousand, by voluntary enlistment, with the consent of their owners, or by conscription, as may be found necessary; and that the committee provide in said bill for the emancipation of said negroes in all cases where they prove loyal and true to the end of the war, and for the immediate payment, under proper restrictions, of their full present value to their owners,

On motion by Mr. Maxwell *[Florida]*,

The Senate resolved into secret legislative session for the consideration thereof.

The having been opened, ...

Secret Session.

The Senate proceeded to consider the resolution submitted to-day in open legislative session, by Mr. Brown *[Mississippi]*, instructing the Committee on Military Affairs to report

A bill to take negro soldiers into the military service of the Confederate States, providing for their emancipation and the payment of their full present value to their owners; and

On motion by Mr. Wigfall *[Texas]*, that the further consideration thereof be in open legislative session,

It was determined in the negative,   {   Yeas..........8
                                                        Nays..........9

On motion by Mr. Orr *[South Carolina]*,

The yeas and nays being desired by one-fifth of the Senators present,

Those who voted in the affirmative are,

Messrs. Graham *[North Carolina]*, Haynes *[Tennessee]*, Orr *[South Carolina]*, Semmes *[Louisiana]*, Simms *[Kentucky]*, Sparrow *[Louisiana]*, Walker *[Alabama]*, and Wigfall *[Texas]*.

Those who voted in the negative are,

Messrs. Baker *[Florida]*, Burnett *[Kentucky]*, Caperton *[Virginia]*, Dortch *[North Carolina]*, Henry *[Tennessee]*, Hunter *[Virginia]*, Maxwell *[Florida]*, Vest *[Missouri]*, and Watson *[Mississippi]*.

On motion by Mr. Sparrow *[Louisiana]*, that the Senate resolve into open legislative session,

It was determined in the negative,

On motion by Mr. Henry *[Tennessee]*, that the resolution lie upon the table,

It was determined in the negative,

On motion by Mr. Burnett *[Kentucky]*, to amend the resolution by striking out "report," line 2, and inserting "inquire into the expediency of reporting,"

It was determined in the negative.

On the question,

Will the Senate agree to the resolution?

It was determined in the negative,   {   Yeas............3
                                                        Nays.........13

On motion by Mr. Orr *[South Carolina]*,

The yeas and nays being desired by one-fifth of the Senators present,

Those who voted in the affirmative are,

Messrs. Brown *[Mississippi]*, Henry *[Tennessee]*, and Vest *[Missouri]*,

Those who voted in the negative are,

Messrs. Baker *[Florida]*, Caperton *[Virginia]*, Graham *[North Carolina]*, Haynes *[Tennessee]*, Hunter *[Virginia]*, Johnson of Missouri, Maxwell *[Florida]*, Oldham *[Texas]*, Semmes *[Louisiana]*, Walker *[Alabama]*, Watson *[Mississippi]*, and Wigfall *[Texas]*.

So the resolution was not agreed to.

On motion by Mr. Brown *[Mississippi]*,

Ordered, That the injunction of secrecy be removed from the proceedings of the Senate on the said resolution.

On motion by Mr. Dortch *[North Carolina]*,

The Senate resolved into open legislative session.

Journal of the House of Representatives [Feb. 7, 1865] p. 549

SEVENTY-SIXTH DAY - TUESDAY, February 7, 1865

Open Session.

A message was received from the Senate, by Mr. Nash, *[South Carolina]*, their Secretary; which is as follows, viz:

Mr. Speaker: The Senate agree to the first, second, fourth, fifth, seventh, eight, ninth, twelfth, thirteenth, fourteenth, and fifteenth, and disagree to the third, tenth, and eleventh amendments of the House of Representatives to the bill [S. 129] to provide for the employment of free negroes and slaves to work upon fortifications and perform other labor connected with the defenses of the country; and they agree to the sixth amendment of the House of Representatives to the said bill, with an amendment; which I am directed to ask concurrence of this House.

SEVENTY-SEVENTH DAY - WEDNESDAY, February 8, 1865

Open Session.

The Chair laid before the House a Senate bill [S. 129] "to provide for the employment of free negroes and slaves to work upon fortifications and perform other labor connected with the defenses of the country;" which had been returned from the Senate with an amendment to the amendments of the House.

Mr. Goode *[Virginia]* moved to suspend the rule requiring the amendments to be referred to a committee.

Mr. Garland *[Arkansas]* demanded the yeas and nays thereon;

Which were ordered,

And recorded as follows, viz: {   Yeas............50
                                            Nays.............6

Yeas: Anderson *[Georgia]*, Batson *[Arkansas]*, Boyce *[South Carolina]*, Bradley *[Kentucky]*, Eli M. Bruce *[Kentucky]*, Chambers *[Mississippi]*, Chilton *[Alabama]*, Clopton *[Alabama]*, Colyar *[Tennessee]*, Conrow *[Missouri]*, De Jarnette *[Virginia]*, Dickinson *[Alabama]*, Dupré *[Louisiana]*, Ewing *[Kentucky]*, Farrow *[South Carolina]*, Foster *[Alabama]*, Funsten *[Virginia]*, Gaither *[North Carolina]*, Garland *[Arkansas]*, Gholson *[Virginia]*, Gilmer *[North Carolina]*, Goode *[Virginia]*, Hanly *[Arkansas]*, Hartridge *[Georgia]*, Hatcher *[Missouri]*, Holder *[Mississippi]*, Holliday *[Virginia]*, Keeble *[Tennessee]*, Lam[p]kin *[Mississippi]*, J. M. Leach *[North Carolina]*, J. T. Leach *[North Carolina]*, Logan *[North Carolina]*, Machen *[Kentucky]*, McMullin *[Virginia]*, Menees *[Tennessee]*, Miller *[Virginia]*, Moore *[Kentucky]*, Murray *[Tennessee]*, Norton *[Missouri]*, Orr *[Mississippi]*, Simpson *[South Carolina]*,
J. M. Smith *[Georgia]*, W. E. Smith *[Georgia]*, Snead *[Missouri]*, Triplett *[Kentucky]*, Turner *[North Carolina]*, Villeré *[Louisiana]*, Wickham *[Virginia]*, Wilkes *[Missouri]*, and Witherspoon *[South Carolina]*.

Nays: Barksdale *[Mississippi]*, Blandford *[Georgia]*, Chrisman *[Kentucky]*, Cluskey *[Tennessee]*, Smith *[Alabama]*, and Mr. Speaker.

Two-thirds having voted in the affirmative, the rule was suspended.

The amendment of the Senate was read as follows, viz:

Strike out all after the word "act," in line 4, sixth amendment of the House, and insert "regulating impressments, approved March twenty-sixth, eighteen hundred and sixty-three."

The question being on concurring in said amendment,

It was decided in the affirmative.

The Senate having refused to concur in the tenth amendment of the House,

Mr. Miles *[South Carolina]* moved that the House recede from its amendment, and called the question; which was ordered.

Mr. McMullin *[Virginia]* demanded the yeas and nays thereon;

Which were ordered,

And recorded as follows, viz: {   Yeas............28
                                              Nays...........45

Yeas: Baylor *[Texas]*, Blandford *[Georgia]*, Boyce *[South Carolina]*, Bradley *[Kentucky]*, Eli M. Bruce *[Kentucky]*, Chilton *[Alabama]*, Chrisman *[Kentucky]*, Clark *[Missouri]*, Conrow *[Missouri]*, Ewing *[Kentucky]*, Gaither *[North Carolina]*, Gholson *[Virginia]*, Hilton *[Florida]*, Holliday *[Virginia]*, Johnston *[Virginia]*, J. T. Leach *[North Carolina]*, Lyon *[Alabama]*, Machen *[Kentucky]*, Miles *[South Carolina]*, Moore *[Kentucky]*, Orr *[Mississippi]*, Pugh *[Alabama]*, Rogers *[Florida]*, Russell *[Virginia]*, Simpson *[South Carolina]*, W. E. Smith *[Georgia]*, Snead *[Missouri]*, and Triplett *[Kentucky]*.

Nays: Akin *[Georgia]*, Anderson *[Georgia]*, Atkins *[Tennessee]*, Baldwin *[Virginia]*, Batson *[Arkansas]*, Horatio W. Bruce *[Kentucky]*, Carroll *[Arkansas]*, Chambers *[Mississippi]*, Clopton *[Alabama]*, Cluskey *[Tennessee]*, Colyar *[Tennessee]*, Conrad *[Louisiana]*, Darden *[Texas]*, De Jarnette *[Virginia]*, Dickinson *[Alabama]*, Dupré *[Louisiana]*, Elliott *[Kentucky]*, Farrow *[South Carolina]*, Foster *[Alabama]*, Garland *[Arkansas]*, Fuller *[North Carolina]*, Gilmer *[North Carolina]*, Goode *[Virginia]*, Gray *[Texas]*, Hanly *[Arkansas]*, Hatcher *[Missouri]*, Holder *[Mississippi]*, Keeble *[Tennessee]*, Lam[p]kin *[Mississippi]*, J. M. Leach *[North Carolina]*, Logan *[North Carolina]*, McMullin *[Virginia]*, Menees *[Tennessee]*, Murray *[Tennessee]*, Norton *[Missouri]*, Ramsay *[North Carolina]*, Sexton *[Texas]*, J. M. Smith *[Georgia]*, Smith *[Alabama]*, Smith *[North Carolina]*, Turner *[North Carolina]*, Villeré *[Louisiana]*, Wickham *[Virginia]*, Wilkes *[Missouri]*, and Witherspoon *[South Carolina]*.

So the House refused to recede from its amendment.

The Senate having refused to concur in the eleventh amendment of the House,

Mr. Miles *[South Carolina]* moved that the House recede from its amendment, and called the question; which was ordered.

Mr. Conrow *[Missouri]* demanded the yeas and nays thereon;

Which were ordered,

And recorded as follows, viz:　　{　　Yeas............31
　　　　　　　　　　　　　　　　　　 Nays...........34

Yeas: Anderson *[Georgia]*, Barksdale *[Mississippi]*, Blandford *[Georgia]*, Boyce *[South Carolina]*, Carroll *[Arkansas]*, Chilton *[Alabama]*, Conrad *[Louisiana]*, Conrow *[Missouri]*, De Jarnette *[Virginia]*, Dickinson *[Alabama]*, Ewing *[Kentucky]*, Funsten *[Virginia]*, Gaither *[North Carolina]*, Gilmer *[North Carolina]*, Hartridge *[Georgia]*, Hatcher *[Missouri]*, Hilton *[Florida]*, Johnston *[Virginia]*, Lam[p]kin *[Mississippi]*, J. M. Leach *[North Carolina]*, Lyon *[Alabama]*, Miles *[South Carolina]*, Moore *[Kentucky]*, Norton *[Missouri]*, Perkins *[Louisiana]*, Pugh *[Alabama]*, W. E. Smith *[Georgia]*, Smith *[Alabama]*, Smith *[North Carolina]*, Villeré *[Louisiana]*, and Wickham *[Virginia]*.

Nays: Akin *[Georgia]*, Atkins *[Tennessee]*, Batson *[Arkansas]*, Bradley *[Kentucky]*, Horatio W. Bruce *[Kentucky]*, Chrisman *[Kentucky]*, Clark *[Missouri]*, Clopton *[Alabama]*, Colyar *[Tennessee]*, Dupré *[Louisiana]*, Farrow *[South Carolina]*, Foster *[Alabama]*, Fuller *[North Carolina]*, Garland *[Arkansas]*, Goode *[Virginia]*, Gray *[Texas]*, Hanly *[Arkansas]*, Holliday *[Virginia]*, Keeble *[Tennessee]*, J. T. Leach *[North Carolina]*, Logan *[North Carolina]*, Machen *[Kentucky]*, McMullin *[Virginia]*, Murray *[Tennessee]*, Ramsay *[North Carolina]*, Sexton *[Texas]*, Simpson *[South Carolina]*, J. M. Smith *[Georgia]*, Snead *[Missouri]*, Triplett *[Kentucky]*, Turner *[North Carolina]*, Wilkes *[Missouri]*, Witherspoon *[South Carolina]*, and Mr. Speaker.

So the House refused to recede from its amendment.

Mr. Miles *[South Carolina]* moved that a committee of conference be tendered to the Senate on the disagreeing votes of the two House on the bill and amendments; which motion prevailed.

Journal of the House of Representatives [Feb. 9, 1865] p. 559

SEVENTY-EIGHTH DAY - THURSDAY, February 9, 1865

Open Session.

The Speaker announced the appointment of

Mr. Chambers *[Mississippi]*

Mr. Baldwin *[Virginia]*

Mr. Sexton *[Texas]*,

as managers on the part of the House on the disagreeing votes of the two Houses on the bill "to provide for the employment of free negroes and slaves to work upon fortifications and perform other labor connected with the defenses of the country."

On motion of Mr. Russell *[Virginia]*,

The House adjourned until 11 o'clock to-morrow.

HOUSE OF REPRESENTATIVES, February 10, 1865.--Read first and second times, referred to a select committee of one from each State, and ordered to be printed.

[By Mr. Barksdale *[Mississippi]*.]

A BILL

To be entitled An Act to increase the military force of the Confederate States.

The Congress of the Confederate States of America do enact, That in order to provide additional forces to repel invasion, maintain the rightful possession of the Confederate States, secure their independence and preserve their institutions, the President be and he is hereby authorized to ask for and accept from the owners of slaves the services of such number of able-bodied negro man as he may deem expedient, for and during the war, to perform military service in whatever capacity the General-in-Chief may direct.

Sec. 2. That the President be authorized to organize the said slaves into companies, battalions, regiments and brigades, under such rules and regulations as the Secretary of War may prescribe and to be commanded by such officers as the President may appoint.

Sec. 3. That while employed in the service the said slaves shall receive the same rations, clothing and compensation as are allowed in the Act approved February 17th, 1864, and the Acts amendatory thereto, "to increase the efficiency of the army by employment of free negroes and slaves in certain capacities," and the compensation so allowed shall be made to the owner or to the slave as the owner thereof may elect.

Sec. 4. That nothing in this Act shall be construed to authorize a change in the relation which the said slaves shall bear towards their owners as property, except by the consent of the States in which they may reside, and in pursuance of the laws thereof.

[Senate Bill, No. 190]

SENATE, February 10, 1865. Read first and second times, referred to Committee on Military Affairs, and ordered to be printed.

[By Mr. Oldham *[Texas]*.]

A BILL

To provide for Raising Two Hundred Thousand Negro Troops.

Section 1. *The Congress of the Confederate States of America do enact,* That the President of the Confederate States be and he is hereby authorized to receive into the military service, any number of negro troops not to exceed two hundred thousand.

Sec. 2. That the President be and he is authorized, to assign officers already appointed, or make appointments of officers, to raise and command said troops; and the same, when raised, shall be organized as provided under existing laws.

Sec. 3. That no negro slave shall be received into the service without the written consent of his owner and under such regulations as may be prescribed by the Secretary of War to carry into effect this act.

Sec. 4. That it is hereby declared, that Congress does not hereby assume to change the social and political status of the slave population of the States, but leaves the same under the jurisdiction and control of the States to which it belongs.

FRIDAY, February 10, 1865.

Open Session.

A message from the House of Representatives, by Mr. Dalton *(Assistant Clerk of House of Representatives):*

Mr. President: The House of Representatives agree to the amendment of the Senate to the sixth amendment of the House to the bill [S. 129] to provide for the employment of free negroes and slaves to work upon fortifications and perform other labor connected with the defenses of the country, insist upon their third, tenth, and eleventh amendments, disagreed to by the Senate to the said bill, ask a conference upon disagreeing votes of the two Houses thereon, and have appointed Messrs. Chambers *[Mississippi],* Baldwin *[Virginia],* and Sexton *[Texas]* managers at said conference on their part...

The Senate proceeded to consider the amendments of the House of Representatives to the bill [S. 129] to provide for the employment of free negroes and slaves to work upon fortifications and perform other labor connected with the defenses of the country, insisted on by the House of Representatives; and

On motion by Mr. Sparrow *[Louisiana],*

Resolved, That the Senate insist on their disagreement to the amendments of the House of Representatives to the said bill, and to agree to the conference asked by the House on the disagreeing votes of the two Houses thereon.

On motion by Mr. Sparrow *[Louisiana],*

Ordered, That the committee of conference on the part of the Senate be appointed by the President pro tempore; and

Mr. Burnett *[Kentucky],* Mr. Graham *[North Carolina],* and Mr. Caperton *[Virginia]* were appointed. *Ordered,* That the Secretary inform the House of Representatives thereof.

Mr. Oldham *[Texas]* (by leave) introduced

A bill [S. 190] to provide for raising 200,000 negro troops;

which was read the first and second times and referred to the Committee on Military Affairs.

Ordered, That it be printed.

Journal of the House of Representatives [Feb. 11, 1865] p. 567

EIGHTIETH DAY - SATURDAY, February 11, 1865

Open Session.

A message was received from the Senate, by Mr. Nash, *[South Carolina],* their Secretary; which is as follows, viz:

Mr. Speaker: ...The Senate insist upon their disagreement to the amendment proposed by this House to the bill [S. 129] to provide for the employment of free negroes and slaves to work upon fortifications and perform other labor connected with the defenses of the country, agree to the conference asked by this House on disagreeing votes of the two Houses thereon, and have appointed Mr. Burnett *[Kentucky],* Mr. Graham *[North Carolina],* and Mr. Caperton *[Virginia]* managers at the said conference on the part of the Senate.

SENATE, February 13, 1865. - Ordered to be printed.

[By Mr. Sparrow *[Louisiana],* from the Committee on Military Affairs.]

Proposed by the Committee on Military Affairs

AMENDMENT
to the Bill [S. 190]
To provide for Raising Two Hundred Thousand Negro Troops.

Strike out the 4th section and insert:

That all slaves received into the service under the provisions of this Act shall be valued and paid for according to existing laws, and that said slaves or any of them, upon a faithful performance of their duties, shall be manumitted by general orders from the War Department, if the consent of the State in which the said slaves may be at the time is given for their manumission.

Journal of the Senate [Feb. 13, 1865] p. 550

MONDAY, February 13, 1865.

Open Session.

Mr. Sparrow *[Louisiana],* from the Committee on Military Affairs, to whom was referred the bill [S. 190] to provide for raising 200,000 negro troops, reported it with an amendment.

Ordered, That the amendment be printed.

EIGHTY-SECOND DAY - TUESDAY, February 14, 1865

Open Session.

Mr. Machen *[Kentucky]* from the same committee *(Quartermaster's and Commissary),* to whom had been referred

A resolution "relative to the feeding of negroes in the employment of the Government," reported back the same with the recommendation that the committee be discharged from its further consideration, and that it do lie upon the table; which was agreed to.

HOUSE OF REPRESENTATIVES, February 14, 1865. --Ordered to be printed.

(By Mr. Swan *[Tennessee]*)

AMENDMENT

To the Negro Soldier Bill.

The Congress of the Confederate States of America do enact, That the General-in-Chief commanding the armies of the Confederate States be and he is hereby invested with the full and complete power to call into the service of the Confederate States, to perform any duty to which he may assign them, so many of the able-bodied slaves within the Confederate States, as in his judgment the exigencies of the public service may require.

Sec. 2. *Be it enacted,* That while said slaves are so employed, whether voluntarily offered for service by their owners or impressed if conformity to any existing or future law, such compensation, clothing and rations shall be allowed to and for said slaves as are allowed, by the Act approved February 17, 1864, and Acts amendatory thereto, to increase the efficiency of the army by the employment of free negroes and slaves in certain cases.

THURSDAY, February 16, 1865.

Open Session.

The Senate proceeded, as in Committee of the Whole, to the consideration of the bill [S. 190] to provide for raising 200,000 negro troops; and

On motion by Mr. Johnson of Georgia,

The Senate resolved into secret legislative session for the further consideration thereof.

The doors having been opened,

Mr. Burnett *[Kentucky]*, from the committee of conference on the part of the Senate on the disagreeing votes of the two Houses on the bill [S. 129] to provide for the employment of free negroes and slaves to work upon fortifications and perform other labor connected with the defenses of the country, reported

That they have met the managers on the part of the House of Representatives, and after full and free conference have agreed to recommend, and do recommend, to their respective House as follows:

That the House of Representative do recede from their third and tenth amendments.

That the Senate do recede from their disagreement to the eleventh amendment of the House of Representatives.

The Senate proceeded to consider the said report; and

On motion by Mr. Burnett *[Kentucky]*,

Resolved, That they concur therein.

Ordered, That the Secretary inform the House of Representatives thereof.

The following message was received from the President of the Confederate States, by Mr. B. N. Harrison, his Secretary:

Richmond, VA., *February 15, 1865.*

To the Senate of the Confederate States:

In partial response to your resolution of the 24th ultimo, I herewith transmit communications from the Secretary of the Navy and the Postmaster-General relating to the number of white men between the ages of 18 and 45, and of negroes, whose services are necessary to their respective Departments.

The Secretary of War has been called to furnish reports on this subject from the several bureaus specified in your resolution, which will be transmitted when received.

JEFFERSON DAVIS

The message was read.

Ordered, That it lie upon the table and be printed.

Journal of the Senate [Feb. 16, 1865] p. 569

THURSDAY, February 16, 1865.

Secret Session.

On motion by Mr. Johnson of Georgia, that the bill [S. 190] to provide for raising 200,000 negro troops be transferred to the Secret Legislative Calendar,

It was determined in the affirmative,　　{　Yeas.........10
　　　　　　　　　　　　　　　　　　　　　　　　　Nays..........7

On motion by Mr. Orr *[South Carolina],*

The yeas and nays being desired by one-fifth of the Senators present,

Those who voted in the affirmative are,

Messrs. Baker *[Florida],* Burnett *[Kentucky],* Dortch *[North Carolina],* Haynes *[Tennessee],* Johnson *[Georgia],* Johnson *[Missouri],* Maxwell *[Florida],* Vest *[Missouri],* Walker *[Alabama],* and Watson *[Mississippi].*

Those who voted in the negative are,

Messrs. Caperton *[Virginia],* Graham *[North Carolina],* Hunter *[Virginia],* Oldham *[Texas],* Orr *[South Carolina],* Semmes *[Louisiana],* and Wigfall *[Texas].*

The Senate resumed the consideration of the said bill; and

On motion by Mr. Oldham *[Texas],*

Ordered, That the further consideration thereof be postponed to and made the special order for to-morrow, at 1 o'clock.

EIGHTY-THIRD DAY - WEDNESDAY, February 16, 1865

Open Session.

A message was received from the Senate, by Mr. Nash, *[South Carolina]*, their Secretary; which is as follows, viz:

Mr. Speaker:...The Senate have agreed to the report of the committee of conference on the disagreeing votes of the two Houses on the bill of the Senate [S. 129] to provide for the employment of free negroes and slaves to work upon fortifications and perform other labor connected with the defense of the country.

Journal of the Senate [Feb. 17, 1865] p. 572

FRIDAY, February 17, 1865.

Secret Session.

The Senate resumed, as in the Committee of the Whole, the consideration of the bill [S. 190] to provide for raising 200,000 negro troops.

On the question to agree to the following reported amendment, to wit: Strike out the fourth section and insert:

That all slaves received in to the service under the provisions of this act shall be valued and paid for according to existing laws, and that said slaves, or any of them, upon a faithful performance of their duties, shall be manumitted by general orders from the War Department, if the consent of the State in which the said slaves may be at the time is given for their manumission,

On motion by Mr. Walker *[Alabama]*, to amend the amendment by striking out the words "upon a faithful performance of their duties," lines 5 and 6,

It was determined in the affirmative.

On motion by Mr. Simms *[Kentucky]*, to amend the amendment by striking out the words " or any of them," line 5,

On motion by Mr. Garland *[Arkansas]*, that the further consideration of the bill be postponed indefinitely,

On motion by Mr. Garland *[Arkansas]*,

Ordered, That the further consideration thereof be postponed until to-morrow.

Journal of the Senate [Feb. 18, 1865] p. 576

SATURDAY, February 18, 1865.

Secret Session.

The Senate resumed, as in Committee of the Whole, the consideration of the bill [S. 190] to provide for raising 200,000 negro troops

The question being on agreeing to the motion submitted by Mr. Garland *[Arkansas]* on yesterday, that the further consideration of the bill be postponed until indefinitely,

After debate,

On motion by Mr. Semmes *[Louisiana]*,

Ordered, That the further consideration of the bill be postponed until Monday next.

Journal of the House of Representatives [Feb. 18, 1865] p. 602

EIGHTY-SIXTH DAY - SATURDAY, February 18, 1865

Open Session.

Mr. Sexton *[Texas]*, from the committee of conference on the disagreeing votes of the two Houses on the bill "to provide for the employment of free negroes and slaves to work upon fortifications and perform other labor connected with the defenses of the country," submitted the following report:

The committee of conference on the part of the House of Representatives on the disagreeing votes of the two Houses on the bill [S. 129] "to provide for the employment of free negroes and slaves to work upon fortifications and perform other labor connected with the defenses of the country," beg leave respectfully to report:

That they have met the managers on the part of the Senate, and after full and free conference, have agreed to recommend, and do recommend, to their respective Houses as follows, viz:

That the House of Representatives do recede from their third and tenth amendments.

That the Senate do recede from their disagreement to the eleventh amendment of the House of Representatives.

All of which is respectfully submitted.

H. C. Chambers *[Mississippi],*
F. B. Sexton *[Texas],*
Managers on the part of the House of Representatives.
H. C. Burnett *[Kentucky],*
W. A. Graham *[North Carolina],*
A. T. Caperton *[Virginia],*
Managers on the part of the Senate.

The question being on agreeing to the report of the committee,

Mr. Carroll *[Arkansas]* demanded the yeas and nays; which was not ordered, and the report was agreed to.

Mr. Smith *[North Carolina]* moved to reconsider the vote by which the report was agreed to.

Mr. Barksdale called the question; which was ordered.

Mr. Marshall *[Louisiana],* demanded the yeas and nays;

Which were ordered,
And recorded as follows, viz: { Yeas............32
                                  Nays...........38

Yeas: Akin *[Georgia],* Baldwin *[Virginia],* Batson *[Arkansas],* Bradley *[Kentucky],* Branch *[Texas],* Bridgers *[North Carolina],* Horatio W. Bruce *[Kentucky],* Burnett *[Kentucky],* Carroll *[Arkansas],* Clark *[Missouri],* Cluskey *[Tennessee],* Colyar *[Tennessee],* Darden *[Texas],* Dupré *[Louisiana],* Farrow *[South Carolina],* Foster *[Alabama],* Fuller *[North Carolina],* Garland *[Arkansas],* Gholson *[Virginia],* Gilmer *[North Carolina],* Hanly *[Arkansas],* Herbert *[Texas],* J. M. Leach *[North Carolina],* J. T. Leach *[North Carolina],* Logan *[North Carolina],* Marshall *[Louisiana],* McCallum *[Tennessee],* Murray *[Tennessee],* Perkins *[Louisiana],* Rogers *[Florida],* Simpson *[South Carolina],* and Smith *[North Carolina].*

Nays: Barksdale *[Mississippi],* Bell *[Georgia],* Blandford *[Georgia],* Chrisman *[Kentucky],* Clopton *[Alabama],* Conrad *[Louisiana],* Cruikshank *[Alabama],* De Jarnette *[Virginia],* Dickinson *[Alabama],* Elliott *[Kentucky],* Ewing *[Kentucky],* Funsten *[Virginia],* Gaither *[North Carolina],* Goode *[Virginia],* Gray *[Texas],* Hartridge *[Georgia],* Hatcher *[Missouri],* Hilton *[Florida],* Johnston *[Virginia],* Keeble *[Tennessee],* Lyon *[Alabama],* Machen *[Kentucky],* Miles *[South Carolina],* Miller *[Virginia],* Pugh *[Alabama],* Ramsay *[North Carolina],* Read *[Kentucky],* Russell *[Virginia],* Sexton *[Texas],* J. M. Smith *[Georgia],* W. E. Smith *[Georgia],* Snead *[Missouri],* Staples *[Virginia],* Triplett *[Kentucky],* Villeré *[Louisiana],* Wickham *[Virginia],* Wilkes *[Missouri],* and Witherspoon *[South Carolina].*

So the motion to reconsider was lost.

A message was received from the Senate, by Mr. Nash, *[South Carolina]*, their Secretary; which is as follows, viz:

Mr. Speaker:. The Senate have passed a bill [S. 195] to authorize the Secretary of War to negotiate with the governors of the several States for slave labor; in which I am directed to ask the concurrence of this House.

Journal of the House of Representatives [Feb. 18, 1865] p. 604

EIGHTY-SIXTH DAY - SATURDAY, February 18, 1865

Secret Session.

Mr. Marshall *[Kentucky]* submitted the following amendment to the amendment of Mr. Swan *[Tennessee]* (in the nature of a substitute):

Strike out the whole thereof and insert the following, viz:

"1. The President shall call into the military service of the Confederate States such number of the male colored population, whether free or slave, between the ages of eighteen and forty-five years, as may be called for by the General-in-Chief commanding the armies of the Confederate States and as the President may deem it expedient and conducive to the public interest to use in defense of the country. He is hereby authorized to incorporate the colored people, so called, into the military service, into the Provisional Army of the Confederate States, and to organize them into companies, squadrons, battalions, regiments, brigades, divisions, or otherwise, as to the General-in-Chief may seem most expedient:

Provided, The said organizations shall be commanded only by white commissioned officers, to be assigned from officers now in service or to be appointed by the President, by and with the advice and consent of the Senate, as to the President may seem best for the public service.

"2. When such troops are mustered into service they shall receive the same clothing, pay, rations, and other allowances as are now given by law to white troops of the Provisional Army, according to the arm of the service to which they may belong, and they shall be subject to such government and discipline as may be prescribed by rules and regulations to be issued by the Secretary of War.

"3. Departmental generals and brigadiers holding separate commands are authorized to receive into the military service as soldiers all free colored men, between the ages of aforesaid, who may offer as volunteers to be mustered into service for the war, and when such volunteer shall have been mustered into service as a soldier, he shall receive the allowances, rations, pay, and clothing given to volunteers who are now in service."

Pending which,
On motion of Mr. Colyar *[Tennessee]*
The House resolved itself into Open Session.

Journal of the House of Representatives [Feb. 20, 1865] p. 604

EIGHTY-SEVENTH DAY - MONDAY, February 20, 1865

Open Session.

The Chair laid before the House a Senate bill [S. 195] "to authorize the Secretary of War to negotiate with the governors of the several States for slave labor:" which was read a first and second time and referred to the Committee on Military Affairs.

Journal of the Senate [Feb. 20, 1865] p. 578-579

MONDAY, February 20, 1865.

Open Session.

A message from the House of Representatives, by Mr. Dalton [*Assistant Clerk of House of Representatives*]:

Mr. President:
.....The House of Representatives have concurred in the report of the committee of conference on the disagreeing votes of the two Houses on the bill [S. 129] to provide for the employment of free negroes and slaves to work upon fortifications and perform other labor connected with the defenses of the country.

Journal of the Senate [Feb. 20, 1865] p. 581

MONDAY, February 20, 1865.

Secret Session.

The Senate resumed, as in Committee of the Whole, the consideration of the bill [S. 190] to provide for raising 200,000 negro troops. The question being on agreeing to the motion submitted by Mr. Garland [*Arkansas*] on Saturday last, that the further consideration of the bill be postponed indefinitely,

After debate,

On motion by Mr. Oldham [*Texas*],

The Senate resolved into executive session.

TUESDAY, February 21, 1865.

Secret Session.

The Senate resumed, as in Committee of the Whole, the consideration of the bill [S. 190] to provide for raising 200,000 negro troops; and

After debate,

On the question to agree to the motion submitted by Mr. Garland *[Arkansas]* on Friday last, that the further consideration of the bill be postponed indefinitely,

It was determined in the affirmative,   { Yeas..........11
                                            Nays..........10

On motion by Mr. Semmes *[Louisiana]*,

The yeas and nays being desired by one-fifth of the Senators present,

Those who voted in the affirmative are,

Messrs. Baker *[Florida]*, Barnwell *[South Carolina]*, Caperton *[Virginia]*, Garland *[Arkansas]*, Graham *[North Carolina]*, Hunter *[Virginia]*, Johnson *[Georgia]*, Johnson *[Missouri]*, Maxwell *[Florida]*, Orr *[South Carolina]* and Wigfall *[Texas]*.

Those who voted in the negative are,

Messrs. Brown *[Mississippi]*, Burnett *[Kentucky]*, Haynes *[Tennessee]*, Henry *[Tennessee]*, Oldham *[Texas]*, Semmes *[Louisiana]*, Simms *[Kentucky]*, Vest *[Missouri]*, Walker *[Alabama]*, and Watson *[Mississippi]*.

So it was.

Ordered, That the further consideration of the bill be postponed indefinitely.

On motion by Mr. Graham *[North Carolina]*,

The Senate resolved into executive session.

NINETY-SECOND DAY - SATURDAY, February 25, 1865

Open Session.

A message was received from the President, by Mr. Harrison, his Private Secretary, notifying the House that on the 23rd instant the President approved and signed:

S. 129 An act to provide for the employment of free negroes and slaves to work upon fortifications and perform other labor connected with the defenses of the country;...

Journal of the House of Representatives [Feb. 28, 1865] p. 666-667

NINETY-FOURTH DAY - TUESDAY, February 28, 1865

Open Session.

Mr. Miles *[South Carolina]*, from the same committee *[Military Affairs]*, to which had been referred a bill [S. 195] "to authorize the Secretary of War to negotiate with the governors of the several States for slave labor," reported back the same with the recommendation that it do pass.

The question being on postponing the bill and placing it on the Calendar.

It was decided in the negative.

Mr. Marshall *[Kentucky]* moved to amend the bill by adding at the end thereof the following words:

Provided, The sum paid to owners for said slaves shall not exceed the wages per month allowed to soldiers in the Army.

Upon which Mr. Marshall *[Kentucky]* demanded the yeas and nays;

And recorded as follows, viz: { Yeas............39
Nays...........17

Yeas: Atkins *[Tennessee]*, Baldwin *[Virginia]*, Barksdale *[Mississippi]*, Batson *[Arkansas]*, Bradley *[Kentucky]*, Branch *[Texas]*, Bridgers *[North Carolina]*, Eli M. Bruce *[Kentucky]*, Burnett *[Kentucky]*, Carroll *[Arkansas]*, Chambers *[Mississippi]*, Clark *[Missouri]*, Cluskey *[Tennessee]*, Conrow *[Missouri]*, Cruikshank *[Alabama]*, De Jarnette *[Virginia]*, Dickinson *[Alabama]*, Foster *[Alabama]*, Fuller *[North Carolina]*, Funsten *[Virginia]*, Gaither *[North Carolina]*, Goode *[Virginia]*, Hanly *[Arkansas]*, Johnston *[Virginia]*, J. T. Leach *[North Carolina]*, Logan *[North Carolina]*, Marshall *[Kentucky]*, McCallum *[Tennessee]*, McMullin *[Virginia]*, Pugh *[Alabama]*, Ramsay *[North Carolina]*, Russell *[Virginia]*, J. M. Smith *[Georgia]*, Smith *[North Carolina]*, Snead *[Missouri]*, Triplett *[Kentucky]*, Turner *[North Carolina]*, Villeré *[Louisiana]*, and Wilkes *[Missouri]*,

Nays: Blandford *[Georgia]*, Boyce *[South Carolina]*, Horatio W. Bruce *[Kentucky]*, Clopton *[Alabama]*, Dupré *[Louisiana]*, Farrow *[South Carolina]*, Gholson *[Virginia]*, Gray *[Texas]*, Hartridge *[Georgia]*, Hatcher *[Missouri]*, Herbert *[Texas]*, Miles *[South Carolina]*, Sexton *[Texas]*, Simpson *[South Carolina]*, W. E. Smith *[Georgia]*, Wickham *[Virginia]*, and Witherspoon *[South Carolina]*.

The amendment was agreed to, and the bill as amended was read a third time.

The question recurring and being put,

Shall the bill pass?

Mr. Miles *[South Carolina]* demanded the yeas and nays thereon;
Which were ordered,

And recorded as follows, viz: {   Yeas............45
                                            Nays.............9

Yeas: Atkins *[Tennessee]*, Baldwin *[Virginia]*, Barksdale *[Mississippi]*, Batson *[Arkansas]*, Boyce *[South Carolina]*, Bradley *[Kentucky]*, Eli M. Bruce *[Kentucky]*, Horatio W. Bruce *[Kentucky]*, Carroll *[Arkansas]*, Chambers *[Mississippi]*, Clopton *[Alabama]*, Cluskey *[Tennessee]*, Conrow *[Missouri]*, Cruikshank *[Alabama]*, De Jarnette *[Virginia]*, Dickinson *[Alabama]*, Foster *[Alabama]*, Gaither *[North Carolina]*, Gholson *[Virginia]*, Gilmer *[North Carolina]*, Goode *[Virginia]*, Hartridge *[Georgia]*, Hatcher *[Missouri]*, Hilton *[Florida]*, Johnston *[Virginia]*, Marshall *[Kentucky]*, McCallum *[Tennessee]*, Miles *[South Carolina]*, Moore *[Kentucky]*, Murray *[Tennessee]*, Pugh *[Alabama]*, Rogers *[Florida]*, Russell *[Virginia]*, Sexton *[Texas]*, Simpson *[South Carolina]*, J. M. Smith *[Georgia]*, W. E. Smith *[Georgia]*, Smith *[North Carolina]*, Snead *[Missouri]*, Swan *[Tennessee]*, Triplett *[Kentucky]*, Villeré *[Louisiana]*, Wickham *[Virginia]*, Wilkes *[Missouri]*, and Witherspoon *[South Carolina]*.

Nays: Dupré *[Louisiana]*, Farrow *[South Carolina]*, Fuller *[North Carolina]*, Gray *[Texas]*, Herbert *[Texas]*, J. M. Leach *[North Carolina]*, J. T. Leach *[North Carolina]*, Logan *[North Carolina]*, and Ramsay *[North Carolina]*.

So the bill passed, and the title was read and agreed to, and a motion to reconsider the vote on the passage of the same did not prevail.

Journal of the Senate [Feb. 28, 1865] p. 607

TUESDAY, February 28, 1865.

Open Session.

Mr. Maxwell *[Florida]*, from the committee *[Military Affairs]*, reported that they had examined and found truly enrolled bills and a joint resolution of the following titles:

H.R. 129. An act to provide for the employment of free negroes and slaves to work upon fortifications and perform other labor connected with the defenses of the country;...

The President pro tempore having signed the enrolled bills and enrolled joint resolution last reported to have been examined, they were delivered to the Secretary of the Senate and by him forthwith presented to the President of the Confederate States for his approval.

Journal of the Senate [Mar. 2, 1865] p. 629

THURSDAY, March 2, 1865.

Open Session.

A message from the President of the Confederate States, by Mr. B. N. Harrison, his *[Private]* Secretary:

Mr. President: The President of the Confederate States, on the 28th ultimo, approved and signed the following acts:

S. 129. An act to provide for the employment of free negroes and slaves to work upon fortifications and perform other labor connected with the defenses of the country;...

Ordered, That the Secretary inform the House of Representatives thereof.

Journal of the House of Representatives [Mar. 2, 1865] p. 676

NINETY-SIXTH DAY - THURSDAY, March 2, 1865

Open Session.

A message was received from the Senate, by Mr. Nash, *[South Carolina]*, their Secretary; which is as follows, viz:

Mr. Speaker:...The Senate have concurred in the amendment of this House to the bill [S. 195] to authorize the Secretary of War to negotiate with the governors of the several States for slave labor.

Journal of the House of Representatives [Mar. 3, 1865] p. 684

NINETY-SEVENTH DAY - FRIDAY, March 3, 1865

Open Session.

A message was received from the Senate, by Mr. Nash, *[South Carolina],* their Secretary; which is as follows, viz:

Mr. Speaker:...The President of the Confederate States has notified the Senate that on the 28th ultimo he approved and signed the following acts:

S. 129. An act to provide for the employment of free negroes and slaves to work upon fortifications and perform other labor connected with the defenses of the country;...

Journal of the House of Representatives [Mar. 3, 1865] p. 689

NINETY-SEVENTH DAY - FRIDAY, March 3, 1865

Open Session.

Mr. Cruikshank *[Alabama],* from the Committee on Enrolled Bills, reported as correctly enrolled

S. 195 An act to authorize the Secretary of War to negotiate with the governors of the several States for slave labor;...

Journal of the Senate [Mar. 8, 1865] p. 670-671

WEDNESDAY, March 8, 1865.

Open Session.

The Senate resumed, as in Committee of the Whole, the consideration of the bill [H.R. 367] to increase the military force of the Confederate States.

On motion by Mr. Caperton *[Virginia],* to amend the bill by inserting at the end of the fourth section the following proviso:

Provided, That not more than twenty-five per cent of the male slaves between the ages of eighteen and forty-five, in any State, shall be called for under the provisions of this act,

It was determined in the affirmative.

No further amendment being proposed, the bill was reported to the Senate and the amendment was concurred in.

Ordered, That the amendment be engrossed and the bill read a third time.

The said bill as amended was read the third time.

On the question,

Shall the bill now pass?

It was determined in the affirmative, { Yeas..........9
                                         Nays.........8

On motion by Mr. Orr *[South Carolina],*

The yeas and nays being desired by one-fifth of the Senators present,

Those who voted in the affirmative are,

Messrs. Brown *[Mississippi],* Burnett *[Kentucky],* Caperton *[Virginia],* Henry *[Tennessee],* Hunter *[Virginia],* Oldham *[Texas],* Semmes *[Louisiana],* Simms *[Kentucky],* and Watson *[Mississippi].*

Those who voted in the negative are,

Messrs. Barnwell *[South Carolina],* Graham *[North Carolina],* Johnson *[Georgia],* Johnson *[Missouri],* Maxwell *[Florida],* Orr *[South Carolina],* Vest *[Missouri],* and Wigfall *[Texas].*

So it was.

Resolved, That this bill pass with an amendment.

Ordered, That the Secretary request concurrence of the House of Representatives in the amendment.

ONE HUNDRED AND FIRST DAY - WEDNESDAY, March 8, 1865

Open Session.

The following messages were received from the Senate, by Mr. Nash, *[South Carolina],* their Secretary:

Mr. Speaker:...The President of the Confederate States has notified the Senate that he did, on the 4th instant, approve and sign the following acts and joint resolutions:

S. 195 An act to authorize the Secretary of War to negotiate with the governors of the several States for slave labor;...

Secret Session.

... The measures passed by Congress during the session for recruiting the Army and supplying the additional force needed for the public defense, have been in my judgment insufficient, and I am impelled by a profound conviction of duty, and stimulated by a sense of the perils which surround our country, to urge upon you additional legislation on this subject.

The bill for employing negroes as soldiers has not yet reached me, though the printed journals of your proceedings inform me of its passage. Much benefit as anticipated from this measure, though far less than would have resulted from its adoption at an earlier date, so as to afford time for their organization and instruction during the winter months....

JEFFERSON DAVIS

THURSDAY, March 16, 1865.

Secret Session.

Mr. Orr *[South Carolina]*, from the select committee to whom was referred that portion of the message of the President of the Confederate States of the 13th instant relating to the action of Congress during the present session, submitted the following report:

The select committee to whom was referred so much of the President's message of the 13th instant as it relates to the action of Congress during the present session, having duly considered the same, respectfully submit the following report:

The attention of Congress is called by the President to the fact, that for carrying on the war successfully, there is urgent need of men and supplies for the Army.

The measures passed by Congress during the present session, for recruiting the Army, are considered by the President inefficient; and it is said that the results of the law authorizing the employment of slaves as soldiers will be less than anticipated, in consequence of the dilatory action of Congress in adopting the measure. That a law so radical in its character, so repugnant to the prejudices of our people and so intimately affecting the organism of society, should encounter opposition and receive a tardy sanction, ought not to exercise surprise, but if the policy and necessity of the measure had been seriously urged on Congress by an Executive message, legislative action might have been quickened. The President, in no official communication to Congress, has recommended the passage of a law putting slaves into the Army as soldiers, and the message under consideration is the first official information that such a law would meet his approval. The Executive message transmitted to Congress on the 7th of November last suggests the propriety of enlarging the sphere of employment of the negro as a laborer, and for this purpose recommends that the absolute title to slaves be acquired by impressment, and as an incentive to the faithful discharge of duty, that the slave thus acquired be liberated, with the permission of the States from which they were drawn. In this connection the following language is used: "If this policy should recommend itself to the judgment of Congress, it is suggested that, in addition to the duties heretofore performed by the slave, he might be advantageously employed as *pioneer and engineer laborer;* and in that event the number should be augmented to 40,000. *Beyond this limit and these employments it does not seem to me desirable, under existing circumstances, to go."* In the same message the President further remarks: "The subject is to be viewed by us, therefore, solely in the light of policy and our social economy. *When so regarded I must dissent from those who advise a general levy and arming of the slaves for duty of soldiers."* It is manifest that the President in November last did not consider that the contingency had then arisen which would justify a resort to the extraordinary policy of arming our slaves. Indeed, no other inference can be deduced from the language used by him, for he says: "These considerations, however, are rather applicable *to the improbable contingency of our need of resorting to his element of resistance than to our present condition."* The Secretary of War, in his report, under date of November 3, seemed to concur in the opinion of the President, when he said: "While it is encouraging to know this resource for further and future efforts is at our command, *my own judgment does not yet either perceive the necessity or approve the policy of employing slaves in the higher duties of soldiers."*

At what period of the session the President or Secretary of War considered the improbable contingency had risen, which required a resort to slaves as an element of resistance, does not appear by any official document within the knowledge of your committee. Congress might well have delayed action on this subject until the present moment, as the President, whose constitutional duty is "to give to the Congress information of the state of the Confederacy," has never asked, in any authentic manner, for the passage of a law authorizing the employment of slaves as soldiers. The Senate, however, did not await the tardy movements of the President. On the 29th December, 1864, the following resolution was adopted by the Senate, in secret session:

Resolved, That the President be requested to inform the Senate, in secret session, as to the state of the finances in connection with the payment of the troops; the means of supplying the munitions of war, transportation and subsistence; the condition of the Army, and the possibility if recruiting the same; the condition of our foreign relations, and whether any aid or encouragement from abroad is expected, or has been sought, or is proposed; so that the Senate may have a clear and exact view of the state of the country and of its future prospects, and what measures of legislation are required."

In response to this resolution the President might well have communicated to the Senate his views as to the necessity and policy of arming slaves of the Confederacy as a means of public defense. No answer whatever has been made to the resolution. In addition to this, a joint committee was raised by Congress, under a concurrent resolution adopted in secret session on the 30th December, 1864. That committee, by the resolution creating it, was instructed "by conference with the President, and by such other means as they shall deem proper. To ascertain what are our reliable means of public defense, present and prospective."

A written report was made by the committee on January 25, 1865; and although it has a conference with the President, no allusion is made in the report to any suggestion by him that the necessities of the country required the employment of slaves as soldiers. Under these circumstances, Congress, influenced no doubt by the opinion of General Lee, determined for itself the propriety, policy, and necessity of adopting the measure in question.

The recommendations of the President -- to employ 40,000 slaves as cooks, teamsters, and as engineer and pioneer laborers -- was assented to, and a law has been enacted at the present session for the purpose, without limit as to number...

The Senate proceeded to consider the said report; and

Resolved, That they concur therein.

On motion by Mr. Maxwell *[Florida]*,

Ordered, That the injunction of secrecy be removed from the report and that it be printed.

On motion by Mr. Barnwell *[South Carolina]*,
The Senate resolved into open legislative session.

HR 418

A Bill to be entitled an act relative to the impressment of slaves.

Sec. The Congress of the Confederate States do enact,

That in executing any law authorizing the impressment of slaves, or under which an enrollment of slaves subject to Government service may be ordered, the Secretary of War may omit any district of counties near the enemy lines, when in his opinion such impressment or enrollment cannot be made without causing slaves to escape in large numbers to the enemy.

passed Senate March 14/65
approved by the President March 16/65

Advertisements

The following advertisements taken from Richmond newspapers during the period of this legislative history demonstrate the efforts to find able-bodied free African Americans to volunteer to perform work in support of the Confederacy. The failure to attract significant numbers of free African Americans to perform the needed labor resulted in the need for African American conscription. They worked on fortifications, in iron works, in hospitals, flour mills and on railroads. Photographs of some of these locations follow the advertisements.

TREDEGAR IRON WORKS,
Richmond, November 28th, 1862

FIVE HUNDRED HANDS WANTED.—We wish to hire for the ensuing year Five Hundred able bodied Negro Men, to be employed by us at our Blast Furnaces in Botetourt county, and at our coal mines, on James River, seventeen miles above this city.

As our works generally are remote from the enemy's lines, and the negroes are well guarded, we think it greatly to the interest of those having hands to dispose of to hire them to us.

The negroes will be supplied with the very best provisions, which have already been secured, and good clothing provided for them at all seasons of the year.

Those of whom we have hands hired, for the present year, will please inform us whether we shall retain these hands at the furnaces until they are re-hired; and if not, to what point they shall be returned, as some of the owners may have changed their places of residence.

Payment for the hire of these hands will be made either at Farmville, Lynchburg, Fincastle, or this city, annually or quarterly, at the option of the owner.

Applications can be made to F. T. Glasgow, Fincastle; Thomas T. Patton, at Clover Dale Furnace; James L. Patton, at Grace Furnace; Thomas Jordan, Alum Springs; John J. Jamieson, Lynchburg; Benj. Holaday, Frederick's Hall, Louisa county; James M. Poindexter, Farmville, or the undersigned at the works.

nov29—tjan15   J. R. ANDERSON & CO

WANTED TO HIRE—TWENTY-FIVE NEGRO LABORERS. Apply to Lieutenant LOUIS ZIMMER, at the office of the Confederate States Arsenal, corner Seventh and Byrd streets, Richmond, Va.   july 29—1w

300 NEGROES WANTED.—Three hundred hands are wanted to work on the grading of the Chatham Railroad, from eight miles west of Raleigh, to B[ear] river, in Chatham county. For No. 1 hands one dollar [per] day will be paid, or they will be hired by the month [for] the rest of the year.

Address the undersigned at Raleigh, North Carolina, [or] Captain JAMES E. ALLEN, Superintendent, Cary, North Carolina.

July 27—2w

KEMP P. BATTLE, President.

Photographs

Chimborazo Hospital, the largest military hospital in the Confederate States. Built by slave labor on an elevated plateau overlooking the James River, its forty acres contained 105-120 buildings. It had its own ice house, soup house, bakery, soap factory, etc., operated its own farms, beef and goat herd, canal trading boat. Civil war casualties came to Richmond, where 76,000 soldiers were treated at the Chimbarazo Hospital, gained the distinction as the largest military hospital to have yet existed. The hospital was named after Mount Chimborazo in Ecuador.
Many free negroes and slaves were employed here as nurses.

Richmond, Virginia May 1865   Reproduced from the Collections of the Library of Congress

Chimborazo Hospital, (Confederate) Richmond, Va.
April. 1865.

Tredegar Iron Works was the center of iron manufacturing in the South. Industrial Negro laborers, both free and slave, played an accelerated role in all operations in Virginia ironworks as the needs of the Confederate armies drastically reduced the number of white laborers. The Iron Works consisted of five acres of buildings between the James River and the Kanawha Canal. At the peak of its productivity, the Tredegar Iron Works employed over 1,200 Negroes, both free and slave.

Richmond, Virginia 1865   Reproduced from the Collections of the Library of Congress

Old Dominion Iron and Nail Works, one of Richmond's most important plants for military production during the Civil War. Negroes, both free and slave, played an important role in the operations of the Iron and Nail Works in Virginia.

Richmond, Virginia 1865   Reproduced from the Collections of the Library of Congress

Haxall and Crenshaw Flour Mill, along the James River, where free negroes were conscripted during the Civil War. In August 1864, the Mill played a pivotal role in the supply of flour to the army when the raid of Wilson and Kautz cut the connection with the South and the army suffered three weeks of bread rations. In less than three weeks, there was an abundance of flour for the army and in less than ninety days, sixty thousand barrels had been secured and stored.[2]

Richmond, Virginia 1865   Reproduced from the Collections of the Library of Congress

---

[2] Richmond, Virginia, Tuesday Morning – December 28, 1875, Obituary, Death of Lewis Dabney Crenshaw, Esq., A public Calamity – Sketch of His Life – Business Education – His Public Spirit and Services to the City. Museum of the Confederacy, Richmond, Va.

Richmond and Danville Railroad Depot where free negroes were employed in the engine shops, and as firemen and brakemen, blacksmiths and helpers during the Civil War. The Richmond and Danville was the fourth major line that was essential to army operations in the Piedmont and southwestern Virginia. By 1864, it was of strategic importance, as General Robert E. Lee's main line was unprepared to assume the burden of heavy and constant transportation of war materials.[3]

Richmond, Virginia April 1865   Reproduced from the Collections of the Library of Congress

---

[3] Brewer, James H. *The Confederate Negro Virginia's Craftsmen and Military Laborers, 1861-1865* Durham, NC: Duke University Press, 1969

Canal and Ruins of Richmond & Danville Railroad Depot.

Richmond, Va., April, 1865.

Ballard T. Edwards

Ballard T. Edwards was a free African American born in 1829, in the town of Manchester or the South of Richmond, Virginia. Edwards was a bricklayer, plasterer and contractor and a descendant of a line of which had been free for several generations. He had a mixture of white and Native American blood. His grandfather, Edward B. Edwards was born in 1763 and his father, Edward B. Edwards, Jr., a carpenter, was born about 1800 and married Mary Trent, a teacher, who was prewar landowner. Some years before the Civil War, Edwards was taught to read and write by his mother. After the war, Edwards conducted a private night school for illiterate freedmen of Chesterfield and he likewise taught many apprentices the brick-laying trade. He was a staunch churchman and became clerk of the First Baptist Church of Manchester in 1847 and served until his death in 1881.[4]

While in the General Assembly he sponsored a bill for the renovation of the Capitol Building that he declared was an eyesore. Others held the same opinion, the rough brick walls being covered with stucco in such a manner that a look of cheapness hung over the structure. Later he was among those responsible for enactment of legislation permitting the erection of the present Ninth Street Bridge in competition with Mayo's Bridge, which was still a private toll structure. In 1870, he was unsuccessful in advocating a law to forbid racial segregation on common carriers.[5]

Lt. Blackford enlisted Ballard Edwards, 36, a bricklayer by occupation, for work on the Richmond and Danville Rail Road. His name is found on page 21 of the Virginia Bureau of Conscription Register of Free Negroes Enrolled and Detailed, May 1864-Jan. 1865. [page 162 in this work.]

---

[4] Jackson, Luther Porter. *Negro Office Holders in Virginia, 1865-1895*, Norfolk, Va.:
Guide Quality Press, 1945, 13-14.
[5] Lutz, Francis Earle. *Chesterfield: An Old Virginia County, Volume I, 1607-1954*
Sponsored by the Bermuda Ruritan Club. Waynesville, N.C.: Don Mills, Inc. 1954, 274-275.

BALLARD T. EDWARDS
House of Delegates
Chesterfield

Documents

Telegraphs and other correspondence clearly demonstrate the implementation of conscription laws and the use of African Americans by the War Department early in the War. Here Alfred Landon Rives requests that the negroes in Petersburg, collected by Captain Turnbull, be sent to Richmond. [Used with permission of the Virginia Historical Society, Richmond, Virginia; Mss1 T1434b 869]

THE SOUTHERN TELEGRAPH COMPANIES.

Office Hours, 7 A. M. to 10 P. M. Sundays, 8½ to 9½ A. M., and 7 to 9 P. M.

Terms and Conditions on which Messages are Received by these Companies for Transmission.

The public are notified that, in order to guard against mistakes in the transmission of messages, every message of importance ought to be repeated by being sent back from the station at which it is to be received to the station from which it is originally sent. Half the usual price for transmission will be charged for repeating the message, and while these Companies will as heretofore, use every precaution to ensure correctness, they will not be responsible for mistakes or delays in the transmission or delivery of repeated messages beyond five hundred times the amount paid for sending the message, nor will they be responsible for mistakes or delays in the transmission of unrepeated messages, from whatever cause they may arise, nor for the delays arising from interruptions in the workings of their telegraphs, nor for any mistakes or omission of any other Company, over whose lines a message is to be sent to reach the place of destination. All messages will hereafter be received by these Companies for transmission subject to the above conditions.

J. R. DOWELL, Gen'l Sup't, PETERSBURG, VA.

W. S. MORRIS, Pres't. LYNCHBURG, VA.

Received at _____ May 21 1862 at _____ o'clock, _____ minutes.

By telegraph from Richmond to Gen'l Huger

It is understood that negroes collected on order of War Department by Capt Turnbull are in Petersburg if so the necessities of the service require that they be sent here immediately

A L Rives
actg chi Eng
Bureau

138

General Robert E. Lee in his 15 March 1863 letter to the Sheriff of Essex County, Virginia requested that in accordance with the 12 February 1863 Act of the Virginia Legislature fifty able-bodied male free African Americans be sent to the Engineering Bureau. "In view of the great want of labor" needed to work on fortifications, General Lee hoped the requisition would be responded to as early as was possible. [Used with the permission of the Virginia Historical Society, Richmond, Virginia; Mss1H8928a 10]

Head Quarters Army of Northern Virginia
March 13ᵗ 1863

To
The Presiding Justice of Essex County, Va

Sir:

In accordance with an Act of the Virginia Legislature "To provide for the enrollment and employment of Free Negroes in the public service" passed Feby 12ᵗʰ 1863, you are earnestly requested to proceed at once to collect and deliver through the Sheriff of your county (who will receive a fair compensation for his services) to Col Wᵐ H. Stevens C. S. Engineers or his Agent at Richmond —

Fifty able bodied male Free Negroes — or such other number as, in your "judgement, may be proper and expedient" to work on the fortifications in this Department.

In view of the great want of labor, it is hoped that this requisition will be responded to as early as possible.

R E Lee
Genl.

Few records of the Conscription Office are extant, although the collection in the National Archives is largest for the Office in Virginia. Only one instance of an Enrolling Office Special Order relating to an individual found on the Register of Free Negroes Enrolled and Detailed, Virginia has been located: the order of Wash Logan detailing him until 1 April 1865 to Captain Wellford. His entry is found on page 63 of the Register [page 182 in this work]. [Used with permission of the Eleanor S. Brockenbrough Library, Museum of the Confederacy, Richmond, Virginia.]

Richmond

ENROLL'G OFFICE THIRD CONG. DISTRICT.

Richmond, Va., *December 29th* 1864.

[EXTRACT.]

SPECIAL ORDERS,

No. *157*

Free negro between 18 and 45 years of age
The following conscripts from .... *Richmond*

....

are hereby detailed *Until 1st April 1865*

and will report to ....

.... *Capt. P. A. Wellford*

....

Department; at the expiration of which time, unless this detail shall be

renewed, they will report at this office, or be considered deserters:

....

Wash Logan

....

....

....

.... *Capt. Cw. N. Wickford* ....
Capt. and E. O. 3d Cong. District.

Capt. P. A. Wellford
a.o.s.

140

CHAPTER I, VOLUME 241

BUREAU OF CONSCRIPTION, VA.

REGISTER OF FREE NEGROES
ENROLLED AND DETAILED.

MAY 1864 - JAN. 1865

Conscript Office
Richmond January 12/64

Sir
Exemption issue on Gov[ernor]'s certificate to John T. Stovall as Commissioner Revenue Henry Co[unty]. has been canceled at this Office. Outside of his being attached to the Service, the Governor in a communication ~~with the~~ to the War Department states that he had inadvertently issued certificates to partys elected in May last giving notice the services would not be required until February 1st/65 and that Military Service ~~should~~ was due from such partys.

1864 №.	Name		Description					Where Born
			Age	Eyes	Hair	Comp	Ht	
533	Scott	John	40	Bck	Bck	Blk	6 —	Richmond
534	Shaver	Henry	25	DK	"	Bck	5 8½	"
535	Smither	J. K.	20	Bck	"	Lt.	5 6	"
536	Strother	Geo W.	19	"	"	"	5 7½	Augusta
	Scott	Harrison	37	"	"	Dk	5 4	Richmond
	Scott	Archer	38	"	"	Yel	5 8	Hanover
	Scott	Miles	17					Do
	Sampson	Henry	28	Bck	Bck	Lt.	6 —	Richmond
	Swan	John	21	"	"	"	5 4	"
	Staunton	B.						"
	Sparrow	B.						"
	Sparrow	John	19					"
	Staunton	Decker	30	Bck	Bck	Lt.	5 6	"
	Stewart	George	27	Bck	Bck	Med	5 8½	Mecklenburg
	Southgate	James	48	DK	DK	bright	5 7	King & Queen
	Staunton	Daniel	20	Bck	Bck	"	5 5	Buckingham
	Spencer	Emmett	17			Lt.	5 4	Petersburg
	Smith	Jacob	29			DK	5 6	Richmond
	Shannon	Jas	29					"
	Slaughter	Albert	47					"
	Smith	J. T.	37					"
	Starr	Isaac	44					Pittsylvania
	Staterwhite	C.	35	Bck	Bck	Lt.	5 6	Essex

Occupation	Enlisted			Assigned		Remarks
	When	Where	By Whom	When	Where	
Messenger	20th Nov	Richmond	Lt Bell	20 Nov		Capt Blackford
Laborer	1 "	"	"	1 "		W. t. M. B.
Messenger	5 "	"	"	5 "		Capt Cooke
			Cfh Matthews			Engineer Dept
						Detailed Navy u tie 1st May /65
						Do Do
						Do Do
						Assd to C Bofs subs. Dept 1st May /65
						" Do " "
						" to J R & K Co tie 1st May /65
						" to Do "
						" to Do "
						" to Do "
Bell Smith						" to 1st May /65 C Renau and Steps
Framer			Lt Dickenson			" to Do to W. F. Bland
						" to J R & K Co 1st May /65
Brain Hand			Lt Bedyford			" to C W Gies
" "			"			" to Do
Boatman						" to Maj J B Harne
"						" Do Do
"						" Do Do
Laborer						" Act Withers Eng Dept
"			St Bumpass			" B. F. Gresham till 1st June

Page	No.	Name	Age	Eyes	Hair	Complex	Feet	In	State	Town or County	Occupation
1	21	Artieu, Lazarus	27	Blk	Blk	Blk	5'	8"	VA	Petersburg	Barber
	22	Archer, Peter	44	"	"	"	5'	6 1/2"	VA	"	"
	23	Adkins, James	22	"	"	"	5'	11"	VA	"	Laborer
	132	Ampy, James	35	"	"	Light	6'	5'	VA	Dinwiddie	"
	133	Ampy, Henry	31	"	"	Dk	6'	5'	VA	"	"
	134	Artis, Lug	22	"	"	Dk	5'	8"	VA	"	"
	135	Ampy, George	22	"	"	Lt	5'	9"	VA	"	"
	155	Allen, Henry	42						VA	Roanoke	Shoemaker
	188	Adkins, Gustus	18	Blk	Blk	Blk	5'	11"	VA	Washington	Laborer
	189	Adkins, Wm	24	Grey	"	Yellow	5'	6 1/2"	VA	Washington	"
	260	Andison, Z	47			Blk	5'	8"	VA	Greensville	
	291	Adams, James	19	Blk	Blk	Brown	5'	9"	VA	Richmond	Blacksmith
	322	Anderson, Wm	37	"	"	Lgt	5'	2"	VA	"	Baker
	323	Anderson, George	45	"	"	Dk	5'	5"	VA	"	Laborer
	334	Austin, Beverly	38	"	"	Lt	5'	6"	VA	"	"
	335	Anderson, Matt H.	39	Grey	"	"	5'	8"	VA	Henrico	Shoemaker
	336	Armstead, James		Dk	"	Dk	5'	6 1/2"	VA	Richmond	Laborer
	347	Anderson, Henry	43	Grey	Lt	Lt	6'		VA	"	"
	371	Anderson, John	21	Dk	Blk	Dk	5'	3"	VA	"	"
	386	Abrahams, Dabney	24	Blue	"	Lt	5'	7"	VA	"	Bar Keeper
	453	Alexander, John	26	Blk	"	Blk	5'	9 1/4"	VA	"	Laborer
	525	Allen, Robt	25		Dk		5'	8"	VA	Prince Ewd.	"
	540	Adkins, Wm	33	Blk	Blk	Copper	5'	10"	VA	Henry	
	541	Armstrong, John	25	"	"	"	5'	6"	VA	Pulaski	
	542	Armstead, Lewis	46	"	"	"	5'	8"	VA	Botetourt	Shoemaker
	615	Adkins, Joseph	22	"	"	Blk	6'		VA	Peterburg	Laborer
	616	Albert, Elias	21	"	"	Brown	5'	9"	VA	"	"
2	687	Ampy, James	48	Dk	Dk	Lgt	5'	8 1/2"	VA	Dinwiddie	Farmer
	688	Ailstork, Wm H	38	"	"	"	6'	2"	VA	Rockbridge	Blacksmith
	689	Asher, James	23	Hazel	Blk	Bright	5'	5"	VA	Culpeper	Laborer
	690	Arrington, James	25	Blk	Blk	Mul	5'	9"	VA	Madison	Blacksmith
	691	Arrington, Ambrose	27	"	"	"	5'	7"	VA	"	Laborer
	692	Arrington, James O.	30	"	"	"	5'	10"	VA	"	"
	693	Aaron, Gray	33	"	"	Dk	5'	8 1/2"	VA	Cumberland	
	694	Atkins, James	45	Dk	Dk	"	6'		VA	Smythe	Shoemaker
	695	Artis, B.	35	Blk	Blk	Copper	5'	7"	VA	Alleghany	
	696	Ailstork, Wm H	38	Dk	Dk	Lt	6'	2"	VA		Blacksmith
	607	Armis, John	36	Bk	Bk	Bk	5'	5 1/2"	VA		
	698	Andis, Simon	21	"	"	"	5'	6 1/4"	VA		
	699	Andis, Jno W.	20	"	"	"	5'	8 1/2"	VA		
	700	Artis, Coleman	28	Dk	Dk	Dk	5'	8"	VA	Pittsylvania	Farmhand
	701	Allen, Jno H	35	Lt	Blk	Lt	5'	7 1/2"	VA	Richmond	Barber
	702	Adams, Richard	23	Dk	Dk	Dk	5'	8"	VA	"	Laborer
	703	Allen, Joe	35	"	"	"	5'	1/2"	Miss		
	704	Armstead, James	20	"	"	"	5'	7"	VA	Richmond	"
	705	Andrews, Hudson	35	Bk	Bk	Bro	5'	8"	VA	Petersburg	Cooper
	706	Abby, William	41	"	"	Blk	5'	5"	VA	"	Laborer
	708	Adison, Thomas	37	"	"	"	5'	7"	VA	"	"
	709	Allen, William	41						VA	Henrico	
	710	Anderson, Henry		Blk	Blk	Mu	5'	5"	VA	Augusta	RR Hand
	711	Ailstork, Harrison	38	"	"	Bk	6'		VA	Rockbridge	Laborer
	1295	Allen, John	23			Lt	5'	3 1/2"	VA	Richmond	Laborer
	1296	Aldin, Chas	22			"	5'	5 1/4"	VA	"	"
	1297	Anderson, James	27			"	5'	7 1/4"	VA	"	"
	1503	Anderson, E	37	Hzl	Blk	Blk	5'	9"	VA		Blacksmith

Enlisted			Assigned		Remarks
When	**Where**	**By Whom**	**When**	**Where**	
03-May	Petersburg	Lt. Hoatte		Eng(ineer) Dept.	B(reast) Works
"	"	"		Do.	B(reast) Works
"	"	"		Detailed Gas Works	Order of C(ommander)
"	Dinwiddie	R G Bosseau		Eng(ineer) Dept.	B(reast) Works
"	"	"		Do.	"
"	"	"		Do.	B(reast) Works
"	"	"		Do.	
01-May	Roanoke	Capt. Clements	April	Do.	
30-Apr	Washington	T M Smith	14-Jun	Q(uarter) M(aster) Dept.	13th District
30-Apr	"		15-Jun	Q(uarter) M(aster) Dept.	
30-Apr	Greensville	D J Godwin			Application for exempt by C O Sanford
06-Apr	Richmond	Capt. Coke			Not accounted for
12-Apr	"	"			Detailed to Surgeon T M Prime
13-Apr	"	"	13-Apr	N(iter) & M(ining) Bureau	
13-Apr	"	"			Light Duty
14-Apr	"	"	25-Apr	N(iter) & M(ining) Bureau	
16-Apr	"	"			Deserter
18-Apr	"	"		Detailed Surg. Manson	
22-Apr	"	"	22-Apr	N(iter) & M(ining) Bureau	
					Order to refront to Eng(ineering) Off(ice)
27-Apr	"	"	April	Eng(ineer) Dept.	Goochland
03-May					
01-Jul	P Ewd	Zimmerman	01-Jul	Eng(ineer) Dept. H. B.	
	Newbern	Lt. Poole		Q(uarter) M(aster) Dept. Dublin	
		"		"	
	Fincastle	Lt. Nowlin	27-Jul	J. R. Anderson & Co.	N(iter) & M(ining)
26-Jul	Petersburg	Lt. Scott	26-Jul	Eng(ineer) Dept.	
27-Jul	"	"	27-Jul	Do.	
04-May	Dinwidee	R G Bosseau	22-Jun	Eng(ineer) Dept.	
30-Jul		Col. Peytorr	01-Aug	Gen Ransom	
19-Aug	Culpeper	Lt. Graves		Eng(ineer) Dept.	
01-Jul	Madison CH	Lt. Adams	10-Jul	to M(edical) Dept.	Gordonsville
"	"	"	"	"	"
"	"	"	"	"	"
15-Jun				"	R B Trent
22-Jun	Marion	Lt. Terry		Not Assigned	Unaccounted
				N(iter) & M(ining) Bureau	
				Eng(ineer) Dept.	
					Detailed till 1st June 65
					"
					"
23-Apr		Lt. McCue			Unaccounted
25-May		Capt. Coke	Gen Kemper		Light Duty
27-Aug		"		N(iter) & M(ining) Bureau	
12-Sep		"			Deserter
15-Sep		"		N(iter) & M(ining) Bureau	
22-Sep	Petersburg	Sgt. Winfree	22-Sep	to M(edical) Dept.	
23-Sep	"		"	"	
					Exempt by Med(ical) Ex(amining) Board
27-Sep	"	"	27-Sep		
Oct				Eng(ineer) Dept.	
"				"	
Nov		Lt. Blackford		R(ichmond) & D(anville) R(ail) R(oad)	
"		"		"	
"		"		"	
					Detailed to Capt. MacMurdo till 1st March

Page	No.	Name	Description						Where Born		Occupation
			Age	Eyes	Hair	Complex	Feet	In	State	Town or County	
3		Anderson, Chas	46	Dk	Dk	Dk	5'	2 1/2"	VA	Henrico	
		Adams, H	35	Blk	Blk	Lt	5'	4"	VA	Richmond	
		Aske, Amos	18			"	5'	6"	VA	"	
		Atkins, A	41	Dk	Dk	"	6'	1"	VA	"	
		Atkins, C	40	"	"	"	5'	11"	VA	"	
		Anderson, Edw	37	Hazel	Blk	Blk	5'	9"	VA	"	
		Anderson, Geo	28							"	Boatman
		Ashton, Rudy								Westmoreland	Farmer
		Adams, Miles									Shoemaker
		Ashton, Richard	25			Blk	5'	6"		Westmoreland	Farmer
		Ashton, Saml	42			"	5'	7"		"	"
4		Chandler, Richard	48	Blk	Blk	Blk	5'	8"	VA	Essex	Laborer
		Chandler, Arch	35	"	"	Lt	5'	10"	VA	"	"
		Cousin, Landy								Henrico Co	
5	1504	Campbell, J	38	Brown	Dk	Lt	5'	6"	VA	Richmond City	Laborer
	1505	Cosby, Wm	32	Dk	Blk	Lt	5'	8"	"	Do.	Blacksmith
	1506	Cunningham, R	32	"	"	"	5'	8"	"	Do.	Engineer Hand
		Cox, George	34	Dk	Dk	"	5'	6'	"	Goochland	
		Clarke, Isaiah	32				5'	1 1/2"	"	Richmond	Laborer
		Cousins, James	28	Blk	Blk	Lt	5'	6"	"	"	"
		Cousins, Wm	17	"	"	"	4'	6"	"	"	"
		Cooper, H							"	"	"
		Carsons, H							"	"	"
		Coy, Bob							"	"	"
		Crump, R.							"	"	"
		Collins, John W	39	Blk	Dk	Dk	5'	8"	"	King & Queen	Shoemaker
		Cole, Alexander	26	"	Blk	Mul	5'	10 1/2"		Mecklenburg Co.	Blacksmith
		Cousins, Elijah	19	"	"	Blk	5'	8 1/2"		"	"
		Cooper, Thomas	30	"	"	Yellow	5'	10"		Rockbridge	Teamster
		Chandler, Loury	30	Blue	Blk	Lt	6'			Essex Co.	Laborer
		Chandler, James	25	"	"	Dk	5'	9"		"	"
		Carter, Charles	22			Lt	5'	6"		Richmond	
		Cooper, Ned	28							"	Boatman

Enlisted			Assigned		Remarks
When	Where	By Whom	When	Where	
				Navy	till 1st May 1865
					Detailed to C Bass Supt Pent(entiar)y to 1st May 1865
					Detailed to O F Manson to 1st May 1865
Jany 2/65		Lt. Blackford		N(iter) & M(ining) Bureau	
"		"		"	
Jany 3/65		"			Detailed to Capt. McMurdo
					Detailed to Maj J. B. Harvie
		Lt. Jenkins			Detailed to Thos Parker 1st May 1865
					Detailed as Shoemaker 1st July 1865
Jan/65		Lt. Jenkins		Eng(ineer) Dept.	
"		"		"	
Dec/64		Lt. Bumpass			Detailed to B F Gresham till 1st June
Feb/65		"			Detailed to Surg. W P Palmer till 1st July/65
					Detailed to Jos R Anderson Co
12-Dec	Richmond	Lt. Blackford	12-Dec	N(iter) & M(ining) Bureau	
07-Dec	"	"	07-Dec	Do.	E H Gill
20-Dec	"	"	20-Dec	R(ichmond) & P(etersburg) Railroad	Detailed to Navy til 1st May '65
					Detailed to Navy til 1st May '65
					Detailed to C Bass Supt Pent(entiar)y to 1st May 1865
					Detailed to C Bass Supt Pent(entiar)y to 1st May 1865
					Detailed to J(ames) R(iver) and K(anawha) Co. "
					Do. "
					Do. "
					Do. "
					Detailed till 1st May 1865
		W. T. Dickinson			Detailed till 1st May Clarksville Ord(nance) Shops
					Do. "
					Detailed till 1st May to Wm Jordan
5-Dec					Detailed to Subsistence Departments
"					Do. "
Jany 3/65		Lt. Blackford			Detailed to R E Blankenship
" 6		"			Detailed to Maj. J B Harvie

Page	No.	Name	Description						Where Born		Occupation
			Age	Eyes	Hair	Complex	Feet	In	State	Town or County	
		Cotrell, David	39							"	"
		Claiborne, A	23							"	"
		Cox, Joe	37	Dk	Dk	Lt	5'	6"		Goochland	Laborer
		Custille, Joe	29			Brown	5'	10 1/2"		Richmond	"
		Campbell, James	25	Blk	Blk	Bright	5'	7"		King & Queen	"
		Cousins, George								Henrico	
		Cousins, Charles								"	
		Coolin, Joe	29	Blk	Blk	Blk	5'	6"		Powhatan	Farmer
		Cooper, Henry	39	"	"	"	5'	8 1/2"		"	"
		Cochran, Brown								Staunton	Shoemaker
7	1	Batt, Drewy	27	Blk	Blk	Ginger	4'	6'	VA	Petersburg	Laborer
	2	Baily, Christopher	38	"	"	"	5'	11"	VA	"	"
	3	Brown, Moses	22	Hazel	"	Yellow	5'	6"	VA	"	Barber
	4	Brown, Albert	20	Blk	"	Blk	5'	8"	VA	"	Laborer
	5	Boone, John	25	"	"	"	5'	3"	VA	"	"
	6	Brandon, John	19	Grey	"	Light	5'	10"	VA	"	"
	7	Brandon, Alexander	28	Blk	"	Brown	5'	10"	VA	"	"
	8	Brandon, Henry	45	Hazel	"	Dark	5'	9"	VA	"	"
	9	Bird, Jesse	29	Blue	"	Light	5'	7"	VA	"	"
	10	Bonner, James	24	Blk	"	Blk	5'	9"	VA	"	"
	11	Berry, John	36	"	"	Brown	5'	7"	VA	"	"
	95	Brockwell, Thomas	21	Hazel	"		5'	8"	VA	"	Barber
	101	Boon, Bradley	36	Dk	Dk	Dk	5'	7"	VA	Dinwiddie	Laborer
	102	Batt, Ben	40	"	"	Light	5'	7 1/2"	VA	"	"
	103	Branch, Wm	32	"	"	"	6'	1"	VA	"	"
	104	Botts, William	25	"	"	Dk	5'	6"	VA	"	"
	105	Bonner, Ben	18	"	"	"	5'	3"	VA	"	"
	106	Bonner, John	37	"	"	"	5'	8"	VA	"	"
	107	Butcher, Willis	40	"	"	"	5'	8 1/2"	VA	"	"
	108	Butcher, George	19	"	"	"	5'	9"	VA	"	"
	204	Beverly, Wm	44	Blk	"	"	5'	9"	VA	Washington	"
	205	Brady, Thomas	24	Grey	Light	Yellow	5'	10"	VA	"	
	206	Brady, Denham	25	"	"	"	5'	10"	VA		
	207	Brady, Rush	25	"	"	"	5'	11"	VA		
	208	Barter, Washington	43	Blue	Blk	"	6'	1"	VA	Washington Co.	
	209	Burcher, Wm	45	"	"	"	5'	8 1/2"	VA	"	
	210	Branch, David	18	"	"	"	5'	9"	VA	"	
	211	Barney, Newell	21	Grey	"	"	5'	8"	VA	"	
8	240	Bailey, Buck	49			Yellow	5'	11 1/2"	VA	Sussex Co.	Laborer
	241	Belcher, Payton	26			Black	5'	3"	VA	"	"
	269	Brown, Elmore	20	Blk	Blk	Lgt	5'	9'	VA	Richmond City	"
	281	Bacchus, Manual	22	"	"	Brown	5'	8"	VA	"	"
	282	Bacchus, Frank	19	"	"	Light	5'	8"	VA	"	
	283	Brooks, Moses	32	"	"	Dk	5'	7"	VA	"	
	300	Brown, William	19	"	Dk	Lt	5'	6"	VA	"	
	301	Brooks, Marcellus	20	"	"	Dk	5'	8 1/2"	VA	"	
	314	Butler, Joseph	22	"	"	"	5'	8"	VA	"	
	343	Brown, Robert	42	Dk	Blk	Lt	5'	7"	VA	Henrico	
	354	Barnes, Wm	30	Brown	"	"	5'	7"	VA	Richmond	Carpenter
	368	Barrow, Joseph	17	Gray	Dk	"	5'	4"	VA	"	Boatman
	369	Butcher, John	18	Blk	Blk	Dk	5'	5 1/2"	VA	"	"
	379	Bird, James H.	21	Gray	"	Lt	5'	6"	VA	"	Cooper
	380	Brown, Hend	43	Dk	"	Dk	5'	8"	VA	"	
	381	Bass, Wm	34	"	"	Light	5'	6 1/2"	VA	"	Laborer
	382	Brown, John H.	21	"	"	Dk	5'	10"	VA	"	"
	394	Bird, Isaiah	20	"	"	Brown	5'	2"	VA	"	"

Enlisted			Assigned		Remarks
When	Where	By Whom	When	Where	
" "		"			Do.
" "		"			Do.
" 9		"			Detailed to Lt. Parker, CSW
" 12		Lt. Blackford			Pending for Lt. Parker, CSW
		Lt. Dickinson			Detailed to John B Morris 1st Msy '65
					Detailed to T C Leake to 1st May '65
					"
					Detailed to Maj. Randolph 1st May '65
					"
		Lt. Matthews			Detailed to J C Hanger till 1st July 1865
03-May	Petersburg	Lt. T Heath		Eng(ineer) Dept.	
"	"	"		Do.	
"	"	"		Do.	
"	"	"		Do.	
"	"	"		Eng(ineer) Dept.	
"	"	"		Do.	
"	"	"		Do.	
"	"	"		Eng(ineer) Dept.	
"	"	"		Do	
"	"	"		Do.	
"	"	"		Do.	
"	"	"		Eng(ineer) Dept.	E H Gill
30-Apr	Dinwiddie	Lt Bosseau		"	
"	"	"		"	
"	"	"		"	
"	"	"		"	
"	"	"		"	
"	"	"		"	
"	"	"		"	
"	"	"		"	
"		P R Hicks	15-Jun	Q(uarter) M(aster) Dept.	13th District
"			"	Do.	"
"			"	Do.	"
"				Q(uarter) M(aster) Dept.	"
"	Washington Co.	Wm M Thompson	15-Jun	Q(uarter) M(aster) Dept.	"
"	"	"			
"	"	"	15-Jun	Q(uarter) M(aster) Dept.	
May & June	Rockingham				
	"				
01-Jul	Mecklenburg	W. Atkins	01-Jul	Detailed to Clarksville to 1st May '65	
	"	"		"	
15-Jun	Prince Edward	Zimmerman	15-Jun	Eng(ineer) Dept. H Bridge	
"	"	"	"	"	
01-Jul	"	"	01-Jul	"	
	Newbern	Lt. Peale		I H Lacy Q(uarter) M(aster) Dept. Dublin	
	"	"		"	
	"	"		"	
	Fincastle	Lt. Nowlin		J(ames) R(iver) C(anal) & C(ompany) N(iter) & M(ining)	
	"	"		"	
	"	"		"	
Detailed to Jno S Wilson till 1st May '65				Detailed By Bass	
04-May	Petersburg	Lt. Scott		Eng(ineer) Dept.	
27-Jul	"	"		"	
28-Jul	"	"		"	
13-Jul	Dinwiddie			"	

Page	No.	Name	Age	Eyes	Hair	Complex	Feet	In	State	Town or County	Occupation
	395	Brooks, John	32	Gray	"	Lgt	5'	5"	VA	"	"
	418	Brown, James	18	"	"	"	5'	11"	VA	"	"
	431	Bird, John	19			Black	5'	8"	VA	Sussex Co.	"
	432	Briggs, Tazewell	20			Copper	5'	8"	VA	Montgomery Co	
	433	Briggs, George	24	"	"	"	5'	9"	VA		Laborer
	458	Briggs, Buford	29						VA	Floyd Co.	"
	460	Burke, Elick	22	Blk	Blk	Blk	6'		VA	Rockingham	"
	461	Burke, Wm	24	"	"	"	5'	10"	VA	"	Cooper
	462	Bundy, Wm	40	"	"	Dk Yellow	5'	6 1/2"	VA	"	
	463	Beard, Wm	20	"	"	Yellow	5'	4 1/2"	VA	"	Blacksmith
	464	Barnett, George	35	"	"	Blk	5'	11"	VA	"	Laborer
10	719	Brown, Jim	34	Blk	Blk	Dk	5'	9"	VA	Nelson Co.	
	720	Bones, William	22	"	"	Lt	5'	5"	VA	"	
	721	Bones, Joseph	17	"	"	"	5'	4"	VA	"	Barber
	722	Billey,	25	"	"	"	6'		VA	Amherst	Carpenter
	723	Branham, M	18	"	"	"	5"	4"	VA		Barber
	724	Branham, R	32	"	"	"	5'	11"	VA	"	Huckster
	725	Beverly, F	18	"	"	"	5'	7"	VA	"	Barber
	726	Beverly, Andrew	37	"	"	"	6'		VA	"	Butcher
	727	Bennit, White	18	"	"	Blk	5'	7"	VA	Buckingham	Blacksmith
	728	Burneal, Robert	45						VA	New Kent	Do.
	729	Braxton, James	44						VA	"	Do.
	730	Brown, William	24	Dk	Dk	Brown	5'	6"	VA	"	Barber
	731	Barlow, Harding	20						VA	"	"
	732	Bundy, Harrison	24	Blk	Blk	Blk	6'		VA	Spottsylvania	Bar Keeper
	733	Bundy, George	33	"	"	"	6'		VA	"	Laborer
	734	Bannister, Henry	39	"	"	Copper	5'	4"	VA	Culpeper	Blacksmith
	735	Bundy, Richard	22	"	"		5'	6"	VA	"	Deck Hand
	736	Beazley, Arthur	20	"	"	Mulatto	5'	9"	VA	Caroline	Blacksmith
	737	Beazley, James	24	Hazel	"	"	5'	9"	VA	"	"
	738	Bruce, John	24	Blk	"	Brown	5'	8"	VA	"	Laborer
	739	Butcher, William	49	"	"	Blk	5'	9"	VA	Petersburg	
	740	Broddy, John	33	Dk	Dk	Dk	5'	9"	VA	Smythe	
	741	Broddy, Charles	35	"	"	"	5'	10"	VA	"	
	742	Brown, Fleming	25	"	"	"	5'	7"	VA	Grayson	
	743	Bickley, Gunaway	23	"	"	Yellow	6'	3"	VA	Russell	Laborer
	744	Black, Thomas	21	"	"	Copper	6'	4"	VA	"	"
	745	Brown, George	20	"	"	Lt	5'	8"	VA	Highland	Blacksmith
	746	Beyer, David	29	"	"	"	5'	9"	VA	"	Laborer
	747	Burns, John	20	Blk	Blk	Dk	5'	11"	VA	Augusta	"
9	465	Barnett, Wm	23	Blk	Blk	Blk	5'	51/4"	VA	Rockingham	Laborer
	466	Broddus, Frank	31	"	"	Yellow	5'	9 1/2"	VA	"	Farmer
	498	Brandon, E	42		"		5'	1"	VA	Mecklenburg	"
	499	Brandon, P	48		"		5'	8"	VA	"	Laborer
	500	Bartlett, D	46		"		5'	9"	VA	Prince Edward	Farmer
	501	Bland, Jas	21		"		5'	8"	VA	"	"
	502	Brown, T H	23		"		5'	4"	VA	"	"
	543	Beverly, S. H.	37	Blk	Blk	Blk	5'	7"	VA	Henry	"
	544	Burks, Hubbert	32	"	"	"	5'		VA	Albemarle	Jobber
	545	Bean, B. M.	36	"	"	Brown	5'	10"	VA	Roanoke	Trader
	546	Brown, Jim	40	"	"	Mulatto	5'	11 1/2"	VA	Botetourt	Fisherman
	547	Brackins, Wm	43	Brown	"	Yellow	5'	10"	VA	"	Trader
	548	Bradley, Wm	26	Blk	"	Blk	5'	10"	VA	"	Blacksmith
	549	Bannister, Wm	22	"	"	"	5'	10"	VA		Laborer
	605	Burke, Robt	48	Blk	Blk	"	5'	7"	VA	Petersburg	Carpenter & Lab
	621	Blizzard, Merritt	45	"	"	"	5'	8"	VA	"	Carpenter
	622	Brown, Wm	23	Hazel	"	Bright	5'	9"	VA	"	Laborer
	626	Butler, Nat	40			Blk	5'	7"	VA	Dinwiddie	"
	627	Bradley, Alfred	25			Dk	5'	10"	VA	Amelia	"
	628	Bailey, Thomas	26				5'		VA	Chesterfield	"

Enlisted			Assigned		Remarks
When	Where	By Whom	When	Where	
27-Jul	Amelia			"	
16-Jun	Chesterfield			"	
06-Jun	Powhatan			"	
30-Jul	Amelia			"	
30-Jul	Dinwiddie	R G Bosseau	27-Jul	"	
28-Jul	Albemarle	Capt. Colston	30-Jun	Maj. Richards	
"	"		"	"	
"	"		"	"	
"	"		"	"	
30-Jun		Lt. Carpenter	01-Jul	"	
30-Apr	Sussex	D J Godwin			
"		"			
05-Apr	Richmond	Capt. Coke	20-Apr	N(iter) & M(ining) Bureau	
06-Apr	"	"	16-Apr	N(iter) & M(ining) Bureau	
06-Apr	"	"	15-Apr	"	
					Discharged Med(ical)
					E(xamining) Board
06-Apr	"	"			Not Accounted for
07-Apr	"	"			
07-Apr	"	"	16-Apr	N(iter) & M(ining) Bureau	
07-Apr	"	"		Eng(ineer) Dept.	
14-Apr	"	"		Eng(ineer) Dept.	
19-Apr	"	"		Eng(ineer) Dept.	
21-Apr	"	"			Deserter
21-Apr	"	"	20-Apr	N(iter) & M(ining) Bureau	
26-Apr	"	"			Deserter
26-Apr	"	"			Deserter
27-Apr	"	"			Do.
27-Apr	"	"		Eng(ineer) Dept.	
28-Apr	"	"			Not Accounted for
28-Apr	"	"	07-May	N(iter) & M(ining) Bureau	
30-Apr	"	"	30-Apr	N(iter) & M(ining) Bureau	
05-May	Sussex	D J Godwin			
07-May	Montgomery	Lt. Sydenstriker		Q(uarter) M(aster) Dept.	Capt. Woodson
07-May	"			Do.	Do.
June	Floyd Co.	Lt. Farrar			
May & June	Rockingham	C A Peyton		Q(uarter) M(aster) Dept.	
"	"			Q(uarter) M(aster) Dept.	
"	"				
"	"			N(iter) & M(ining) Bureau	
"	"				
02-Jul	Nelson	Lt. Carpenter	03-Jul	Maj. Richard	
"	"	"	"	"	
"	"	"	"	"	
04-Jul	Amherst	Lt. Roane	06-Jul	"	
08-Jul	"	"	11-Jul	Gen. Ransom	
"	"	"	"	"	
"	"	"	"	"	
"	"	"	"	"	
10-Jun		A T Mosely	14-Jun	Col. Scott	High Bridge
Oct		T Taylor	Oct	N(iter) & M(ining) Bureau	
"		"	"	"	
					To LC Crawford transfer
"		"	"	"	till 1st May '65
"		"	"	"	
04-Apr		Lt. Williams		Unassigned	Petersburg for Detail
"		"		"	"
27-Aug	Culpeper	Lt. Graves			
04-Sep	"	"			
19-Jul	Bowling Green	Lt. Hancock	20-Jul	Gen. Ewell	Richmond
"	"	"	"	"	"
"	"	"	"	"	"

Page	No.	Name	Description						Where Born		Occupation
			Age	Eyes	Hair	Complex	Feet	In	State	Town or County	
	629	Bently, S	40				5'		VA	Powhatan	"
	656	Bailey, Washington	36			Dk	5'	9"	VA	Amelia	Farmer
	702	Bounis, Charles	44	Blk	Blk	Blk	5'	7"	VA	Dinwiddie	"
	713	Bowles, Peter	22	"	"	Dk	5'	7"	VA	Albemarle	"
	714	Bowles, Zack	25	"	"	"	5'	8"	VA	"	"
	715	Bowles, E	54	"	"	Lt	6'		VA	"	"
	716	Banks, A	40	"	"	"	6'	2"	VA	"	Laborer
	717	Barber, James	25	"	"	"	5'	8"	VA	"	"
	718	Brown, John	23	"	"	Dk	5'	8"	VA	Nelson	Farmer
11	748	Burns, Moses	32	Blk	Blk	Mulatto	6'		VA	Augusta Co.	Farmer
	749	Banks, Thorton	25	Dk	Dk	Blk	5'	5"	VA	"	"
	750	Bailey, William	22	Gr	Dk	Copper	5'	9"	VA	Greenville	Laborer
	751	Belchers, Peyton	26	"	"	"	5'	11"	VA	"	"
	752	Bowers, Robert	45	Blue	Blk	Blk	5'	9"	VA	"	"
	753	Barrett, James	33	"	"	Yellow	5'	8"	VA	Pittsylvania Co.	Blacksmith
	754	Barber, Elijah	23	"	"	"	5'	8"	VA	"	Farm Hand
	755	Bowman, Henry	35	"	"	Blk	5'	7"	VA	"	Shoemaker
	756	Bowman, Bob	29	"	"	"	5'	8"	VA	"	Boatman
	757	Bowman, Joe	19	"	"	"	5'	4"	VA	"	"
	758	Bowser, Everett	47	"	"	Bro	5'	11"	VA	"	"
	759	Bartlett, Ben	42	"	"	Yellow	5'	11"	VA	"	"
	760	Bowman, Milton	35	"	"	Blk	5'	4"	VA	"	"
	761	Bowman, Henry	35	"	"	Dk	5'	7"	VA	"	Farm Hand
	762	Brown, Carrington	18	Dk	"	Lt	5'	4 1/2"	VA	Richmond	Barber
	763	Barker, Dick	49	"	Dk	Lt	5'	5"	VA	Manchester	"
	764	Brown, Eli	33	"	"	Blk	5'	6"	VA	Faquier	House Servant
	765	Banks, Alexander	20	Lt	Blk	Dk	5'	3"	VA	Henrico	Laborer
	766	Byrd, J H	20	Dk	Dk	Lt	5'	7"	VA	Richmond	"
	767	Byrd, William	23	Dk	"	Dk	5'	8"	VA	"	"
	768	Black, John	34	"	"	"	5'	8 1/2"	VA	Hanover	Farmer
	769	Beasly, S H	39	Bl	Blk	Copper	6'		VA	Franklin	"
	770	Branch, James	30	Dk	Dk	Blk	5'	7 1/2"	VA	Dinwiddie	Shoemaker
	771	Banister, W F	22						VA		
	772	Beverly, Douglas	44						VA		
	773	Beverly, John	40						VA		
	774	Bonner, William	48	Blk	Blk	Blk	5'	10"	VA	Petersburg	Blacksmith
	775	Brander, Theopholous	27	"	"	"	5'	6"	VA	"	Laborer
	777	Bishop, Jeff	35	"	"	"	5'	8"	VA	"	"
12	778	Burrows, Frank	25	Blk	Blk	Blk	5'	4"	VA	Petersburg	Laborer
	779	Beard, Tom	18	"	"	Yellow	5'	7"	VA	"	"
	780	Bowling, John	30	"	"	Blk	5'	6"	VA	"	"
	781	Brander, Jria	28	"	"	Brown	5'	11"	VA	"	"
	782	Boon, B	22	"	"	"	5'		VA	"	"
	783	Burris, Henry	27				5'		VA	Richmond	Cartman
	784	Bazell, Jas	40				5'		VA	"	Groom
	785	Brown, Richard	22	Blk	Blk	Mulatto	5'	8 1/2"	VA	Augusta	House Servant
	786	Baily, Irving	32	"	"	Ginger	5'	6"	VA	Surry	Distiller
	787	Bailey, Nat	35	"	"	Dk	5'	5"	VA	"	Laborer
	788	Bailey, Thomas	26	"	"	"	5'	5"	VA	"	"
	789	Barber, James	40	Hz	"	Mulatto	5'	5"	VA	Chesterfield	"
	790	Bailey, George	23	Blk	Blk	Blk	5'	8"	VA	Dinwiddie	Fireman
	791	Bird, Samuel	21	Y	Grey	"	5'	6 1/2"	VA	Rockbridge	Teamster
	792	Beverly, Alexander	20	"	"		5'	7 1/2"	VA	"	Laborer
	793	Brice, James	25	"	Blk	"	5'	6"	VA	"	Tanner
	794	Bird, Alexander	24	Blk	"	"	5'	10"	VA	Lynchburg	"
	795	Byers, Wyatt	18	"	"	"	5'	11"	VA		
	1398	Bradley, Evans	48	"	"	Lt	6'	2"	VA	King William	Farmer

Enlisted			Assigned		Remarks
When	Where	By Whom	When	Where	
13-Jul				Eng(ineer) Dept.	
22-Jun	Marion	Lt. Terry			Unaccounted
"	"	"			"
					Discharged Med(ical)
02-Jun		Lt. Hammer			Ex(amining) Board
11-Jun		Lt. Sawyer			Unaccounted
"		"			"
					Detailed to J. Majors till
01-Jul					1st May '65
					Detailed til 1st January
"					'65
15-Jul					Unaccounted
15-Jul				To M(edical) Dept.	
26-Aug				"	
May	Hucksford	Lt. Holland			Unaccounted
"	"	"			"
"	"	"			Deserted
19-Apr		Lt. McCue			Unaccounted
					Detailed to Henry
23-Apr		"			Ramsey
"		"		Eng(ineer) Dept.	
28-Apr		"		To M(edical) Dept.	
"		"		"	
"		"		"	
"		"		"	
30-Apr		"			Unaccounted
06-Oct		Lt. Williams		Eng(ineer) Dept.	
07-Jun		Capt. Coke		N(iter) & M(ining) Bureau	
03-Aug		"			Unaccounted
30-Aug		"		N(iter) & M(ining) Bureau	
30-Sep		"		"	
13-Sep		"		"	
17-Sep		"		"	
24-Sep		"		"	
01-May		Capt. Bernard			Unaccounted
04-May	R G Bosseau				"
		Lt. Newlon		N(iter) & M(ining) Bureau	"
		"		"	
		"			Deserted
20-Sep	Sgt Winfree	Sgt. Winfree	20-Sep	To M(edical) Dept.	
22-Sep		"	22-Sep	"	
					Exempted by Med(ical)
24-Sep		"	24-Sep		Ex(amining) Board
26-Sep	Petersburg	Sgt. Winfree	26-Sep	To M(edical) Dept.	
27-Sep	"	"	27-Sep	Ordered to Hospital by Med(ical) Board	
28-Sep	"	"	28-Sep	To M(edical) Dept.	
					Ex(empt) by Med(ical)
29-Sep	"	"	29-Sep		Ex(amining) Board
29-Sep	"	"	"	Sent to Hospital for treatment	
Oct	"	"		Eng(ineer) Dept. N(iter) & M(ining) Bureau	
"	"			N(iter) & M(ining) Bureau	
				Eng(ineer) Dept.	
20-Apr		Lt. Spencer			
"		"		Eng(ineer) Dept.	Unaccounted
"		"		"	
01-May				Discharged by Med(ical) Ex(amining) Board	
"				Eng(ineer) Dept.	
				To M(edical) Dept.	
				"	
				Detailed till 1st November '64	
27-Jun				Eng(ineer) Dept.	
				To M(edical) Dept.	
19-Nov		Lt. Haw	20-Nov	Eng(ineer) Dept.	

Page	No.	Name	Age	Eyes	Hair	Complex	Feet	In	State	Town or County	Occupation
						Description			Where Born		
	1399	Bradley, Delaware	37	"	"	"	5'	6"	VA	"	"
	1400	Bradley, Thomas	35	"	"	"	5'	6"	VA	"	"
	1401	Bradley, Pleasant	35	"	"	"	5'	6"	VA	"	"
	1402	Barly, Kiah					5'		VA	Richmond	Fireman
	1403	Biliu, James	22			Lt	5'	5"	VA	"	"
	1404	Baker, Robt	25			Dk	5'	5 1/2"	VA	"	Eng Cleaner
	1405	Banks, John	42			Lt	5'	5 3/4"	VA	"	Laborer
	1406	Brooks, Joe	20			Dk	6'		VA	"	"
	1407	Bryant, Wm	25			Lt	5'	5"	VA	"	"
	1408	Bird, Ben	22			Dk	5'	4 1/2"	VA	"	"
		--See page 93--									
13	53	Crocker, Benjamin	34	Gray	Blk	Blk	5'	8"	VA	Petersburg	Laborer
	54	Colston, J	34	Blk	Blk	Brown	5'	8"	VA	"	Shoemaker
	55	Cooley, Charles	37	"	"	"	5'	8"	VA	"	Carpenter
	56	Carter, James	31	Brown	"	Light	5'	11"	VA	"	"
	57	Cohen, John	25	Blk	"	Blk	5'	9"	VA	"	Laborer
	58	Crowder, Henry	38	Blue	"	Yellow	5'	4"	VA	"	"
	59	Cowin, Isham	46	Blk	"	"	5'	2"	VA	"	"
	60	Cholsom, James	29	"	"	Blk	5'	7"	VA	"	"
	61	Coleman, Cornilus	35	"	"	"	5'	10"	VA	"	"
	62	Chivers, John	23	Blue	Bushy	Dark	5'	3"	VA	"	"
	63	Coleman, Andrew	40	Blk	Blk	Dark	5'	8"	VA	"	"
	136	Catnick, John	30	"	"	"	5'	6"	VA	Dinwiddie	"
	168	Coff, Henry	22	Hazel	"	Bright	5'	9"	VA	Roanoke	"
	223	Craig, David	25	"	"	Yellow	5'	7 1/2"	VA	Washington	Blk
	224	Clarke, Mitchell	25	"	"	"	5'	8"	VA	Do.	
	225	Coleman, William	25	Blue	"	"	5'	10"	VA	Washington Co.	
	226	Clarke, R. J.	25	Gray	"	Blk	5'	5"	VA	"	
	227	Crawford, Chas. W.	25	"	"	"	5'	10"	VA	Scott Co.	
	233	Clark, Thomas	20	Dk	Dk	Brown	5'	9 1/2"	VA	Washington Co.	
	261	Cain. T. S.	29			Blk	5'	5"	VA	Greenville Co.	
	262	Cain, Wm Son	30			"	5'	5"	VA	"	
	292	Cole, William	29	Blk	Blk	Lgt	5'	9"	VA	Richmond	Blacksmith
	294	Cox, Albert	32	Blk	Dk	Lgt	5'	7"	VA	Goochland Co.	Carpenter
	295	Cosby, William	32	"	Blk	Lgt	5'	8"	VA	Richmond	Blacksmith
	296	Crow, Albert	40	"	"	"	5'	4"	VA	"	Carpenter
	316	Coy, Pleasant	40	Dk	Dk	Dk	5'	2"	VA	"	Laborer
	326	Cox, George	38	"	"	Lgt	5'	5"	VA	Goochland	"
	364	Clay, Archer	40	"	"	Blk	5'	5"	VA	Richmond	Blacksmith
	365	Cousins, James	32	"	"	Dk	5'	3 1/2"	VA	"	Nurse
14	366	Cole, Thomas	46	Dk	Blk	Dk	5'	8 1/2"	VA	Richmond	Machinist
	377	Causway, Matt	23	Gray	"	Lgt	5'	5"	VA	"	Blacksmith
	409	Cunningham, R	27	Dk	"	Blk	5'	4 1/2"	VA	"	Fireman RR
	412	Cowan, James	33	"	"	"	5'	1/2"	VA	Albemarle	Brakeman
	413	Cosby, Andrew	40	Blue	"	Bright	5'	8"	VA	Richmond	Laborer
	428	Cypress, John	29			Yellow	5'	3"	VA	Sussex Co.	
	439	Campbell, John	40	Gray	Blk	Copper	5'	11"	VA	Montgomery Co.	
	505	Cousins, G	35				5'	6"	VA	Mecklenburg	Carpenter
	506	Cousins, Jas	28				5'	8"	VA	"	"
	507	Curtis, R	32				5'	8"	VA	"	"
	508	Chavis, Jas	35				5'	6"	VA	"	"
	509	Cousins, M	26				5'	5"	VA	"	Laborer
	510	Chavis, John	30				5'	7"	VA	"	Carpenter
	511	Casey, Benj.	30				5'	6"	VA	"	"
	512	Carter, Clem	25				5'	7"	VA	Prince Edward	Laborer
	513	Cooper, Jas	40				5'	4"	VA	Do.	"
	550	Callender, Louis	22	Blk	Blk	Blk	5'	11"	VA	Botetourt	
	551	Callender, Harrison	20	"	"	Brown	5'	11"	VA	"	
	552	Coleman, Burbridge	33	"	"	"	5'	11"	VA	Roanoke	Wagoner
	553	Cooper, Jas	18	Blk	"	Light	5'	8"	VA	Botetourt	Collier
	554	Coleman, Pleasant	35	"	"	Blk	5'	10"	VA	"	Chopper
	556	Copeland, John	37	"	"	"	5'	7"	VA	"	Boatman

Enlisted			Assigned		Remarks
When	Where	By Whom	When	Where	
"		"	"	"	
"		"	"	"	
"		"	"	"	
Nov		Lt. Blackford		R(ichmond) & D(anville) Railroad	
"		"		"	
"		"		"	
"		"		"	
"		"		"	
"		"		"	
"		"		"	
03-May	Petersburg	Lt. Heath		Eng(ineer) Dept.	
"	"	"		"	
"	"	"		27th August exempted by Board	
"	"	"		Eng(ineer) Dept.	
"	"	"		"	
"	"	"		"	
"	"	"		"	
"	"	"		"	
"	"	"		Eng(ineer) Dept.	
"	"	"		Do.	
"	"	"		Do.	
"	Dinwiddie	R G Bosseau		Do.	
01-May	Roanoke	Capt. Clements	April	Capt. Morton N(iter) & M(ining)	
30-Apr			15-Jun	Q(uarter) M(aster) Dept.	
"			Do.	Do.	
"	Washington	W. M. Thompson		Do.	
"	"	"		Do.	
"	Scott Co.	"			Unassigned
"	Washington Co.	"		Q(uarter) M(aster) Dept.	
"	Greenville Co.	D J Godwin			
"	"	"			
06-Apr	Richmond	Capt. Coke	15-Apr	Col. Carter CAV	
06-Apr	"	"		Navy Dept.	
07-Apr	"	"			Not accounted for
07-Apr	"	"			Do.
09-Apr	"	"		Navy Ord(nance) Dept.	
12-Apr	"	"	05-May	Eng(ineer) Bureau	
20-Apr	"	"		Detailed A F Harvie	Not accounted for
20-Apr	"	"		Detailed to James Penitentiary	
21-Apr	Richmond	Capt. Coke	April	Navy Dept.	
26-Apr	"	"	"		Deserter
29-Apr	"	"	"	Va Central (Railroad)	R(ail) R(oad)
29-Apr	"	"	"	Do.	Detailed till 1st May '65
29-Apr	"	"			Deserter
					Discharged Med(ical) Board
05-May	Sussex Co.	D J Godwin			Board
06-May	Montgomery Co.	Lt. Sydenstriker		To M(edical) Dept.	Capt. Woodson
01-Jul	Mecklenburg	W. Atkins	01-Jul	Order Dept. Clarkesville till 1st May '65	
"	"	"	"	"	
"	"	"	"	"	
"	"	"	"	"	till 1st May '65
"	"	"	"	"	till 1st May '65
"	"	"	"	"	till 1st May '65
15-Jun	Prince Edward	Zimmerman	15-Jun	Eng(ineer) Dept.	High Bridge
01-Jul	"	"	01-Jul	"	
	Newbern	Lt. Poole		Q(uarter) M(aster) Dublin	
"	"	"		"	
18-Apr	Salem	Capt. Clements		"	
27-Jul	Fincastle	Lt. Nowlin		J(ames) R(iver) & (Kanawha) C(anal) C(ompany) N(iter) & M(ining)	
"	"	"		"	
"	"	"		"	

Page	No.	Name	Description						Where Born		Occupation
			Age	Eyes	Hair	Complex	Feet	In	State	Town or County	
	557	Callender, Robt							VA	"	Farmer
	590	Colson, James	34	Blk	Blk	Brown	5'	8"	VA	Petersburg	Shoemaker
	596	Coleman, John	25	"	"	Blk	5'	9"	VA	Do.	Laborer
	597	Crowder, Henry	38	Blue	"	Yellow	5'	4"	VA	Do.	"
	598	Conn , Isham	46	Blk	"	"	5'	2"	VA	"	"
	599	Cohen, James	29	"	"	Blk	5'	7"	VA	"	
	600	Coleman, Jas	30	"	"	"	5'	7 1/2"	VA	"	
15	606	Campbell. Austin	30	Blk	Blk	Dk	5'	10"	VA	Petersburg	Carpenter
	607	Christian, Wm	19	"	"	Blk	6'		VA	"	Laborer
	608	Cary, Chas	23	"	"	Brown	5'	6 1/4"	VA	"	"
	618	Campbell, Jas	19	"	"	Blk	5'	11"	VA	"	"
	796	Cooper, Frank	53	Dk	"	Dk	6'		VA	Albemarle	Supt D H
	797	Cooper, Dick	21	Blue	Blk	Lt	5'	8"	VA	"	Laborer
	798	Cooper, Frank	25	"	"	"	5'	8"	VA	"	"
	799	Cox, R	21	"	"	"	5'	8"	VA	"	Farmer
	800	Clim, John	37	"	"	Dk	5'	9"	VA	Nelson Co.	Laborer
	801	Church, William	22	"	"	Lt	5'	6"	VA	"	Farmer
	802	Cashwell, W	24	"	"	"	6'		VA	"	"
	803	Cashwell, Peter	18	"	"	Dk	6'	1"	VA	Amherst	"
	804	Clark, N M	24	"	"	Lt	5'	7"	VA	"	"
	805	Cotrell, Jueab	48	"	"	Blk	5'	8"	VA	Buckingham	
	806	Cumber, Jno	27				5'	6"	VA	New Kent	Farmer
	807	Cambill, A	49	Dk	Blk	Blk	5'	7 1/2"	VA	Orange	Laborer
	808	Campbell, Wm	18	"	"	"	5'	5 1/2"	VA	"	"
	809	Cambill, G	49	"	"	"	5'	6 1/2"	VA	"	"
	810	Cambill, Wm	47	Hazel	"	Yellow	5'	6"	VA	"	"
	811	Clark, James	23	Blk	"	"	5'	1 1/2"	VA	Rockingham	"
	812	Cook, Harry	24	"	"	Blk	5'	7 1/2"	VA	"	"
	813	Clatterbuck, Beverly	42	"	"	Lt	5'	10 1/4"	VA	Caroline	"
	814	Clatterbuck, John	25	"	"	"	5'	5 1/2"	VA	"	"
	815	Chenault, Hezekiah	29	"	"	Copper	5'	10 1/2"	VA	"	"
	816	Clark, James H.	16	Gray	Reddish	Light	5'	5 1/2"	VA	"	"
	817	Cash, M	47	Blk	Blk	Blk	5'	4"	VA	"	"
	818	Carpenter, Albert	30	"	"	Dk	6'		VA	Madison	"
	819	Cook, Henry	45	"	"	Mu	5'	10"	VA	"	Shoemaker
	820	Cobler, Walker	30	"	"	Dk	6'	3"	VA	"	Farmer
16	821	Carpenter, George	20	Blk	Blk	Blk	5'	6"	VA	Madison	Laborer
	822	Coleman, Dick	55	"	"	"	5'	7"	VA	Cumberland	
	823	Cato, Dick	49	"	"	Mu	5'	7"	VA	"	
	824	Cooley, J	27						VA	Powhatan	
	825	Cato, David	36	Dk	Dk	Dk	6'		VA	Smythe	Farmer
	826	Collins, Wm	35	Gr	Blk	Brn	5'	6"	VA	"	
	827	Campbell, Wm	30	Dk	Dk	Dk	5'	4"	VA	Augusta	Barber
	828	Cooper, John	37	"	Blk	Mul	6'		VA	"	Farmer
	829	Colly, Nathan	41	"	"	Yellow	5'	9 1/2"	VA		
	830	Colly, Isiah	21	"	"	"	6'	1/2"	VA		
	831	Cook, William	34	Blk	"	"	5'	3"	VA		
	832	Cochran, Brown	23	"	"	M	6'	1"	VA	Augusta	Shoemaker
	833	Curtis, Henry	35	"	"	Dk	5'	4"	VA	"	Farmer
	834	Clark, George	36	Dk	Dk	M	5'	7"	VA	"	"
	835	Collins, George	40	Lt	Blk	"	5'	7"	VA	"	"
	836	Carter, Samuel	33	Dk	Dk	Yellow	5'	10"	VA	Pittsylvania	Tanner
	837	Carter, Cornelius	40	"	"	Blk	6'		VA	"	Boatman
	838	Cole, John	28	"	"	"	5'	6"	VA	"	"
	839	Cook, James	41	"	"	"	5'	10"	VA	"	Farm hand
	840	Carter, Sanford	32	"	"	Yellow	6'	1"	VA	"	
	841	Carter, Richd	31	Lt	"	Blk	5'	11"	VA	Richmond	Fisherman

156

Enlisted			Assigned		Remarks
When	Where	By Whom	When	Where	
30-Aug	"	Detailed to S. Moftsinger till 1st May 1865			
	Petersburg	Lt. Scott			
25-Apr	"	"			
02-May	"	"			
"	"	"			
"	"	"			
04-May	"	"			
25-Jul	Petersburg	Lt. Scott	25-Jul	Eng(ineer) Dept.	
"	"	"	"	Do.	
28-Jul	"	"	28-Jul	Do.	
26-Jul	"	"	26-Jul	Do.	
27-Jun	Albemarle	Capt. Colston	29-Jun	Maj Richards	
"	"	"	"	"	
"	"	"	"	"	
28-Jun	"	"	30-Jun	"	
29-Jun		Lt. Carpenter	"	"	
02-Jul	Nelson	"	03-Jul	"	
04-Jul	"	"	06-Jul	"	
04-Jul	Amherst	Lt. Roane	06-Jul	"	
08-Jul		"	11-Jul	Eng(ineer) Dept.	
10-Jun		A T Moseley	14-Jun	Col. Scott	High Bridge
Oct		T Taylor	Oct	N(iter) & M(ining) Bureau	Detailed to 1st May 1865
25-Jun	Orange	Lt. Lewis	25-Jun	Gordonsville	Maj. Richards
"	"	"	"	"	"
					Detailed J A Taliaferro
"	"	"	"	Orange C(ourt)ho(use)	till 1st Jan(uary) '65
04-Jul	"	"	05-Jul	"	"
05-Jul	"	"	22-Jul	Gordonsville	Maj. Richards
"	"	"	11-Aug	"	"
19-Jul	Caroline	Lt. Hancock	20-Jul	Gen. Ewell	Richmond
"	"	"	"	"	"
"	"	"	"	"	"
"	"	"	"	"	"
"	"	"	"	"	"
01-Jul	Mad CHo	Lt. Adams	10-Jul	To M(edical) Dept. Gordonsville	
01-Jul	"	"	"	"	
"	"	"	"	"	
			"		
01-Jul			10-Jul	To M(edical) Dept. Gordonsville	
30-Jun				Col. J. Scott	
15-Jun				"	
06-Jun				To M Ag(en)t Powhatan	
21-Jun		Lt. Terry			Unaccounted
				N(iter) & M(ining) Bureau	
	Staunton			"	
31-Aug	"			To M(edical) Dept	Capt. Bell
					Detailed till 1st January '65
					Unaccounted
				Eng(ineer) Dept.	
18-Aug				To M(edical) Dept.	
					Detailed J Showalter till
"				"	1st April '65
24-Aug				"	
					Detailed till 17th
20-Jul					December '64
23-Apr	Lt. McCue				Deserted
28-Apr	"			To M(edical) Dept.	
"	"			Eng(ineer) Dept.	
					Ex(empt) by Med(ical)
26-May	"				Board
06-Oct	Lt. Williams			Eng(ineer) Dept.	
06-Jun	Capt. Coke			"	

Page	No.	Name	Age	Eyes	Hair	Complex	Feet	In	State	Town or County	Occupation
	842	Cunningham, I	23	Dk	Blk	Brown	5'	8"	VA	Manchester	Breaksman
	843	Cawling, Ottoway	25	Blk	"	Blk	5'	5"	VA	Richmond	Cook
	844	Clark, Saml	34	"	"	Dk	5'		VA	"	Laborer
	845	Clayton, Jno	36	Lt	Dk	"	5'	5"	VA	"	Shoemaker
	846	Cousins, Thos	26	Dk	"	"	5'	2"	VA	"	"
	847	Clayton, Benj	48	"	"	"	5'	8"	VA	New Kent	"
	848	Carter, Richd	40	"	"	"	5'	11 1/2"	VA	Richmond	
	849	Clark, William	36	"	"	Lt	5'		VA	Hanover	Laborer
17	850	Compton, Cornelius	26						VA		Blacksmith
	851	Carney, John	48	Blk	Blk	Blk	5'	6"	VA	Petersburg	Laborer
	852	Cousins, Archer	33	"	"	Bro	5'	6"	VA	"	Boat Hand
	853	Cousins, Smith	37	"	"	Blk	5'	6"	VA	"	Blacksmith
	854	Coleman, Isiah	29	"	"	"	5'	8"	VA	"	Laborer
	855	Chafers, Bob	46	"	"	Brn	5'	5"	VA	"	Shoemaker
	856	Cohen, James	33	"	"	Dk	5'	7"	VA	"	
	857	Cousins, W H	44	"	"	Bro	5'	6"	VA	"	Boatman
	858	Cooper, Jno		"	"	Dk	5'	6"	VA	Augusta	R R Hand
	859	Cousins, Henry J.	25	"	"	Yellow	5'		VA	Henry	Farmer
	860	Carler, Sanford	33	"	"	"	6'	4"	VA	"	"
	861	Crane, Nat	36	"	"	Dk	6'	-	VA	Powhatan	Laborer
	862	Coghill, J	20	"	"	M	5'	7"	VA	Chesterfield	Cooper
	863	Clark, Alexander	23	Y	"	Blk	5'	10"	VA	Rockingham	Laborer
	864	Crenshaw, Wm	24	Bro	Blk	Lt	5'	8"	VA	Halifax	"
	865	Christian, Wm	35	"	"	Blk	5'	11"	VA	Appomatox	Cooper
	1409	Carter, James	39	Dk	Dk	Mu	5'	6"	VA	Orange	Cook
	1410	Custalow, Norment	33	Blk	Blk	Lt	5'	7"	VA	King William	Brick Layer
	1411	Coy, Moses	36			Dk	5'	6 3/4"	VA	Richmond	Laborer
	1412	Cousins, German	27			"	5'	9 3/4"	VA	"	"
	1413	Cousins, Clarence	17			"	5'	3"	VA	"	"
	1414	Coghill, Richard	26			Lt	5'	4 1/4"	VA	"	"
	1415	Cousins, Ben	17			"	5'	5"	VA	"	"
	1416	Columbus, R	22			Dk	5'	8"	VA	"	"
	1417	Cheatom, Bruch	22			Lt	5'	7"	VA	"	"
	1418	Cousins, Phoenix	33			"	5'	9"	VA	"	"
	1507	Coy, Chas	38	Blk	Blk	Blk	5'	9"	VA	"	Blacksmith

Carried to page 4

Page	No.	Name	Age	Eyes	Hair	Complex	Feet	In	State	Town or County	Occupation
18	86	Day, Lebulone P.	21	Blue	Blk	Brown	5'	6"	VA	Petersburg	Laborer
	87	Diggins, Robert	35	"	"	Yellow	6'	-	VA	"	Carpenter
	88	Diggins, Charles	31	"	"	"	6'	1"	VA	"	Laborer
	89	Day, Robert	39	"	"	Blk	5'	6"	VA	"	"
	111	Diggs, George	34	Dk	Dk	Dk	6'	1/2"	VA	Dinwiddie	"
	112	Dinkin, Septimous	26	"	"	Light	6	2 1/2"	VA	"	"
	141	Day, Henry	34	Brown	"	Yellow	6'	3"	VA	Spottsylvania	Carpenter
	142	Day, Lemuel	18	"	"	"	5'	8"	VA	"	House Servant
	159	Dunn, John	28	Brown	Blk	Bright Mulatto			VA	Roanoke	Laborer
	160	Day, David	35	Blk	Blk	Dk M	5'	1"	VA	"	Wagoner
	175	Dickerson, Nathaniel	32	Blue	Blk	Yellow	5'	9"	VA	Russell	Laborer
	176	Dom, Charles	18	Blk	"	"	5'	7"	VA	Wythe	
	177	Dunsed, Alexander	39	Grey	"	Blk	5'	10"	VA	Scott Co.	
	341	Dixon, James	47	Dk	"	Dk	5'	7 1/2"	VA	Richmond	Blacksmith
	370	Dodson, Manuel	45	"	"	"	5'	4"	VA	"	"
	396	Drew, George	28	Grey	"	Bright	5'	5"	VA	"	Huskster
	416	Duvall, Charles	43	Dk	Blk	Dk	5'	7 1/2"	VA	"	Laborer
	434	Dobbins, Floyd	41	Blue	"	Copper	5'	8"	VA	Montgomery	Blacksmith
	484	Duiguid, C H	47		Dk		5'	7"	VA	Appomatox	Laborer
	485	Dimock, N	33		"		5'	8"	VA	"	"
	514	Drew, G W	35		"		5'	7"	VA	Meck County	Carpenter

Enlisted			Assigned		Remarks
When	Where	By Whom	When	Where	
22-Jun	"				Unaccounted
02-Jul	"			N(iter) & M(ining) Bureau	
28-Jul	"			"	
03-Aug	"				Unaccounted
27-Aug	"			N(iter) & M(ining) Bureau	
06-Sep	"			To M(edical) Dept.	
					Detailed till 1st April 1865
07-Sep	"			"	
10-Sep	"			N(iter) & M(ining) Bureau	
		Lt. Noland	19-Sep	Applied for detail as Blacksmith	
19-Sep	Petersburg	Sgt. Winfree	"	To M(edical) Dept.	
"	"	"	"	"	
22-Sep	"	"	"	"	
					Ex(empt) by Med(ical) Board
"	"	"	"		
"	"	"	"	To (Quarter) Mas(ter) Dept.	
27-Sep	"	"	27-Sep	"	
19-Sep	"	"	18-Sep	"	
Oct				Eng(ineer) Dept.	
05-May	Henry CH	Lt. Hawthorn	15-May	To M(edical) Dept.	
"	"	"	05-Jul	Eng(ineer) Dept.	
					Ex(empt) by Med(ical) Board
"		Lt. Spencer			Detailed 1 Nov(ember) '64
01-Jul		"			Unaccounted
06-Sep		Capt. E. J. Anderson			
12-Aug		"			
29-Nov	O. CHo	Lt. W H T Lewis		Eng(ineer) Dept.	
19-Nov		Lt. G P Haw	20-Nov	"	
"	Richmond	Lt. Blackford		R(ichmond) & D(anville) R(ail) R(oad)	
"	"	"		"	
"	"	"		"	
"	"	"		"	
"	"	"		"	
"	"	"		"	
"	"	"		"	
"	"	"		"	
				Detailed to Capt. MacMurdo till 1st March	
03-May	Petersburg	Lt. Heath		Eng(ineer) Dept.	
"	"	"		Do.	
"	"	"		Do.	
"	"	"		Do.	
"	Dinwiddie	R G Bosseau		Do.	
"	"	"			
01-May	Spottsylvania	Lt. H S Williams			
"	"	"			
"	Roanoke	Capt. Clements	April	Capt. Wade ACS	
					Ex(empt) by Med(ical) Board
"	"	"			
30-Apr		W M Thompson	15-Jun	R. M. Dept	
"	"	"	"	Do.	
"		"			Deserter
14-Apr	Richmond	Capt. Coke		Naval Ord(nance) Dept.	
22-Apr	"	"		Do. till 1st May 1865	
29-Apr	"	"	29-Apr	N(iter) & M(ining) Bureau	
29-Apr	"	"		Detailed to Lt. Blackford	
09-Apr	Montgomery	Lt. Sydenstriker			
06-Jun	Appomatox	Lt. Fantross	08-Jun	Do. Engineer Dept. Richmond	
"	"	"	"		
01-Jul	Mecklenburg	W Atkins	01-Jul	Ord(nance) Dept. Clarksville till 1st May 1865	

Page	No.	Name	Description						Where Born		Occupation
			Age	Eyes	Hair	Complex	Feet	In	State	Town or County	
	515	Davis, R	40		"		5'	9"	VA	Prince Edward	Laborer
	531	Dooley, Dennis								Craig Co.	
	569	Daniel, Henry							VA	Roanoke	Wagoner
	570	Daniel, John	25	Blk	Blk	Blk	5'	10"		"	Farmer
	571	Day, Caleb	35	"	"	"	5'	10"		Botetourt	Cooper
	572	Dennis, Lang	43	"	Grey	Brown	5'	9"		"	Blacksmith
	620	Dangerford, Joseph	24	Grey	Blk	Bright	5'	7"		Petersburg	Laborer
19	866	Dabney, Henry	21	Dk	Dk	Lg	5'	6"	VA	Dinwiddie	Farmer
	867	Dabney, Ben	24	"	"	"	6'	2"	VA		
	868	Dove, Henry	52	"	"	"	5'	11"	VA	Albemarle	Blksmith
	869	Dobbins, W	31	Blk	Blk	Lt	5'	10"	VA	Nelson	"
	870	Donning, James	19	"	"	"	5'	4"	VA	Nelson	Farmer
	871	Desmul, S	23	Dk	Dk	Blk	5'	5"	VA	Buckingham	Groom
	872	Derris, Jno	20							New Kent	Blksmith
	873	Day, Henry	34	Bro	Blk	Yellow	6'	3"	VA	Spottsylanvia	Carpenter
	874	Day, Samuel	18	"	"	"	5'	8"	VA	"	House Servant
	875	Dandridge, Byrd	44	"	"	Bright	6'	-	VA	Caroline Co.	Laborer
	876	Deer, William	28	"	"	Mul	5'	10"	VA	Madison "	"
	877	Davis, Daniel	22	"	"	Blk			VA	Petersburg,Chesterfield	"
	878	Dunkin, Jas	30			M	5'	6"	VA	Cumberland	
	879	Douglas, M	23	Dk	Dk	Lt	5'	10"	VA	Highland	
	880	Dunning, Ociata							VA		
	881	Dinwiddie, Jackson	39	Blk	Blk	Mu	6'	1/4"	VA	Augusta	Laborer
	882	Davis, Chas	47	Dk	Dk	Blk	5'	10"	VA	Pittsylvania	Farmer
	883	Davis, George	40	"	"	Yellow	5'	7 1/2"	VA	"	"
	884	Dodson, Jno	22	"	"	Blk	5'	3"	VA	"	"
	885	Day, Edward	21	"	"	"	5'	8"	VA	"	"
	886	Day, Wesley	32	"	"	Yellow	6'	-	VA	"	Carpenter
	887	Dear, Henry	46	"	"	"	5'	11"	VA	"	Laborer
	888	Day, Abner	19	"	"	Bro	5'	4"	VA	"	Teamster
	889	Davis, Moses	28	"	"	Yellow	5'	8"	VA	"	Farm Hand
	890	Davis, Samuel	21	"	"	"	5'	11"	VA	"	"
	891	Davis, James	34	"	"	Blk	5'	8"	VA	"	"
	892	Davis, Wm		"	"	Yellow	5'	6"	VA	"	"
	893	Davis, James	25	"	"	Blk	5'	6"	VA	Hanover	Blksmith
	894	Davis, Nelson	24	Blk	Blk						
20	895	Darby, John	39	Dk	Dk	Dk	5'	4"		Richmond	Laborer
	896	Dunning, Stephen	33	Dk	Blk	Yell	5'	9"		Franklin	Shoe Maker
	897	Dunning, John	41	Dk	Blk	Yell	5'	7"		"	Farmer
	898	Dennis, Fertian	23								
	899	Dodson, Amos	18	Blk	Blk	Yell	5'	7"		Petersburg	Laborer
	900	Day, Bryant	47	"	"	Blk	5'	6 1/2"		"	"
	901	Diggs, William	26	"	"	"	5'	2"		"	"
	902	Dusky, Jno	39							Richmond	
	903	Duncan, WIlliam	27	Blk	Blk	Blk	5'	6"		Rockbridge	Blacksmith
	904	Deane, Julius	45	Dk	Dk	Mul	5'	6"			Shoe Maker
	905	Deane, William	20			Bk	5'	6"			Farm Hand
	1419	Day, William	45			Yellow	5'	6"		Charlotte	-
	1420	Dixon, Bob	27			Lt	5'	9 1/4"		Richmond	Laborer
	1421	Dangerfield, David	28			"	5'	61/2"	VA	"	Fireman
	1508	Deane, W	44	Dk	Dk	Dk	5'	8"			Blksmith
	1509	Dixon, Geo									
	1510	Diggs, Robt	36	"	"	Yellow					
		Davenport, Emual	45	Dk	Dk	Lt	5'			Richmond	
	See	Davenport, John	27	"	"	"	5'	8"		"	
	Page	Douglas, John	18	"	Blk	Mul	5'	7"		Mecklenburg Co.	Blksmith
	25	Doors, Jas								Rappahannock	Farmer
		Doors,								"	"
		Drew, Huston	28			Bright	6'	2"		Bedford Co.	"
		Davis, Isaac	25	Blk	Dk	Dk	5'	11"		King & Queen	"
		Davis, James	18	"	"	"	5'	9"		" & "	"

Enlisted			Assigned		Remarks
When	Where	By Whom	When	Where	
15-Jun	Prince Edward	Zimmerman	15-Jun	Eng(ineer) Dept. High Bridge	
05-Aug		Lt. Oakhaim	05-Aug	Buchanan Q(uarter) M(aster) Dept.	
18-Apr	Salem	Capt. Clements		Q(uarter) M(aster) T J Jenkins	
27-Jul	"	"		" Maj. Mahon	
24-Jun	Fincastle	Lt. Nowlin		Detailed till 1st May 1865 Jon S Wilson	
01-Jul	"				
27-Jul	Petersburg	Lt. Scott		Dept. Navy till 1st May 1865	
22-Jul	DinCHo	R G Bosseau	02-Aug	Capt. Dinnock	Eng(ineer) Dept.
	"		"	"	"
26-Jun		Capt. Colston	27-Jun	Maj. Richard	
02-Jul		Lt. Carpenter	02-Jul	"	
04-Jul		Lt. Roane	05-Jul	Gen. Ransom	
10-Jun		AT Mosely	13-Jun	Col. Scott	High Bridge
Oct		T. Taylor	Oct	N(iter) & M(ining) B(ureau)	
04-Apr	Fredbg	Lt. Williams		Unassigned	Petition for detail
"	"	"		"	"
19-Jul	Bow Green	Lt. Hancock	19-Jul	Gen. Ewell	
"	CHo	Lt. Adams	09-Jul	To M(edical) Dept. Gordonsville	
7-19				Capt. Dinnock	
15-Jun				Col. J. Scott	
				Detailed to 1st May 1865	
				To M(edical) Dept.	Capt. Bell
	Staunton			"	
20-Apr		Lt. McCue			Not accounted
06-Jul		Lt. Williams		Danville Arsenal	
"		"		Eng(ineer) Dept.	
"		"		"	
"		"		"	
"		"		"	
"		"		"	
19-Apr		Lt. McCue			Unaccounted
23-Apr		"		Eng(ineer) Dept.	
"		"		"	
"		"			Unaccounted
"		"			"
01-Sep		"		To M(edical) Dept.	
12-Sep	Capt. Coke			N(iter) & M(ining) B(ureau)	
					Det(ailed) by or(der) B of C
12-Jul	Capt. Berman				
25-Jul	"			Eng(ineer) Dept.	
	Lt. Nowlin			N(iter) & M(ining) B(ureau)	
23-Sep	Sgt. Winfree		23-Sep	To M(edical) Dept.	
					Ex(empt) by Med(ical) Board
26-Sep	"		26-Sep		
27-Sep	"		27-Sep	To M(edical) Dept.	
12-Sep				N(iter) & M(ining) B(ureau)	
					Unaccounted
				To M(edical) Dept.	
				"	
23-Nov	Lt. Graves			Eng(ineer) Dept.	
"	" Blackford			R(ichmond) & D(anville) R(ail) R(oad)	
"	"			"	
				Detailed to S Farmers till July	
				1st/65 detailed to A. P. Rahmul 1st Mar(ch)	
				Detailed to T. Timberlake 1st May	
				Detailed to Navy til 1st May/65	
				"	
				Detailed to 1st May/65 Clarksville Ord(nance) Shop	
				Detailed to 1st May/65 M. P. Scott Surgeon CS.	
				"	
				Detailed to A. M. Stevens til 1st May 1865	
	Lt. Dickinson			Detailed to Dudley til 1st May 1865	
	"			"	

Page	No.	Name								Occupation
					Description			Where Born		
			Age	Eyes	Hair	Complex	Feet	In	State	Town or County	

Page	No.	Name	Age	Eyes	Hair	Complex	Feet	In	State	Town or County	Occupation
		Desmal, John	17							Richmond	Boatman
		Dungy, Geo	26							"	"
		Dailey, Wm	40			Blk	5'	5"		Henrico	Laborer
		Denson, Wm									
		Dixon, B	45	Dk	Dk	Bro	5'	7"		New Kent	
21	90	Evans, Nat	40	Blk	Blk	Yellow	6'	4"	VA	Petersburg	Laborer
	91	Evans, Nat	26	"	"	Blk	5'	5 1/2"	VA	"	"
	143	Eskridge, Frank	35	Brown	"	Brown	5'	10"	VA	Spottsylvania	Farmer
	192	Epperson, Wyatt	25	Blk	"	Yellow	5'	7"	VA	Mecklenburg Co.	
	193	Estill, Allen	40	"	"	"	5'	8"	VA	Washington Co.	
	194	Early, Charles	25	Black	"	"	6'	4"	VA	"	
	242	Evans, Bob	30			Black	5'	4"	VA	Sussex Co.	
	243	Estes, William	30			Yellow	5'	10"	VA	Greenville Co.	
	526	Ellison, Davy	23				5'	9"	VA	Prince Edw	Laborer
	527	Estes, M	47		"		6'	-	VA	Lunenburg	Shoe Maker
	578	Early, Robt	33	Blk	Blk	Light	5'	11"	VA	Botetourt	Driver
	579	Evans, John	45	Blk	"	Blk	5'	9"	VA	Petersburg	Shoe Maker
	580	Ellis, James	20	"	"	Brown	5'	7"	VA	"	Laborer
	906	Evis, N	25	"	"	Lt	5'	7"	VA	Albemarle	Shoe Maker
	907	Essex, W	44	"	"	"	5'	9"	VA	Nelson	Farmer
	908	Eskridge, Frank	35	"	"	Bro	5'	10"	VA	Spottsylvania	"
	909	Edwards, William	28	Dk	Dk	Lt	5'	10"	VA	Louisa	Laborer
	910	Ellis, J	38						VA	Powhatan	
	911	Edmonds, H	21						VA	"	
	912	Evans, Jesse	46	Dk	Dk	Brown	5'	11"	VA	Pittsylvania	
	913	Evans, William	35	"	"	"	6'	-	VA	"	
	914	Edmuson, W H	26	"	"	"	5'	8"	VA		
	915	Evans, William	48	"	"	"	5'	6"	VA	Petersburg	Laborer
	916	Epps, Woodson							VA		
	917	Ellis, John	21						VA	Richmond	Carpenter
	918	Ellis, J W H	18	Bk	Bk	Bk	5'	5"	VA	Hanover	Laborer
	919	Edmonds, Jos	35						VA	Lunenburg	
	1422	Edwards, Ballard	36				5	10"	VA	Richmond	Bricklayer
	1537	Eves, George	18	Blk	Blk	Yellow	5'	7"	VA	Augusta	
22		Evans, Edmund	35	Blk	Blk	Mul	5'	10 1/2"		Mecklenburg	Blksmith
		Evans, Jordan	35	"	"	"	5'	7 1/2"		"	Laborer
		Edward, Thos									
25		Davis, W									
		Davis, W	40			Lt	5'	10"	VA	Essex Co.	
26	71	Farley, John	20	Blk	Blk	Brown	5'	7"	VA	Petersburg	Cooper
	72	Frills, William	27	"	"	Blk	5'	7"	VA	"	Laborer
	73	Friend, William	30	"	"	"	5'	8"	VA	"	"
	238	Fry, John	28	Grey	"	"	5'	8 1/2"	VA	Washington Co.	
	248	Ferguson, James	21			Yellow	5'	6 1/2"	VA	Greenville Co.	
	249	Ferguson, Frank	26			Blk	5'	9 1/2"	VA	"	
	250	Ferguson, Levy	28			Brown	5'	7"	VA	"	
	251	Ferguson, Urquhart	20				5'	5 1/2"	VA	"	
	252	Ferguson, Bynum	34				5'	5 1/2"	VA	"	
	271	Francis, Robert	37	Brown	Blk	Lgt	5'	8"	VA	Richmond Cty	Barber
	284	Foster, George	21	Blk	"	Lgt	4'	9"	VA	"	Painter
	285	Ferguson, William	24	"	"	"	5'	10 1/2"	VA	"	Barber
	331	Ford, Jas	33	"	"	"	5'	9"	VA	"	Amb Driver
	407	Freeman, Jordan	20	"	"	Blk	5'	5"	VA	"	Wood House Hand
	417	Fields, Wm	36	Lt	"	Lt	5'	7"	VA	Henrico	Sho Last M

Enlisted			Assigned		Remarks
When	Where	By Whom	When	Where	
Jan 6 /65				Detailed to Maj. Harvie	
"				"	
Jan 12 /65				Pending CSW	
			"	Jos. R Anderson & Co.	
			"	Mrs. Julia E. Rickson til 1st/July	
03-May	Petersburg	Lt. J E. Heath		Eng(ineer) Dept.	
"	"	"		"	
01-May	Spottsylvania	Lt. H. Williams			
30-Apr	Washington	G M Smith	14-Jun	Q(uarter) M(aster) Dept.	13th District
"	"	W M Thompson		Detailed til 1st Jan(uary)/65	
"	"	"			Unassigned
"	Sussex Co.	D J Godwin			
"	Greenville	"			
01-Jul	P Edw	Zimmerman	30-Jun	Eng(ineer) Dept. HB	
					Detailed til 1st Jan(uary)/65
	Fincastle	Lt. Nowlin	28-Aug	N(iter) & M(ining) J(ames) R(iver) A.and C.	
23-Apr	Peterburg	Lt. Heath	22-Apr	Eng(ineer) Dept.	
		"	26-Aug	"	
26-Jun	Capt. Colston		27-Jun	Maj. Richard	
04-Jul	Nelson	Lt. Roane	05-Jul	"	
04-Apr					
04-Sep	Louisa CHo	Lt. Vaughan	03-Sep	N(iter) & M(ining) Bureau	
06-Jun				To M Ag(en)t Powhatan	to 1st May/65
"				"	
28-Apr		Lt. McCue		"	
"		"			Unaccounted
					Detailed to M(edical)
07-Sep		Capt. Coke			Dept. till 1st May/65
27-Sep	Peterburg	Sgt. Winfree	26-Sep	To M(edical) Dept.	
				Eng(ineer) Dept.	
				N(iter) & M(ining) B(ureau)	
28-Apr		Lt. Spencer		Eng(ineer) Dept.	
06-Jul					
Nov	Richmond	Lt. Blackford		R(ichmond) & D(anville) R(ail) R(oad)	
Dec				Engineer Dept	
					Detailed till 1st May/65
					Clarksville Ord(nance)
					"
					Jos R Anderson & Co.
				Detailed to Mrs. Pollard till 1st July	
Jan-65	Essex Co.	Lt. Perkins		Eng(ineer) Dept.	
03-May	Petersburg	Lt. Heath		Eng(ineer) Dept.	
"	"	"		Do.	
"	"	"		Do.	
30-Apr	Washington	W M Thornton		Q(uarter) M(aster) Dept.	
"	Greenville	D J Godwin		Detailed to E H Gill January 5/65	
"	"	"			
"	"	"			
"	"	"			
"	"	"			
05-Apr	Richmond	Capt. Coke		Eng(ineer) Dept.	
					Detailed Capt. MacMurdo till 1st Mar(ch)/65
06-Apr	"	"			
06-Apr	"	"	20-Apr	Col. Shields	
15-Apr	"	"		Med(ical) Dept. till 1st May 1865	
29-Apr	"	"		Detailed to Central (Rail) Road	
					Detailed Capt. MacMurdo till 1st Mar(ch)/65
29-Apr	"	"	29-Apr	N(iter) & M(ining) Bureau	

Page	No.	Name	Description						Where Born		Occupation
			Age	Eyes	Hair	Complex	Feet	In	State	Town or County	
	450	Fontaine, Wm	18	Grey	"	Dk	5'	8"	VA	Richmond	Laborer
	452	Folk, Jacob	24	Blk	Blk	Brown	5'	5"	VA	Suffolk	"
	483	Fadely, Westly	34	"	"	Yellow	5'	7"	VA		
	486	Ferguson, S	32		"		5'	9"	VA	Appomattox	Laborer
	487	Fields, Wm	40				5'	9"	VA	"	"
	630	Flowers, John	45				5'	9"	VA	Dinwiddie	"
	631	Friend, A	30						VA	Powhatan	"
	632	Ford, I	32						VA	"	"
	633	Friend, B	25						VA	"	"
	634	Flemming, Geo	26						VA	"	"
	635	Friend, I	19						VA	"	"
	920	Fisher, Herum	36	Blk	Blk	Lt	5'	8"	VA	Albemarle	Shoe Maker
	921	Farris, James	19	"	"	"	5'	7"	VA	"	Carpenter
	922	Fitzgerald, W	19	Brown	"	Yellow	5'	6"	VA	Nelson Co.	Laborer
27	923	Fortune, R	21	Blk	Blk	Dk	5'	6"	VA	Nelson Co.	Laborer
	924	Foster, Pollard	18	"	"	Lt	5'	6"	VA	Amherst "	Farmer
	925	Foster, F	34	"	"	"	5'	7"	VA	"	"
	926	Foster, John	24	"	"	Dk	6'	-	VA	"	"
	927	Fortune, Eugine	22	"	"	Mu	5'	9"	VA	Caroline	Laborer
	928	Fortune, John Henry	32	"	"	"	5'	11 1/2"	VA	"	"
	929	Fox, John Thos	29	"	"	Blk	5'	5"	VA	"	"
	930	Fox, Thomas	45	"	"	"	5'	5"	VA	"	"
	931	French, James	39	"	"	Mu	5'	10"	VA	Madison	"
	932	Freeman, E	24	"	"	Blk	5'	10"	VA	Botetourt	
	933	Freeman, George	22	"	"	"	5'	8"	VA	Alleghany	
	934	Freeman, John	25	"	"	"	5'	9 1/2"	VA		
	935	Furgerson, Urquhart	27	"	"	"	5'	10"	VA	Greenville	Laborer
	936	Furgerson, Frank	39	Blue	"	"	5'	10"	VA	"	"
	937	Furgerson, James	35	"	"	"	5'	11"	VA	"	"
	938	Furgurson, B	34	"	"	"	6'	-	VA	"	"
	939	Freeman, Dick	39	"	"	"	5'	9"	VA	Pittsylvania	Bksmith
	940	Freeman, John	39	"	"	"	5'	10"	VA	"	"
	941	Forrow, Lewis I.	19						VA		
	942	Freeman, Robert	18	Blk	Blk	Yellow	5'	5"	VA	Petersburg	Laborer
	943	Fox, Punch	24	"	"	M	5'	8"	VA	Augusta	Farm Hand
	944	Frazier, George	40	Bk	Bk	Bk	5'	7"	VA	Rockbridge	Laborer
	1423	Fortune, Mac	29			Lt	5'	6 1/2"	VA	Richmond	Fireman
	1424	Freeman, Tom	34			"	5'	6 3/4"	VA	"	Laborer
	1425	Fox, Henry	32			"	5'	6 1/4"	VA	"	"
	1426	Francis, Robt									
	1511	Fowler, Jim								Richmond	Train Hand
28 1864											
	1512	Freeman, A	26	Brown	Dk	Lt	6'			Richmond Cty	Farmer
	1513	Fleming, John	21	Blk	Dk	Dk	6'			Orange Co.	Laborer
		Foster, Thomas	30	Blue		Brown	5'	6"		Richmond Cty	Striker
		Freeman, Jim	34				5'	6"		Caroline	Laborer
		Ford, Wilson	30	Dk	Dk	Dk	5'	10"		Culpeper	"
		Friend, I					5'	8"		Richmond	"
		Fox, Wm	40	Dk	Dk	Lt	5'	8"		"	Barber
		Faggan, Robt	44							"	Boatman
		Fox, Thomas	36	Dk	Dk	Yellow	5'	7"		New Kent	Farmer
		Fortune, Ben								King Wm Co.	Laborer
		Freeman, Dick									
33	82	Green, William	48	Grey	Blk	Dark	5'	7"		Petersburg	Laborer
	83	Gilliam, Gladwell	29	"	"	Light	6'	2"		"	"
	84	Goode, Thomas	28	Blk	Dark	Dark	5'	7"		"	"
	162	Goings, Washington	25	"	Blk	Blk	5'	8"		Roanoke	"
	236	Gray, William	29	Blk	Blk	Yellow	5'	9"		Washington	
	253	Granger, E T	18			Brown	5'	7"		Greensville Co.	
	254	Granger, James	19			"	5'	5 1/2"		"	

Enlisted			Assigned		Remarks
When	Where	By Whom	When	Where	
05-May	"	"	05-May	"	
02-May	"	"			Deserter
	Harrisonburg	Lt. Col. Peyton			
06-Jun	Appomatox	Lt. Fantross	08-Jun	Engineer Dept Richmond	
					Detailed til 1st January 1865
22-Jun	Dinwiddie			Eng(ineer) Dept.	
12-Jun				"	
"				"	
"				"	
"				"	
25-Jun		Capt. Colston	26-Jun	Maj. Richard	
27-Jun		"	29-Jun	"	
30-Jun		Lt. Carpenter	01-Jul	"	
02-Jul	Nelson	Lt. Carpenter	03-Jul	Maj. Richard	
08-Jul		Lt. Roane	"	Gen. Ransom	
"		"	"	"	
"		"	"	"	
19-Jul	BGreen	Lt. Hancock	20-Jul	Gen. Ewell	
"	"	"	"	"	
"	"	"	"	"	
"	"	"	"	"	
01-Jul	M CHo	Lt. Adams	10-Jul	To M(edical) Dept. Gordonsville	
				N(iter) & M(ining) B(ureau)	
				"	Unaccounted
May		Lt. Holland	28-May	Eng(ineer) Dept.	
"		"			Unaccounted
"		"	23-May	Q(uarter) M(aster) Dept.	
"					
19-Apr		Lt. McCue			
"		"			
		Lt. Nowlin		N(iter) & M(ining) B(ureau)	
26-Sep		Sgt. Winfree	26-Sep	Q(uarter) M(aster) Dept.	
Oct				Eng(ineer) Dept.	
					Deserter
Nov		Lt. Blackford		R(ichmond) & D(anville) R(ail) R(oad)	
"		"		"	
"		"		"	
				Messenger	Col. Withers
03-Jan				R(ichmond) & P(etersburg) R(ail) R(oad)	E H Gill Supt.
24-Dec	Richmond	Lt. Blackford	24-Dec	N(iter) & M(ining) B(ureau)	
03-Sep	Orange	Lt. Lewis	20-"	Detailed to I. T. Gentry	
			Jan 7/65	Detailed to A W Robinson til 1st May/65	
				Navy til 1st May/65	
				Detailed to Mrs. S. R. Thomas till 1st May/65	
				Detailed to R & K Co. til 1st May/65	
				Detailed to A/C Public Necessity	
				Detailed to Maj. J B Harvie	
				Detailed to G T Rumley 1st January 1865	
				Detailed to Mrs McDowell til 1st January 1865	
				Detailed to Jos R Anderson & Co.	
03-May	Petersburg	Lt. Heath		Eng(ineer) Dept.	
"	"	"		Do.	
"	"	"		Do.	
01-May	Roanoke	Capt. Clements	April	T J Jenkins Maj & Q(uarter) M(aster)	
30-Apr	Washington	W M Thompson			
"	Greensville Co.	D J Godwin			
"	"	"			Exempt til January '65

Page	No.	Name	Description						Where Born		Occupation
			Age	Eyes	Hair	Complex	Feet	In	State	Town or County	
	255	Grain, W L	19			Yellow	5'	10"		"	
	256	Graves, Lewis	36			Blk	5'	6"		"	
	257	Graves, James	49			"	5'	6"		"	
	258	Graves, Stephen	47			"	5'	8"		"	
	259	Graves, Frank	31	Grey	Blk	"	5'	1"		"	
	274	Gray, Arthur	18	Brown	Brown	Light	5'	8"		Richmond Cty	Barber
	275	Gilpin, Joseph	40	Blk	Blk	Dk	5'	5"		"	Shoe Maker
	276	Grimes, Henry	22	"	Brown	Lgt	5'	7 1/2"		"	"
	319	Gaines, Alexander	29	Dk	Dk	"	5'	8"		"	
	320	Griffin, Valentine	40	"	"	Dk	5'	5 1/2"		"	Blacksmith
	356	Garrett, Benjamin	27	Blk	Blk	"	5'	6"		Henrico	"
	378	Gray, Wm	36	Dk	"	"	5'	8"		Amelia	
	392	Gardner, William	17	Gray	"	Lt	5'	6"		Richmond	Barber
	419	Green, James	22	Blk	"	Blk	5'			"	Laborer
	441	Griffin, Giles	18	"	"	"	5'			Montg. Co.	
	478	Gibson, Marsel	38	"	Red	Yellow	5'			Rockingham	Laborer
	479	Goins, James	26	"	Blk	"	5'			"	Cooper
	480	Goins, Benjamin	19	Gray	"	"	5'			"	Laborer
	481	Gibson, John	47	Blk	Blk	"	5'			"	Wagon Maker
	482	Grady, Chls D	18	Hazel	Lt	"	5'				
	496	Green, James	49				5'			Appomatox	Laborer
	530	Graves, W	43		Dk		5'			Mecklenburg	
34	552	Goins, Josephus	21	Blk	Blk	Blk	5'	10"	VA	Patrick Co.	
	553	Goins, Bartley							VA	Roanoke	Wagoner
	592	Griffin, James	47	"	"	"	5'	11"	VA	Petersburg	Cooper
	593	Gilliam, Henry	36	"	Lt	Lt	5'	11"	VA	"	Laborer
	594	Green, Wm	42	"	Blk	Blk	5'	2"	VA	"	"
	595	Goins, Henry	19	"	"	"	5'	6"	VA	"	"
	652	Green, Allen	24			M	5'	9"	VA	Amelia	"
	653	Gortney, Ewd	44				5'		VA	Chesterfield	"
	654	Gortney, Jno	35				5'		VA	"	"
	655	Graves, Seith	40				5'	6"	VA	Cumberland	
	945	Graves, Robert	30				5'	4 1/2"	VA	Dinwiddie	Farmer
	946	Goins, Jesse	23	Blk	Blk	Gin	5'	8"	VA	Albemarle	Blksmith
	947	Goins, William	48	"	"	Lt	5'	8"	VA	"	Farmer
	948	Goins, Elix	17	"	"	"	5'	6"	VA	"	"
	949	Goins, S	54	"	"	"	5'	6"	VA	"	"
	950	Goins, Skelson	33	"	"	"	5'	6"	VA	"	Laborer
	951	Goins, Ben	22	"	"	"	6'		VA	"	Farmer
	952	Goins, J T	14	"	"	"	6'		VA	"	"
	953	Goins, Henry	60	"	"	Bro	6'	-	VA	"	Blksmith
	954	Green, Jesse	28	"	"	Lt	5'	8"	VA	"	Cooper
	955	Goins, Thomas	16	"	"	Dk	5'	6"	VA	Nelson Co.	Farmer
	956	Grange, George	18	"	"	Lt	5'	6"	VA	Buckingham	Huckster
	957	Gray, Elas	40	"	"	Bro	5'	7"	VA	"	Farmer
	958	Goins, Ben	18	"	"	Lt	5'	10"	VA	Rockingham	"
	959	Gray, John	25	Bro	"	Blk	5'	7"	VA	Spottsylvania	Laborer
	960	Grimes, James	36	Yl		Lt	5'	4 1/2"	VA	Caroline	Laborer
	961	Grimes, James	20	Blk	"	Mul	5'	7"	VA	"	"
	962	Grimes, Hiram	24	Gray	"	"	5'	9"	VA	"	"
	963	Gibson, Peter	27	Blk	Blk	"	5'	6"	VA	Smythe	Barber
35	964	Gordon, W H	23	Blk	Blk	Blk	5'	8"	VA		
	965	Goings, Michael	25	"	"	Dk	5'	6"	VA	Augusta Co.	Cooper
	966	Green, Lovell	30	"	"	"	5'	7"	VA	Greenville	Laborer
	967	Garnes, Wm	20	Dk	Dk	Blk	5'	10"	VA	Pittsylvania	Boatman
	968	Garnes, James	38	"	"	Yellow	5'	6"	VA	"	"
	969	Garnes, George	22	"	"	Blk	6'	-	VA	"	"

Enlisted			Assigned		Remarks
When	Where	By Whom	When	Where	
"	"	"			
"	"	"			Deserter
"	"	"			Deserter
"	"	"			Deserter
"	"	"			Detailed til 1st May /65
05-Apr	Richmond	Capt. Coke		Q(uarter) M(aster) Dept.	Deserter
05-Apr	"	"	15-Apr	N(iter) & M(ining) Bureau	
05-Apr	"	"	Do.	Do.	
12-Apr		"			Not accounted for
12-Apr		"			Deserter
19-Apr		"	03-May	N(iter) & M(ining) Bureau	
26-Apr		"			Deserter
28-Apr		"	17-May	N(iter) & M(ining) Bureau	
30-Apr		"	30-Apr	N(iter) & M(ining) Bureau	
28-May	Montg. Co.	Lt. Sydenstriker	31-May	Maj. McMaken	
May & June	Rockingham	Col. C S Peyton			Detailed til 1st Jan(uary) /65 Priv(ate) Nec(essity)
"	"	"			Deserter
"	"	"	01-Aug	Eng(ineer) Dept. Richmond	
"	"	"			Detailed til 1st Jan(uary) /65 Priv(ate) Nec(essity)
"	"	"		Detailed to Fracis Niswander til 1st May/65	
01-Jul	Appomatox	Lt. Fantross	01-Jul	Eng(ineer) Dept. H(igh) Bridge	
01-Aug	Mecklenburg	W T Atkins			
	NewBern	Lt. Poole		Q(uarter) M(aster) Dept. I H Lacy	
18-Apr	Salem	Capt. Clements		" " " T. J. Jenkins	
25-Apr	Petersburg	Lt. Scott		Eng(ineer) Dept.	
02-May	"	Do.		Do.	
"	"	"		Do.	
27-Jul	"	"		Do.	
23-Jul	Amelia			Do.	
19-Jun	Chesterfield			Do.	
"	"			Do.	
14-Jul	Cumberland			Do.	
24-May	Dinwiddie	R G Bousseau	22-Jul	Do.	
25-Jun		Capt. Colston	28-Jun	Maj. Richard	
21-Jun		"	"	"	
"		"	"	"	
"		"	"	"	
"		"	"	"	
"		"	"	"	
"		"	"	"	
28-Jun		"	"	"	
30-Jun		Lt. Carpenter	01-Jul	"	
10-Jun		A T Moseley	14-Jun	Col. Scott	High Bridge
10-Jun		"	"	"	"
30-Jul		Col. C S Peyton	01-Aug	Gen. Ransom	
04-Apr	Fredericksburg	Lt. Williams		unassigned	
19-Jul	Bowl Green	Lt. Hancock	20-Jul	Gen. Ewell	Richmond
"	"	"	"	"	"
"	"	"	"	"	"
22-Jun		Lt. Terry			unaccounted
					unaccounted
				To M(edical) Dept.	
May			23-May	R(ichmond) & P(etersburg) R R	to E H Gill
26-Apr		Lt. McCue			
28-Apr		"		To M(edical) Dept.	
28-Apr		"		"	

Page	No.	Name	Age	Eyes	Hair	Complex	Feet	In	State	Town or County	Occupation
	970	Garnes, Thomas	37	"	"	"	6'	3 1/2"	VA	"	"
	971	Gray, C	45	"	"	Dk	5'	8"	VA	Powhatan	Laborer
	972	Green, Robert	19	"	"	Blk	5'	-	VA	Petersburg	"
	973	Goings, Morgan	26	"	"	"	5'	7"	VA	Augusta	Farm Hand
	974	Gardiner, Thomas	21	"	"	"	6'	-	VA	Chesterfield	Fireman
	975	Gwinn, William	33	Yellow	Gray	Blk	5'	5 1/2"	VA	Rockbridge	Cooper
	976	George, Charles	45	Hz	Blk	Lt	5'	8"	VA	Lynchburg	Butcher
	977	Garland, William	17	Bk	Bk	Bro	5'	8"	VA		
	1427	Gallimore, Jacob	28	"	"	"	5'	8"	VA	Charlotte	Laborer
	1428	Graham, Peter	30			Dk	5'	9 1/2"	VA	Richmond	Eng cleaner
	1429	Green, Alfred	46			"	5'	6"	VA	"	Laborer
	1430	Garner, Jim	21			"	5'	10"	VA	"	Boatman
	1431	Gray, Roth	44			"	6'	2"	VA	"	Helper
	1514	Griffin, V	44	Blk	Blk	Coffee	5'	7"	VA		
	1515	Gallimon, Pleasant	39	Blk		"	6'	-	VA	Charlotte	Blk Smith
		Gray, Harrison	33	Dk	Dk	Blk	5'	8"	VA	Amelia	"
		Gray, Wm	29	"	"	"	5'	11"	VA	"	"
		Gray, George	27	"	"	"	5'	10"	VA	"	"
		Gray, Chastone	26	"	"	"	5'	9"	VA	"	Laborer
		Green, Lem	26	"	"	"	5'	6 1/2"	VA	Chls City	
		Goins, Henry	24	Dk	Blk	Lt	5'	9"		Richmond	Farmer
		Gordon, W H	23	Blk	"	Yellow	5'	8"		Rockingham	Baker
		Graves, Jim	23	Dk	"	Dk	5'	8"		Richmond	
		Gilpin, Peter	34							"	
36		Gray, Joe	25							Richmond	Boatman
		Gray, Peter	30							"	"
		Giles, John	37	Blk	Blk	Blk	5'	10"		Powhatan	Farmer
		Giles, Daniel	48	"	Dk	Brown	5'	4 1/2"		"	"
		Gibson, John	47	"	Blk	Yellow	5'	8 1/2"		Rockingham	Wagon Maker
		Green, Abler	28	Blue	"	"	5'	1"		Essex	Laborer
		Green, Peter	30	Blue	"	"	5'	1"			"
40	34	Hill, Robert	43	Blk	Blk	Ginger	5'	10"	VA	Petersburg	Laborer
	35	Hill, John	46	Hazel	"	Light	5'	7"	VA	"	"
	36	Hearns, J H	18	Blk	"	Blk	5'	8"	VA	"	"
	37	Hargrove, Ben R	46	"	"	"	5'	7"	VA	"	"
	38	Hargrove, Ben	23	"	"	"	5'	6"	VA	"	"
	39	Heath, Cornelius	23	"	"	Dark	5'	6"	VA	"	"
	80	Harper, Wyatt	38	Blue	"	Brown	4'	8"	VA	"	"
	81	Hastings, Thomas	20	Blk	Blk	Blk	5'	6"	VA	"	"
	117	Hill, Hed	27	"	"	"	5'	8 1/2"	VA	Dinwiddie	"
	118	Hill, Mike	25	"	"	"	5'	7 1/2"	VA	"	"
	119	Hill, Willis	28	"	"	"	5'	9"	VA	"	"
	120	Harper, Jim	20	"	"	"	5'	2"	VA	"	"
	121	Harper, Wilkins	26	"	"	"	5'	6 1/2"	VA	"	"
	122	Hollida, Robert	37	Gray	Light	Light	5'	8 1/2"	VA	"	"
	144	Hearn, Horace	35	Brown	Blk	Yellow	5'	5"	VA	Spottsylvania	Farmer
	156	Hughes, A. N.	32	Blk	"	Bright	5'	5"	VA	Roanoke	Shoe Maker
	157	Henderson, David	22	Blk	Blk	Bright	5'	6"	VA	"	Wagoner
	167	Harris, James G	18	"	"	"	6'	-	VA	"	Cooper
	200	Hofman, Wm	44	Blk	Blk	Yellow	5'	10"	VA	Russell	Blksmith
	201	Howell, W. E.	18	Grey	"	"	5'	9 1/2"	VA	Washington	
	203	Hearn, Elbert	21				5'	10"	VA	Bland	
	228	Hand, Jefferson	28	Blk	Blk	"	5'	7"	VA	Washington	Laborer
	244	Hargrove, W. T.	21			Light	5'	10"	VA	Sussex Co.	
	245	Hill, John	18			Black	5'	10"	VA	Greensville	
	270	Hill, Joseph G.	42	Blk	Blk	Lgt	5'	8"	VA	Richmond Cty	Barber
	303	Hudson, Edward	45	"	Dk	Brown	5'	8"	VA	"	Laborer
	308	Hill, William	21	"	"	Lgt	5'	9"	VA	"	Carpenter
	327	Harris, Benjamin	46	Grey	"	"	5'	5"	VA	"	"
	328	Harris, Sam	45	Dk	Lt	Dk	5'	9 1/2"	VA		Bricklayer
41	350	Harris, James	45	Dk	Blk	Dk	5'	5"	VA	Richmond	Laborer
1864	362	Harris, Peter	24	"	"	"	5'	8 1/2"	VA	"	Blksmith

Enlisted			Assigned		Remarks
When	Where	By Whom	When	Where	
"		"		"	
09-Sep		Capt. Coke		N(iter) & M(ining) B(ureau)	
26-Sep	Petersburg	Sgt. Winfree	26-Sep	30 Days Furlough by Med(ical) Ex(amining) B(oar)d	
Oct				Eng(ineer) Dept.	
					Capt(ure)d by enemy unaccounted
25-Aug		Capt. Anderson			
23-Nov				To M(edical) Dept.	
"		Lt. Graves		Eng(ineer) Dept.	
"		Lt. Blackford		R(ichmond) & D(anville) R(ail) R(oad)	
"		"		"	
"		"		"	
				N(iter) & M(ining) B(ureau)	
		Lt. Graves		Detailed to Capt MacMurdo till 1st March/65	
				Engineer Dept.	
				Navy till 1st May 1865	
				"	
				"	
				"	
				Detailed to C Bass Supt. Pent(entiar)y to 1st May 1865	
Jan 5/65				Detailed to T C Brubaker til 1st May1865	
				Detailed to N(iter) & M(ining) B(ureau)	
				Detailed to J B Harvie	
				Detailed to J B Harvie	
				"	
				Detailed to Maj. Randolph til 1st May 1865	
				"	
				Detailed til 1st July 1865	
		Lt. Myers		Detailed to B F Gresham till 1st June	
		Lt. Bumpass		"	
03-May	Petersburg	Lt. Heath		Eng(ineer) Dept.	
"	"	"		Do.	
"	"	"		Do.	
"	"	"		Do.	
"	"	"			Exempted by Board
"	"	"		Do.	
"	"	"		Do.	
"	"	"		Do.	
"	Dinwiddie	R G Bosseau		Do.	
"	"	"		Do.	
"	"	"		Do.	
"	"	"		Do.	
"	"	"		Do.	
"	"	"		Do.	
01-May	Spottsylvania	Lt. H S Williams		Do.	
"	Roanoke	Capt. A Clements	April	Maj. King C.S.	
"	"	"	April	T J Jenkins Q(uarter) M(aster)	
"	"	"			No information
30-Apr		J M Smith	11-Jun	Q(uarter) M(aster) Dept	13th District
"		Wm M Thompson		"	
"		"			
"	Washington	"	15-Jun	Q(uarter) M(aster) Dept	13th District
"	Sussex Co.	D J Godwin			
"	Greensville Co.	"			
05-Apr	Richmond	Capt. Coke	15-Apr	N(iter) & M(ining) Bureau	
07-Apr	"	"			Deserter
07-Apr	"	"			Do.
12-Apr	"	"		Private Necessity	
13-Apr	"	"	13-Apr	N(iter) & M(ining) Bureau	
18-Apr	Richmond	Capt. Coke	05-May	Eng(ineer) Bureau	
20-Apr	"	"			Not Accounted for

Page	No.	Name	Age	Eyes	Hair	Complex	Feet	In	State	Town or County	Occupation
	363	Harris, Jim	38	"	"	"	5'	8"	VA	"	"
	372	Hope, Wm	32	Grey	Dk	Lt	5'	5"	VA	"	Laborer
	414	Harris, Dennis	39	"	"	"	5'	6"	VA	"	Train Hand
	415	Hicks, Henry	30	"	"	"	5'	8"	VA	"	Brick Layer
	421	Hamblin, Henry	25			Blk	5'	6"	VA	Sussex Co.	
	422	Hamblin, James	35			"	5'	9"	VA	"	
	423	Hamblin, Wm	29			"	5'	6"	VA	"	
	424	Hamblin, Henry T.	23			Yellow	5'	7 1/2"	VA	"	
	446	Hall, Thomas	39	Grey	Blk	Lgt	5'	6"	VA	Richmond	Carpenter
	457	Harris, James	30	Dk	Dk	Brown	5'	10"	VA	"	Butcher
	488	Hamblin, Robert	36			"	5'	8"	VA	Appomatox	Laborer
	489	Homes, E	33			"	5'	9"	VA	Prince Edward	"
	524	Hill, Booker	40			"	6'	-	VA	Do.	"
	554	Harris, Wm	31	Blk	Blk	Blk	5'	11"	VA	Patrick	
	555	Harris, John	18	"	"	Bright	5'	6"	VA	Henry	
	556	Harris, Levi	28	"	"	Blk	5'	8"	VA	"	
	557	Holmes, Boyer	17	"	"	Brown	5'	10"	VA	Bedford	
	558	Harvey, Wm	23	"	"	Blk	5'	10"	VA	Craig	
	559	Harris, Edwin							VA	Roanoke	
	560	Hargrove, Benj	36	Blk	Blk	Blk	5'	8 1/4"	VA	Botetourt	Chopper
	568	Henderson, Elijah							VA	Roanoke	Wagoner
	604	Hill, Thomas	49	"	"	"	5'	6"	VA	Petersburg	Laborer
	612	Hargrove, J	31	"	"	Dk	5'	11"	VA	"	"
	613	Hinton, John	28	"	"	Brown	5'	4 1/2"	VA	"	"
	657	Holeman, Wm	22			Yellow	6'	-	VA	Powhatan	"
	658	Hughes, H	32						VA	"	
	659	Holeman, Wm	38						VA	"	
42	660	Howell, D	24						VA	Powhatan	
	661	Holeman, Jackson	35			Dk	5'	7"	VA	Cumberland	
	662	Hicks, Jesse	36						VA	Powhatan	
	978	Hullin, Frank	40	Bk	Bk	Bk	5'	8"	VA	Albemarle Co.	Farmer
	979	Howell, John	23	"	"	Dk	5'	7"	VA	Nelson Co.	"
	980	Hill, James	24	Bro	"	Bro	5'	8"	VA	Spottsylvania	Carpenter
	981	Hawkins, Ambrose	25	Blk	Blk	Blk	5'	6 1/2"	VA	Culpeper	Wheelwright
	982	Hailstock, John	26	"	"	"	5'	5 3/4"	VA	Caroline	Laborer
	983	Hudson, James	27	"	"	Mulatto	5'	8"	VA	"	"
	984	Harris, David		"	Dk	Dk	5'	10"	VA	Louisa	Carpenter
	985	Hale, John	27	"	Blk	M	6'	2"	VA	Russell	Tanner
	986	Hale, George	22	"	"	"	5'	10"	VA	"	Laborer
	987	Hash, Jacob	20	"	"	Copper	5'	8"	VA	Washington	Farmer
	988	Holly, Jeff	22	"	"	Blk	5'	7"	VA		
	989	Hughes, Wm	43	"	"	"	5'	7 1/2"	VA		
	990	Hackley, Gabrill	36	"	"	"	5'	11"	VA		
	991	Hall, Curtis	22	"	"	Yellow	5'	9 1/2"	VA		
	992	Hackley, Jacob	42	"	"	Dk	5'	10"	VA	Rockingham	
	993	Hackley, John	40	"	"	"	5'	9"	VA		
	994	Hargrove, Wm	29	"	Dk	Blk	5'	10"	VA	Greensville	Laborer
	995	Hill, John	19	"	Blk	"	5'	10"	VA	"	"
	996	Harris, Dock	23	"	Dk	Blk	5'	-	VA	Pittsylvania	Waiter in Army
	997	Harris, Ned	25	"	"	Yellow	5'	4"	VA	"	Cook in Hosp
	998	Hendrick, Thos	21	"	"	Blk	5'	6"	VA	"	Boatman
	999	Hendrick, William	24	"	"	Yellow	5'	7"	VA	"	
	1000	Hendrick, A	33	"	"	Blk	5'	4"	VA	"	"
	1001	Hull, James	19	"	"	Yellow	5'	8"	VA	"	Farm Hand
	1002	Harris, N.	22	Lt	"	Blk			VA	Charles City Co.	Fisherman
43	1003	Harris, Stephen	18	Dk	Blk	Brown	5'	4"		Richmond	Laborer
	1004	Harris, Lewis	36	"	"	Brown	5'	5"		"	"
	1005	Harris, Lewis	36	Dk	"	"	5'	8"		"	Messenger
	1006	Henry, Jas	33	Blk	"	Blk	5'	8"		"	Laborer
	1008	Hollinger, Chas	23	"	"	"	5'	6"		"	"
	1009	Henry, Wm	25	Dk	Dk	"	5'	7"		Henrico	"

Enlisted			Assigned		Remarks
When	Where	By Whom	When	Where	
21-Apr	"	"			
25-Apr	"	"		Detailed in Enrolling Office	
29-Apr	"	"		Detailed VA Central R(ail) Road	
30-Apr	"	"			Deserter
05-May	Sussex Co.	D J Godwin			
"	"	"			
"	"	"			
"	"	"			
02-May	Richmond	Capt. Coke	02-May	N(iter) & M(ining) Bureau	
05-May	"	"			Deserter
06-Jun	Appomatox	Lt. Fantross	08-Jun	Eng(ineer) Dept. Richmond	
15-Jun	Prince Edward	Zimmerman	15-Jun	Do. H(igh) Bridge	
01-Jul	"	"	01-Jul	Do. H(igh) Bridge	
	Newbern	Lt. Poole		Q(uarter) M(aster) Dept. I H Lacy Dublin	
	"	"		Do.	
	"	"		Do.	
	"	"		Do.	
	"	"		Do.	
18-Apr	Salem	Capt. Clement		" T J Jenkins	
27-Jul	Fincastle	Lt. Nowlin		J(ames) R(iver) & (Kanawha) C(anal) Co(mpany) N(iter) & M(ining)	
13-Apr	Salem	Capt. Clement		Q(uarter) M(aster) T J Jenkins	
04-May	Petersburg	Lt. Scott		Eng(ineer) Dept.	
25-Jul	"	"		"	
26-Jul	"	"		"	
15-Jul	Powhatan			Do.	
12-Jun	Do.			Do.	
"	"			Do.	
12-Jun	Powhatan			Eng(ineer) Dept.	
15-Jun	Cumberland			Q(uarter) M(aster) Agent (Cumberland)	
06-Jun	Powhatan			Q(uarter) M(aster) Agent (Powhatan)	
25-Jun	Albemarle Co.	Capt. Colston	24-Jun	Maj. Richard	
30-Jun	Nelson Co.	Lt. Carpenter	01-Jul	"	
04-Apr		Lt. Williams			Unassigned
19-Aug	Culpeper	Lt. Graves		Eng(ineer) Dept.	
19-Jul	Bowl Green	Lt. Hancock	20-Jul	Gen. Ewell	Richmond
"	"	"	"	"	"
04-Sep	Louisa CHo	Lt. Vaughan	04-Sep	N(iter) & M(ining) Bureau	
11-Jun		Lt. Sawyer			Unaccounted
"		"			"
15-Jun		W M Thompson			"
					Deserter
					Detailed till 1st Jan(uary)/65
					Unaccounted
					Detailed till 1st Jan(uary)/65
					Detailed till May/65
					"
May					Unaccounted
"					"
19-Apr		Lt. McCue			"
"		"		Eng(ineer) Dept.	"
28-Apr		"		To M(edical) Dept.	
"		"		"	
"		"			Unaccounted
"		"		Eng(ineer) Dept.	
06-Jun		Capt. Coke		"	
06-Jun		Capt. Coke		Eng(ineer) Dept.	
16-Jun		"		Detailed to Parker Smith	
08-Jul		"		Med(ical) Dept.	
11-Jul		"		N(iter) & M(ining) B(ureau)	
09-Sep		"		"	
28-Sep		"		"	

Page	No.	Name	Description						Where Born		Occupation
			Age	Eyes	Hair	Complex	Feet	In	State	Town or County	
	1010	Hix, John	23	"	"	Lt	5'	9 1/2"		Richmond	Plaster
	1011	Hill, Daniel	36								
	1012	Hawkins, Charles	42								
	1013	Hill, Williams	29								
	1014	Holmes, Benj	45								
	1015	Howard, John	38								
	1016	Harrison, Joseph	20	Dk	Dk	Dk	5'	11"		Augusta	Blk Smith
	1017	Hill, Samuel	18	Blk	Blk	Blk	5'	6"		Petersburg	Laborer
	1018	Howard, Yudar	36	"	"	"	5'	7"		"	Boat Hand
	1019	Hill, Jack	20	"	"	Yellow	5'	6"		"	Laborer
	1020	Hill, Alexander	30	"	"	"	5'	5"		"	Plasterer
	1021	Hastings, W T	27	"	"	Brown	5'	-		"	Laborer
	1022	Hailstock, Geo	27	"	"	M	5'	8 1/2"		Augusta	Blk Smith
	1023	Harris, George	38	"	"	Yellow	5'	10"		Henry	"
	1024	Hall, William	30	"	"	"	5'	10 1/2"		"	Farmer
	1025	Hall, John	26	"	"	"	5'	10"		"	"
	1026	Hickman, Jas M	33	"	"	"	6'	-		Patrick	Shoemaker
	1027	Humbles, Richard	35	"	"	Bk	5'	8"		Rockbridge	Laborer
	1028	Hays, Nelson	33	"	"	"	5'	8 1/2"		"	Teamster
	1432	Hill, Robert	20	"	"	Lt	5'	5"		King William	Laborer
	1433	Hill, William	18	"	"	Bright	5'	7"		"	"
	1434	Holt, Williams	30	"	"	Lt	5'	6"		"	Farmer
	1435	Howell, Wm	32							Goochland	"
44	1436	Howlett, Robt	18			Lt	5'	5 1/2"		Richmond Cty.	Fireman
	1437	Hicks, Beverly	32			"	5'	7"		"	"
	1438	Howlett, Wm	20			"	5'	7 1/2"		"	"
	1439	Hickman, Jesse								"	"
	1440	Hickman, Jas	20			Dk	5'	6 1/2"		"	En Cleaner
	1441	Hill, John	17			Lt	4'	10 3/4"		"	Laborer
	1442	Harris, James	34			Dk	5'	5 1/2"		"	"
	1443	Harrison, Emit	32			Lt	5'	10 3/4"		"	Fisherman
	1516	Hill, Robt	24	Brown	Blk	Dk	5'	11"		"	
	1517	Harris, Ben	48	Bro	"	Lt	5'	6"		"	Drayman
		Hanley, John	35	Dk	Dk	Blk	5'	7 1/2"		York	Laborer
		Henderson, Wm	43	"	"	"	5'	10"		New Kent	"
		Hill, Jas H	16	"	"	"	5'	1"		Richmond	
		Harris, Geo	25	Blk	Blk	Lt	5'	6"		"	
		Harrison, W H	35	Dk	Dk	Lt	5'	7"		Buckingham	Blk Smith
		Hubard, Josephus	35				5'	7"			Blk Smith
		Hanley, J								Richmond	Laborer
		Hadley, Wm	36	Blk	Blk	Yellow				Tazwell Co.	Tanner
		Harrison, Lee	47	"	"	Lt	5'	8"		Lynchburg	
		Harris, John	40	"	"	Blk	5'	8"		Mecklenburg	Laborer
		Howlett, Thos	49			Dk	5'	10"		Richmond	Blk Smith
		Howell, Thos	35			Lt	5'	10"		"	Packer
		Homes, Jas	31			Dk	5'	7"		Surrey Co.	Fireman
		Harris, Chls	20							Richmond	Boatman
		Hamlin, Geo	27							"	"
		Harris, Jas								King & Queen Co.	Farmer
		Hackley, John	40	Dk	Dk	Dk	5'	9"		Rockingham	Laborer
		Howard, Eli	21	"	"	Yellow	5'	10"		Bath Co.	Tanner
		Harris, Peter	25	Blk	Blk	Dk	5'	6"		King & Queen	Farmer
		Harris, Littleton	35	Dk	Dk	Blk	5'	5"		New Kent	Blk Smith
45		Homes, Patrick								King Wm Co.	
		Homes, Wm								Essex Co.	
		Howard, Festus								Augusta	
		Henry, Chas	18			Blk	5'	10"		Westmorland Co.	Farmer
50	48	Jenkins, William	30	Blk	Blk	Blk	5'	7"	VA	Petersburg	Barber
	49	Jackson, Abraham	18	"	"	"	5'	7"	VA	"	
	50	Jarrola, Thomas	46	"	"	Lgt	5'	9"	VA	"	Carpenter

Enlisted			Assigned		Remarks
When	Where	By Whom	When	Where	
28-Sep		"		"	
		Lt. Nowlin		"	
		"			Unaccounted
		"			"
		"		Detailed for WW Boyd till 1st Jan/65	
		"			Deserter
01-Sep		Capt. Mathews		Ord(nance) Dept.	
19-Sep	Petersburg	Sgt. Winfree	19-Sep	To M(edical) Dept.	
"	"	"	"	C(onfederate) S(tates) Dept.	
21-Sep	"	"	21-Sep	To M(edical) Dept.	
					Exempt by Med(ical)
24-Sep	"	"	24-Sep		Ex(amining) B(oar)d
27-Sep	"	"	27-Sep	To M(edical) Dept.	
Oct				Eng(ineer) Dept.	
05-May	Henry CHo	Lt. Hawthorn	05-Jul	"	
"	"	"	"	"	
"	"	"	"	"	
					Exempt by Med(ical)
"	"	"	"		Ex(amining) B(oar)d
				To M(edical) Dept.	
				"	
19-Nov		Lt. Haw	20-Nov	Cm Office	
"		"	"	Eng(ineer) Dept.	
"		"		"	
16-Nov		Lt. Wright		"	
Nov	Richmond	Lt. Blackford		R(ichmond) & D(anville) R(ail) R(oad)	Detailed to
"	"	"		"	"
"	"	"		"	"
"	"	"		"	"
"	"	"		"	"
"	"	"		"	"
"	"	"		"	"
"	"	"		"	"
20-Dec	"	"		Engineer Dept	
12-Dec	"	"		Med(ical) Dept.	
				Navy Dept	til 1st May/65
				"	"
				"	"
				Detailed to C Bass Supt. Pent(inentiar)y to 1st May 1865	
				Exempt till 1st July 1865	
				Detailed to J(ames) R(iver) & K(anawha) Co(mpany) til 1st May 1865	
		J M Smith		Detailed til 1st May 1865	
Aug				Detailed to Capt. Anderson	
				Detailed til 1st May 1865 Cl(ar)ksville Ord(nance) Shops	
Jany 3/65				Detailed to R.E. Blankenship	
"				"	
Jany 6/65				Detailed to E H Gill	
"				Detailed to Maj Harvie	
"				Do.	
				Detailed to J G Bland 1st May/65	
		Lt. Myers		Detailed to Silas Henton 1st May/65	
				Detailed to T R Wallace 1st May/65	
				Detailed to Maj. Benton til 1st May/65	
				Detailed to Public Necessity til 1st May/65	
		Lt. G P Haw		to James G White 1st July/65	
		Lt. Bumpass		to B.F. Gresham 1st June	
				to Henry Gunsh 1st July	
May/65	Westmoreland	Lt. J P Jenkins		En(gineer) Dept.	
03-May	Petersburg	Lt. Heath		Eng(ineer) Dept.	
"	"	"		Do.	
"	"	"		Do.	

Page	No.	Name	Description						Where Born		Occupation
			Age	Eyes	Hair	Complex	Feet	In	State	Town or County	
	51	Jones, Henry	18	"	"	Blk	5'	6"	VA	"	Laborer
	92	Johnson, Thomas	35	"	"	Dark	5'		VA	"	"
	109	Jones, John	32	"	"	Lght	6'	2 1/2"	VA	Dinwiddie	"
	110	Jackson, Joseph	35	"	"	Dark	5'	6 1/2"	VA		"
	163	Johnson, Bentley	19	"	"	Blk	5'	8"	VA	Roanoke	Wagoner
	239	Jackson, John	18				5'	9"	VA	Washington Co.	
	268	Jenkins, Thomas	24	Blk	Blk	Brown	5'	5"	VA	Richmond Cty	Barber
	302	Jordan, Henry	25	"	"	"	5'	10"	VA	"	Laborer
	329	James, Matthew	18	Gray	"	Lt	5'	5"	VA	Henrico	Mechanic
	342	Judah, John	24	Dk	"	Blk	5'	7"	VA	Richmond	Laborer
	344	James, Wm T	35	"	"	Lt	5'	7"	VA	Henrico	"
	372	Joiner, Wm	38	"	"	Dk	5'	2"	VA	Richmond	Shoe Maker
	389	Johnson, Andy	36	Gray	"	Lt	5'	7"	VA	"	Laborer
	398	Jones, Charles	21	Dk	Dk	Blk	5'	3"	VA	Hanover Co.	Fireman
	424	Jones, Thad	18			Brown	5'	8"	VA	Sussex Co.	
	427	Judkins, Harrison	40			"	5'	7"	VA	"	
	523	Johnson, Jos	40		Dk		5'	10"	VA	Prince Ewd	
	561	Johnson, Solomon	34	Blk	Blk	Blk	5'	8"	VA	Patrick	
	562	Jenkins, Wm	45	"	"	"	6'	-	VA	Pulaski	
	563	Jackson, Wm	39	Dk	Dk	Mulatto	5'	10"	VA	Botetourt	Boatman
	564	Jupiter, Jim	35	Blk	Blk	Blk	5'	5"	VA	"	Driver
	601	Johnson, Saml	39	"	"	"	5'	6"	VA	Petersburg	Laborer
	602	Jones, Henry	18	"	Lt	"	5'	6"	VA	"	
	603	Johnson, Jos	25	"	Blk	Dk	5'	6"	VA	"	
51	609	Jenkins, Joseph	32	Blk	Blk	Dark	5'	10"	VA	Petersburg	Laborer
	610	Jones, Thomas	33	"	"	Blk	5'	9"	VA	"	Driver
	611	Jackson, Cornelius	30	"	"	Dk	5'	10"	VA	"	Laborer
	668	Johnson, Claiborne	46			Dk	5'	11"	VA	Amelia	"
	669	James, H	26			"			VA	Powhatan	
	670	James, J	48			"			VA	"	"
	671	Jackson, S	39			"			VA	"	
	672	Jenkins, Peter	43			"	5'	9 1/2"	VA	Cumberland	
	673	Jackson, Alexander	18			"	5'	7 1/2"	VA	"	
	674	Jenkins, Sam	42			"	6'	-	VA	"	
	675	Jenkins, Geo							VA	"	
	676	Jenkins, Lewis	40			Blk	5'	10"	VA	"	
	677	Jackson, J	43						VA	Powhatan	
	678	Jackson, Chls	44						VA	"	
	1029	Jackson, M	36	Bl	Blk	Blk	5'	8"	VA	Albemarle	Shoe Maker
	1030	Johns, Q S	20	"	"	Lt	5'	9"	VA	Amherst	Farmer
	1031	Johns, Charles	33	"	"	"	5'	11"	VA	"	"
	1032	Johns, Josh	22	"	"	"	6'	-	VA	"	"
	1033	Johns, Preston	18	"	"	"	5'	7"	VA	"	"
	1034	Johns, Philip I	19	"	"	"	5'	-	VA	"	"
	1035	Johns, E	25	"	"	"	5'	4"	VA	"	"
	1036	Johns, Talten	19	"	"	"	5'	6'	VA	"	"
	1037	Johns, W C	27	"	"	"	5'	10"	VA	"	"
	1038	Jones, Albert	18	"	"	"	5'	8"	VA	"	Jobber
	1039	John, W	25	"	"	"	5'	5"	VA	"	Farmer
	1040	John, W V	30	"	"	"	6'	-	VA	"	"
	1041	Jones, Walter	47	Dk	Dk	Lt	5'	9"	VA	Rockingham	"
	1042	Johnson, Lewis	49	Blue	Sandy	Yl	5'	4 1/2"	VA	Orange	"
	1043	Jones, Charles	18	Hz	Blk	Mulatto	5'	6"	VA	Caroline	Shoe Maker
	1044	Jeter, Henry	23	Blk	"	"	5'	7 1/2"	VA	"	Laborer
52	1045	Jeter, John	20	Blk	Blk	Mul	5'	7"	VA	Caroline Co	Laborer
	1046	Jordan, Abram	24	Dk	"	Dk	5'	7"	VA	Goochland Co	"
	1047	Jordan, Ben	21	Hz	"	Lt	5'	7"	VA	Louisa "	"
	1048	James, Fortune	45	"	Lt	Dk	5'	5"	VA	Hanover "	"
	1049	Jackson, Andrew	23	Blk	Blk	Blk	5'	6"	VA	Washington "	Brick Mason
	1050	Jones, Walter	42	Dk	Dk	Lt	5'	9"	VA		Farmer
	1052	Jackson, Samuel							VA		
	1052	Johnson, Abram	21	Gray	Blk	Yl	6'	-	VA		

Enlisted			Assigned		Remarks
When	Where	By Whom	When	Where	
"	"	"		Do.	
"	"	"		Eng(ineer) Dept.	
30-Apr	Dinwiddie	R G Bosseau		Do.	
03-May	"	"		Do.	
01-May	Roanoke	Capt. Clement		-	
30-Apr	Washington Co.	W M Thompson	15-Jun	Q(uarter) M(aster) Dept.	
05-Apr	Richmond Cty	Capt. Coke	15-Apr	N(iter) & M(ining) Bureau	
					Exempt by Secretary of War
07-Apr	"	"		-	
13-Apr	"	"		Eng(ineer) Dept.	
14-Apr	"	"		-	Deserter
16-Apr	"	"		-	Light Duty
25-Apr	"	"	05-May	N(iter) & M(ining) Bureau	
27-Apr	"	"		Q(uarter) M(asterl) Dept	Deserter
29-Apr	"	"		-	
05-May	Sussex Co.	D J Godwin		-	
"	"	"		-	Discharged by Board
01-Jul	P Ewd	Zimmerman	01-Jul	Eng(ineer) Dept.	High Bridge
	Newbern	Lt. Poole		Q(uarter) M(aster) Dept I H Lacy	
	"	"		Do.	
	Fincastle	Lt. Nowlin	27-Jul	N(iter) & M(ining) J(ames R(iver) & (Kanawha Canal) Co(mpany)	
	"	"	27-Jul	N(iter) & M(ining) J(ames R(iver) & (Kanawha Canal) Co(mpany)	
02-May	Petersburg	Lt. Scott		Eng(ineer) Dept.	
"	"	Do.		Do.	
25-Jul	"	Do.		Do.	
25-Jul	Petersburg		25-Jul	Eng(ineer) Dept.	
26-Jul	"		26-Jul	Do.	
27-Jul	"		27-Jul	Do.	
27-Jul	Amelia		27-Jul	Do.	
12-Jun	Powhatan		12-Jun	Do.	
"	"		"	Do.	
"	"		"	Do.	
23-Jun	Cumberland		23-Jun	Do.	
19-Jun	"		19-Jun	Do.	
19-Jun	"		"	Do.	
19-Jun	"		"	Do.	
15-Jun	"		15-Jun	Q(uarter) M(aster) Dept. (Cumberland)	
06-Jun	Powhatan		06-Jun	Q(uarter) M(aster) Dept. (Powhatan)	
06-Jun	"		06-Jun	"	
25-Jun	Albemarle	Capt. Colston	02-Jun	Maj Richard	
08-Jul	Amherst	Lt. Roane	11-Jul	Gen Ransom	
"	"	"	"	Private Necessity Detailed til 1st May 1865	
"	"	"	"	"	
"	"	"	"	"	
"	"	"	"	"	
"	"	"	"	"	
"	"	"	"	"	
"	"	"	"	"	
10-Jun		AT Moseley	14-Jun	Col. Scott	High Bridge
"		"	"	"	"
"		"	"	"	"
30-Jul		Col. C S Peyton	01-Aug	Gen Ransom	
25-Jun	Orange	Lt. Lewis	25-Jun	Orange CH Detailed J F Taliafero til 1st January 1865	
19-Jul	Bowl Green	Lt. Hancock	20-Jul	Gen. Ewell	Richmond
"	"	"	"	"	"
19-Jul	Bowl Green	Lt. Hancock	20-Jul	Gen. Ewell	Richmond
01-Sep		Lt. Vaughan	04-Sep	N(iter) & M(ining) B(ureau)	
01-Sep		"	"	"	
02-Sep		"	"	"	
15-Sep	Abingdon	Wm Thompson			Unaccounted for
				Eng(ineer) Dept.	
				N(iter) & M(ining) B(ureau)	
				To M(edical) Dept.	

Page	No.	Name	Age	Eyes	Hair	Complex	Feet	In	State	Town or County	Occupation
	1053	Jones, Morrison	40	Blk	Blk	Blk	6'		VA		
	1054	Johnson, Walker	39	"	"	Yel	5'	7"	VA		
	1055	Johnson, Nelson	23	"	"	M	5'	9"	VA	Augusta Co.	Tanner
	1056	Jackson, John	26	"	"	Blk	6'	-	VA	"	"
	1057	Jones, Joshua	24	"	"	"	5'	3"	VA	"	
	1058	Jones, George	22	"	"	"	5'	9"	VA	"	
	1059	Jenkins, Wyatt	46	"	"	Dk	5'	8"	VA	Pittsylvania	Shoe Maker
	1060	Jackson, Samuel	26	Blue	Dk	"	5'	6"	VA	"	Striker
	1061	Jonathan, A	27	Lt	Bk	Bk	5'	10"	VA	Henrico Co	Fisherman
	1062	James, S	40	"	"	"	5'	6"	VA	" "	"
	1063	Jackson, Anderson	33	Dk	"	Dk	5'	7"	VA	Richmond	
	1064	Johnson, C	34	"	"	"	5'	6"	VA	"	Bl Smith
	1065	James, Wm	27	"	"	"	5'	5"	VA	Henrico	Carpenter
	1066	Jones, Wm	45	"	"	"	5'	9"	VA	"	Laborer
	1067	Jackson, Henry	48	"	"	"			VA	"	
	1068	James, Robert	41	"	"		5'	9"	VA	"	Farmer
	1069	Jentry, W H	23	"	"	"	6'	-	VA	Richmond	Laborer
	1070	Jeter, Ben	27	"		Lt	5'	6"	VA	"	"
	1071	Jackson, James	22	"		Bk	5'	5 1/2"	VA	Dinwiddie	Farmer
	1072	Jubilee, Lully	24							Au	
	1073	Jackson, Samuel	36	Lt	Dk	M	6'	-		Augusta	Tanner
	1074	Johnson, Abraham	21	Bk	Dk	Bro	5'	11"		"	Cooper
53	1075	Johnson, James	43	Blk	Blk	Blk	5'	7"		Petersburg	Laborer
	1076	Jones, J H	28	"	"	"	6'	-		"	Carpenter
	1077	Jones, John	25	"	"	Brown	6'	-		"	Laborer
	1078	Isaacs, Jno	40							Richmond	"
	1079	Jeter, James	24	Blk	Blk	Yellow	5'	11"		Henry	Manf Tobacco
	1080	Johnson, Lee	40	"	"	"	5'	9"		"	Farmer
	1081	Johnson, George	21	"	"	Blk	5'	10"		"	Laborer
	1082	Johnson, William	30	"	"	"	6'	1"		"	Farmer
	1083	James, Thomas	35							Richmond	
	1084	Jackson, Giles	32	Yel	Blu	Bk	5'	10 1/2"		Rockbridge	Grave Digger
	1085	Jackson, William	25	Bk	Bk	"	5'	5"			Engineer
	1086	Jackson, Richard	23	"	"	Brown	6'	-			Waiter
	1087	Johnson, Robert	18	"	"	Bk	5'	-			Mason
	1444	Jackson, M	25	"	"	Mu	5'	10"		Orange	Laborer
	1445	Jackson, James		-	-	-				Charlotte	
	1446	Jones, William G	30	Blk	Blk	Blk	5'	9"		"	
	1447	Jackson, Thomas	24			Dk	5'	3"		Richmond	Eng Cleaner
	1448	Jeffries, James	25			"	5'	6 1/4"		"	Laborer
	1449	Jackson, William	26			Lt	5'	6"		"	"
	1450	Johnson, Elix	31			Dk	5'	9 1/4"		"	"
	1451	Jackson, Henry	36			Lt	5'	5 1/2'		"	"
	1452	Johnson, Andrew								"	"
	1453	Johnson, Alex	38			Blk	5'	3"		"	Blk Smith
	1454	Jones, Geo	34			Dk	5'	1"		"	Eng Cleaner
	1518	Johnson, Wm	25	Bro	Blk	Blk	5'	9"		"	Sawyer
	1519	Jackson, J	24	Blk	"	Blk	5'	5"		"	Engine Hand
	1520	Jackson, A	24	"	"	"	5'	5"		"	Laborer
	1521	Jones, Chls	24	"	"	"	5'	3 1/2"		"	Laborer
	1522	Johnson, A	28	"	"	"	5'	8"		"	Do.

See Page 56

Page	No.	Name	Age	Eyes	Hair	Complex	Feet	In	State	Town or County	Occupation
54	74	King, Benj	48	Blk	Blk	Brown	5'	7"	VA	Petersburg	Shoe Maker
	75	King, Wm H	28	Gray	"	Light	5'	8"	VA	"	Carpenter
	76	King, William	21	Blk	Bushy	Ginger	5'	7"	VA	"	Laborer
	140	King, Aron	33	Dk	Dk	Dk	5'	9 1/2"	VA	Dinwiddie	"
	145	King, Robert	28	Brown	Blk	Blk	5'	7"	VA	Spottsylvania	Farmer

Enlisted			Assigned		Remarks
When	Where	By Whom	When	Where	
					Unaccounted
					"
15-Jul					"
19-Jul				To M(edical) Dept.	
19-Jul					Detailed till 1st January/65
19-Jul				To M(edical) Dept.	
23-Apr		Lt. McCue			Detailed till 1st January/65
06-Jul		Williams		Armory	*
06-Jun		Capt. Coke		Eng(ineer) Dept.	
"		"		"	
08-Jun		"		"	
					Detailed to Capt. MacMurdo till 1st Mar(ch)
03-Aug		"		To M(edical) Dept.	
05-Aug		"		N(iter) & M(ining) B(ureau)	
06-Sep		"		"	
07-Sep		"			Unaccounted
19-Sep		"		N(iter) & M(ining) B(ureau)	
22-Aug		"		To M(edical) Dept.	
22-Sep		"		N(iter) & M(ining) B(ureau)	
04-May		R G Bosseau			Unaccounted
		Lt . Nowlin			Deserter
20-Sep		Capt. Mathews		To M(edical) Dept.	
"		"		"	
19-Sep	Petersburg	Sgt. Winfree	Petersbg	To M(edical) Dept.	
23-Sep	"	"	23-Sep	"	
"	"	"	"	"	
05-May				N(iter) & M(ining) B(ureau)	
"	Henry CHo	Lt. Hawthorn		Rec(commeded) for light duty by Ex(aming) B(oar)d	
"	"	"	05-Jul	Eng(ineer) Dept.	
"	"	"	"	"	Detailed 1 January/65 Ex(empt) by Med(ical) B(oar)d
"	"	"	"		
13-Sep				N(iter) & M(ining) B(ureau)	Unaccounted
				Detailed 1st July/65 this office	
27-Jun				Eng(ineer) Dept.	
"				"	
01-Nov	O CHo	Lt. W H Lewis		"	
23-Nov		Lt. Graves		"	
"		"		"	
"		Lt. Blackford		R(ichmond) & D(anville) R(ail) R(oad)	
"		"		"	
"		"		"	
"		"		"	
"		"		"	
"		"		Messenger	Maj. Bailey
"		"		N(iter) & M(ining) B(ureau)	
"		"		R(ichmond) & D(anville) R(ail) R(oad)	Detailed to
"		"		Detailed to Capt. MacMurdo till 1st Mar	
03-Dec		"		N(iter) & M(ining)	
20-Dec		"		R(ichmond) & P(etersburg) R(ail) R(oad)	
06-Dec		"		N(iter) & M(ining)	
28-Dec		"		Detailed to Surg. Palmer	
03-May	Petersburg	Lt. J. E. Heath		Detailed til 1st Nov(ember)/64	
"	"	"		Eng(ineer) Dept.	
"	"	"		Do.	
"	Dinwiddie	R G Bosseau		Do.	
01-May	Spottsylvania	Lt. H. S. Williams			

Page	No.	Name	Description						Where Born		Occupation
			Age	Eyes	Hair	Complex	Feet	In	State	Town or County	
	146	King, Albert	25	"	"	"	6'	-	VA	"	"
	229	Kendrick, Wm	39	Blue	"	Yellow	5'	8"	VA	Washington	
	230	Kilgore, Wilson	46	Gray	Blk	Blk	5'	4"	VA	Scott Co.	
	231	Kilgore, Henry S	28	"	"	"	5'	6"	VA	"	
	232	Kilgore, Henry	19				5'	9"	VA	"	
	324	Kailes, Clay	27	Dk	Dk	Dk	5'	5 1/2"	VA	Richmond	Laborer
	345	Kenny, George	20	"	"	"	4'	11 1/2"	VA	"	
	397	Kenny, Wm	28	"	"	Blk	5'	11 1/2"	VA	Albemarle	Farm Hand
	577	Kidd, Alexd	47	"	Blk	Yellow	5'	11"	VA	Botetourt	
	1088	Kinney, Horace	26	"	"	Lt	5'	9"	VA	Albemarle	Blk Smith
	1089	King, Peter R.	44	Dk	"	Dk	6'	2"	VA	Louisa	Laborer
	1090	Keith, S. P.	32	Blk	Blk	Yellow	6'	3"	VA	Russell	"
	1091	Kinney, Wm	45	"	"	Dk	5'	6"	VA	Augusta	Bk Smith
	1092	Keeling, Edw	29	"	"	"	5'	9"	VA	Pittsylvania	Farm Hand
	1093	King, Edward	23	Dk	Dk	Dk	5'	8"	VA	Richmond	Laborer
	1094	King, William	18						VA	Henrico	
	1095	King, Thomas	18						VA	"	
	1096	Kelly, John	35						VA	Lunenberg	
	1455	Key, Austin	48	Bk	Bk	Dk	6'	-	VA	King Wm	Laborer
	1456	Key, Wm A	26	"	"	Bk	5'	7"	VA	" "	"
	1457	Kinney, William	30			Dk	6'	-	VA	Richmond	Farm Hand
	1523	King, Robt	36	"	"	Blk	5'	10"		"	
		Kinney, Jim								Richmond	
		Kingrey, Wm	28			Blk	5'	11 1/2"		"	
		Key, John	31				5'	10"		Essex	Laborer
55		Kersey, Benj	36	Dk	Blk	Mul	5'	7"		Mecklenburg	Wood Worker
		Kaughman, John	48	Blk	Blk	Blk	5'	6"		King & Queen	Farmer
		Kaughman, Jeremiah	32	Blk	Blk	Lt	5'	7"		"	"
56		Jones, Elijah	46	Dk	Dk	Lt	5'	8"		Henrico	
		James, W F	20	Blk	Blk	Brown	5'	6"		Do.	
		Jonathan, Alexd	28	Dk	Dk	Dk	5'	9"		Do.	
		Jonathan, James	46	"	"	"				Do.	
		Jackson, B								Richmond	Farmer
		Johns, Eskridge	25	Gray	Dk	Yellow	6'	-		Amherst	Farmer
		Jackson, Marshall	24	Dk	Bro	Blk	5'	8"		Louisa	Laborer
		Jones, Elias	47			Mul	5'	10"		Lancaster	"
		Jackson, Andrew	35			Dk	5'	6"		Richmond	Fireman
		Jefferson, Wm	22							Pittsylvania	Boatman
		Jordan, George	48	Dk	Lt	Brt	5'	10"		King & Queen	Farmer
		Jenifer, Julius	50							Pittsylvania	Laborer
		Jones, Augustine	25	Dk	Dk	Dk				Middlesex	"
		Jordan, Theodore	21	Blk	Blk	Bro	6'	1"		Essex	
		Jones, Pleasant									
		Jackson, Thos	25			Dk	5'	9"		Richmond Co.	Farmer
		Jackson, Wm	23			Blk	5'	8"		"	"
		Johnson, Oliver	22			"	5'	9"		"	"
		Jackson, Edward	20			"	5'	4"		"	"
		Johnson, Lewis	28			"	6'	4"		Westmorland	"
		Johnson, Joe	35			Lt	5'	10"		"	"
60	79	Lee, Oliver	23	Brown	Blk	Blk	5'	11"	VA	Petersburg	Ostler
	147	Long, Atwell	22	"	"	Yellow	6'	3"	VA	Spottsylvania	Farmer
	161	Lovely, Griffin	27						VA	Roanoke	Farmer
	181	Levi, Jesse	30	Blk	Blk	Yellow	5'	9 1/2"	VA	Russell	
	182	Lester, Anderson	34	"	"	Brown	5'	10 1/2"	VA	"	
	183	Lester, Gordon	49	"	"	Yellow	5'	6"	VA	"	
	184	Lethco, W J	25	Blue	"	"	5'	11"	VA	Washington Co.	
	185	Lethco, A H	25				5'	9"	VA	Washington Co.	
	186	Lester, John	26				5'	8"	VA	"	
	187	Lester, Alexander	18				5'	9 1/2"	VA	"	
	246	Lester, William	26			Yellow	5'	7"	VA	Sussex Co.	
	267	Lyons, W B	26	Blk	Blk	Lgt	5'	6"	VA	Richmond Cty.	Barber
	289	Lilly, Andrew	24	"	"	Brown	5'	9"	VA	"	"

Enlisted			Assigned		Remarks
When	Where	By Whom	When	Where	
"	"	"			
30-Apr	Washington Co.	Wm M Thompson			Unassigned
"	Scott Co.	Do.			Unassigned
"	"	Do.			Deserter
"	"	Do.			Deserter
12-Apr	Richmond	Capt. Coke			Deserter
16-Apr	"	"	Nov	R(ichmond) & D(anville) R(ail) R(oad)	
29-Apr	"	"		Va Central (Rail) Road	
27-Jul	Fincastle	Lt. Nowlin		N(iter) & M(ining) J(ames) R(iver) & Kanawha Canal Co(mpany)	
30-Jun		Capt. Colston	01-Jul	Maj Richard	
01-Sep		Lt. Vaughan	04-Sep	N(iter) & M(ining) Bureau	
11-Jun		Lt. Sawyer		Exempt by Med(ical) Ex(amining) B(oar)d	13th Dist(rict)
					Detailed 1st January/65
03-Oct		Lt. Williams		Eng(ineer) Dept	
13-Sep		Capt. Coke		N(iter) & M(ining) B(ureau)	
				Eng(ineer) Dept.	
				" "	
06-Jul					
19-Nov		Lt. G P Haw	20-Nov	Eng(ineer) Dept.	
12-Jul		"	"	" "	
Nov		Lt. Blackford		R(ichmond) & D(anville) R(ail) R(oad)	
				Detailed to	
				Detailed to J(ames) R(iver) & K(anawha) Canal Co(mpany) till 1st May/65	
				Detailed to Va Central (Rail Road) till 1st May/65	
Dec/64		Lt. Bumpass		Detailed to B F Gresham 1st June	
				Detailed till 1st May/65 Cl(ar)ksville Ord(nance) Shops	
		Lt. Dickinson		Detailed till 1st July/65	Dr. Bland
		"		"	"
January 1865				Navy detailed till 1st May/65	
"				Do.	
"				Do.	
"				Do.	
"				Detailed to J(ames) R(iver) & K(anawha) Co. till 1st May/65	
"				Detailed till 1st July 1865	
"				Detailed to J C Meeks 1st May/65	
"				Public & Private Necessity till July 1865	
"				Detailed to E H Gill	
11-Jan				Col Withers Eng(ineer) Dept.	
Dec 3/64				Detailed till 1st July/65	Dr. Bland
				Detailed to Ord(nance) Dept. till 1st July/65	
				Detailed to T B Evans till 1st July/65	
				"	
				Detailed to Jos. R Anderson Co.	
January/65				Eng(ineer) Dept.	
"				"	
"				"	
"				"	
"				"	
03-May	Petersburg	Lt. J. E. Heath		Eng(ineer) Dept.	
01-May	Spottsylvania	Lt. H. S. Williams			
01-May	Roanoke	Capt. Clements	April	Capt. Wade A.C.S.	
30-Apr		W M Thompson	15-Jun	Q(uarter) M(aster) Dept.	
"		"	"	Do.	
"		"			
"		"	15-Jun	Q(uarter) M(aster) Dept.	
"		"	"	Do.	
"		"	"	Do.	
"			"	Q(uarter) M(aster) Dept.	
"	Sussex Co.	D J Godwin			
05-Apr	Richmond	Capt. Coke		Exempted to Private Necessity	
06-Apr	"	"		Detailed to Hospital No. 9	

Page	No.	Name	Description						Where Born		Occupation
			Age	Eyes	Hair	Complex	Feet	In	State	Town or County	
	290	Ligon, Cornelius	30	"	"	Dk	5'	2 1/2"	VA	"	Shoe Maker
	304	Lee, Samuel	36	"	Dk	Brown	5'	7"	VA	"	Cooper
	330	Logan, John	20	Dk	"	Lt	5'	6 1/2"	VA	"	Cook
	355	Lawrence, John	45	Brown	"	"	5'	8"	VA	"	Black Smith
	367	Lewis, Henry	46	Dk	Blk	Dk	6'	-	VA	"	"
	376	Logan, Robert	39	"	Blk	Lt	5'	9"	VA	Chesterfield	Cooper
	387	Levell, James	44	Grey	"	"	5'	7"	VA	Richmond	Laborer
	388	Liggon, Fleming	45	"	"	"	5'	7"	VA	"	Barber
	404	Lucas, John	24				5'	11 1/2"	VA	"	RR Employee
	435	Lester, John	27	Blk	Blk	Blk	5'	9"	VA	Montgomery	
	447	Lookadoo, Wm	49	Grey	Lght	Bright	5'	7"	VA	Richmond	Shoe Maker
	454	Lynch, Wm	31	"	Blk	Lt	5'	7"	VA	Goochland	Carpenter
	520	Ligan, R T	22		"		5'	-	VA	Mecklenburg	Laborer
	521	Lewis, Green	22				5'	4"	VA	Prince Edwd	"
	538	Lac, Jacob	44	Blk	Blk	Blk	5'	4"	VA	Patrick	
	591	Lowry, Archer	44	Brown	"	"	5'	8"	VA	Petersburg	
61	617	Lockett, Wm	21	Blk	Dk	Yellow	5'	7"	VA	Petersburg	Laborer
	679	Logan, W	45						VA	Powhatan	"
	680	Logan, H	22						VA	"	Shoe Maker
	681	Logan, Isaac	48						VA	"	
	682	Lockett, Geo	49				5'	9 1/2"	VA	Cumberland	
	683	Lynch, Geo	29				5'	9"	VA	"	
	684	Lynch, Madison	45				5'	6"	VA	"	
	685	Logan, James	47						VA	Powhatan	
	686	Lipscomb, S	27						VA	"	
	1097	Lewis, James	58	Blk	Blk	Lt	5'	7"	VA	Albemarle	Carpenter
	1098	Lewis, William	21	"	"	"	5'	6"	VA	"	Laborer
	1099	Lewis, James	32			Dk	6'	-	VA	"	Carpenter
	1100	Logan, John	25	"	"	"	5'	6"	VA	"	Farmer
	1101	Logan, S	23	Dk	Dk	Blk	5'	8"	VA	Buckingham	Blk Smith
	1102	Logan, William	34	"	"	"	5'	7"	VA	"	Jobber
	1103	Lewis, George	22	"	Blk	Bro	5'	10 1/2"	VA	Orange	Laborer
	1104	Lawson, Joseph	38	Bro	"	Yellow	5'	11"	VA	Spottsylvania	Drayman
	1105	Lewis, William	45	Blk	"	Bro	5'	7"	VA	"	Cooper
	1106	Lewis, David	27	Bro	"	Yellow	5'	7"	VA	"	Shoe Maker
	1107	Lewis, Solomon	21	Blk	Yel	Bright	5'	9 1/2"	VA	Culpeper	Buck Sawyer
	1108	Lacy, John	22	Blk	Blk	Blk	5'	8"	VA	"	Laborer
	1109	Lucus, Phil	40	"	"	Bro	5'	3 1/2"	VA	Spottsylvania	Drayman
	1110	Lucus, William	25	"	"	Yellow	5'	10"	VA	"	
	1111	Logan, Joseph	46	"	"	Dk	5'	9 3/4"	VA	"	
	1112	Lee, Robert	21	Dk	Dk	Yel	5'	9"	VA	"	
	1113	Lundige, Greenberry	21	"	Blk	Dk	5'	7"	VA	Augusta	Striker
	1114	Lundige, Wm	24	"	"	Blk	5'	4"	VA	"	Laborer
	1115	Lester, Wm	20	"	"	"	5'	9"	VA	Greensville	"
62	1116	Lawson, John	26	Blk	Blk	Bro	5'	5"	VA	Petersburg	Bk Smith
	1117	Leech, Wash	30	"	"	Blk	5'	5"	VA	Augusta	R R Hand
	1118	London, Olm	26	"	"	"	5'	5"	VA	"	Farm Hand
	1119	London, Jno	30	"	"	"	4'	2"	VA	"	"
	1120	Liggon, Joseph	22	Yellow	"	"	5'	10"	VA	Rockbridge	
	1121	Long, Henry	21	Bk	"	Yellow	5'	10"	VA	Halifax	Carpenter
	1458	Langston, John	39	"	"	Lt	5'	6"	VA	King William	Farmer
	1459	Langston, Hath	37	"	"	Cop	5'	6"	VA	"	"
	1460	Langston, Thos W	26	"	"	Lt	5'	7"	VA	"	"
	1461	Lipscomb, James	30			"	5'	9 3/4"	VA	Richmond	Laborer
	1462	Logan, Royall	35			Dk	5'	7"	VA	"	Farmer
	1463	Lancy, James	22			Lt	5'	4"	VA	"	Laborer
	1464	Lee, Isiah	19			"	5'	8"	VA	"	"
	1465	Lewis, Jos	24			"	5'	8"	VA	"	"
	1466	Lawrence, Edmund	29			Blk	5'	6"	VA	"	"
	1467	Laney, John T	18			Lt	5'	7 1/2"	VA	"	"
	1468	Lipscomb, Olway	43			"	5'	7 1/2"	VA	"	"
		Lewis, Fleming	35	Blk	Blk	Mul	5'	8"	VA	New Kent	Farmer
		Langley, Jno B.	45	Gray	Dk	"	5'	6"	VA	"	Miller

Enlisted			Assigned		Remarks
When	Where	By Whom	When	Where	
06-Apr	"	"	18-Apr	N(iter) & M(ining) Bureau	
07-Apr	"	"		Commissary Dept.	
13-Apr	"	"	13-Apr	N(iter) & M(ining) Bureau	
19-Apr	"	"		Naval Ord(nance) Dept.	
21-Apr	"	"		Navy Dept.	
25-Apr	"	"		Do.	
27-Apr	"	"		Discharged by Secretary of War	
28-Apr	"	"	08-May	N(iter) & M(ining) Bureau	
29-Apr	"	"		Detailed to Va Central (Rail) Road	
11-Apr	Montg Co.	Lt. Sydenstriker			
02-May	Richmond	Capt. Coke	16-May	N(iter) & M(ining) Bureau	
04-May	"	"			Deserter
01-Jul	Mecklenburg	W. Atkins	30-Jun	Ord(nance) Dept. Cl(ar)ksville	
"	Prince Edwd	Zimmerman	"	Eng(ineer) Dept. H. B.	
	Newbern	Lt. Poole		Q(uarter) M(aster) Dept I H Lacy	
02-Aug				Q(uarter) M(aster) Dept til Nov 1864	
26-Jul	Petersburg	Lt. Scott	26-Jul	Eng(ineering) Dept	
12-Jun	Powhatan		12-Jun	Do.	
"	"		"	Do.	
"	"		"	Do.	
19-Jun	Cumberland		19-Jun	Do.	
15-Jun	"		15-Jun	Q(uarter) M(aster) Dept Ag(en)t (Cumberland)	
15-Jun	"		15-Jun	Do.	
06-Jun	Powhatan		06-Jun	Q(uarter) M(aster) Dept Ag(en)t (Powhatan) til 1st May/65	
06-Jun	"		06-Jun	Do.	
27-Jun		Capt. Colston	29-Jun	Maj. Richard	
27-Jun		"	"	"	
28-Jun		"	30-Jun	"	
"		"	"	"	
10-Jun		A T Moseley	14-Jun	Col. Scott	High Bridge
"		"	"	"	"
23-Jun		Lt. Lewis	18-Aug	Gordonsville	To Maj. Richard
14-Apr		Lt. Williams			Unassigned
"		"			"
"		"			"
19-Aug		W Graves		Eng(ineer) Dept	"
				"	
04-Apr		Lt. Williams			Unassigned
				Col. Shields detailed til 1st January/65	
					Unaccounted
					"
				To M(edical) Dept.	
				"	
May					Unaccounted
28-Sep	Petersburg	Sgt. Winfree	28-Sep	To M(edical) Dept.	
Oct				Eng(ineer) Dept.	
"				"	
"				"	
					Detailed as Farmer
21-Sep		Capt. Anderson			
19-Nov		Lt. Haw	20-Nov	Eng(ineer) Dept.	
"		Lt. Haw	"	"	
"		Lt. Haw	"	"	
"		Blackford		R(ichmond) & D(anville) R(ail) R(oad)	
"		"		"	
"		"		"	
"		"		"	
"		"		"	
"		"		N(iter) & M(ining) B(ureau)	
"		"		R(ichmond) & D(anville) R(ail) R(oad)	Detailed to
"		"		"	"
		T Taylor		Detailed til 1st April/65 this office	
		"		Detailed til 1st July/65 this office	

Page	No.	Name	Description						Where Born		Occupation
			Age	Eyes	Hair	Complex	Feet	In	State	Town or County	
		Lowndes, Tom	28	Dk	Dk	Yellow	5'	11"	VA	Prince George	Laborer
		Logan, Robt	38	"	"	Dk	5'	7 1/2"	VA	Chesterfield	"
		Lockley, Jim	37	Blk	Blk	Dk	5'	6"	VA	Essex Co.	"
		Logan, J A							VA	Richmond	
		Lipscomb, H							VA	"	
		Lynch, Washington	26	Blk	Blk	Brown	5'	8"	VA	Powhatan	Blk Smith
		Lynch, Robt	28	"	"	"	5'	7"	VA	"	"
		Lewis, Henry	46	"	"	Blk	5'	11"	VA	Richmond	4th Class Merchant
		Logan, John							VA	Washington Co.	
		Lewis, John	36	Dk	Dk	Yellow	5'	5"	VA	New Kent	Farmer
63		Lawson, Mayo	22							Pittsylvania	Laborer
		Lewis, John	38	Blue	Dk	Yellow	6'	-		Powhatan	Farmer
		Lucas, Arnold	19			Blk	6'	-		Westmoreland	"
		Logan, Washington	41	Blk	Blk	Blk	5'	9"			
66	12	McRae, Jos	23	Blk	Blk	Ginger	4'	6"	VA	Petersburg	Laborer
	13	Maye, William	28	"	"	Bro	5'	5"	VA	"	Blacksmith
	14	Miam, James W.	19	"	"	Light	5'	4"	VA	"	Laborer
	15	Merit, John	18	"	"	"	5'		VA	"	"
	16	McKaey, John	20	"	"	Dark	5'	4"	VA	"	"
	17	McKing, Andrew	25	"	"	Light	5'	6"	VA	"	"
	18	Mason, Thomas	23	"	"	"	5'	5"	VA	"	"
	85	Map, Benj Tom	32	Blk	Bushy	Yellow	6'	6"	VA	"	Gardner
	94	Maple, Joe	19	Blk	Bushy	Blk	5'	8"	VA	"	Laborer
	126	Malory, Daniel	19	Dk	Dk	Dk	5'	6 1/2"	VA	Dinwiddie	"
	127	Malone, Andrew	22	"	"	"	5'	5"	VA	"	"
	128	Miles, Morrie	48	"	"	"	5'	7 1/2"	VA	"	Blacksmith
	129	Mumford, Edward	25	"	"	Light	5'	4"	VA	"	Laborer
	130	Myrick, John	21	"	"	Dk	5'	5"	VA	"	"
	158	Mays, Osborne	22	Blk	Blk	Dk	5'	8"	VA	Roanoke	Shoemaker
	234	McCrackin, Chls R	23	Blk	Blk	Yellow	5'	9"	VA	Washington Co.	
	235	Martin, Frank	18	"	"	"	5'	6"	VA	"	
	247	Mabry, Henry	35			Brown	5'	3"	VA	Greensville Co.	
	267	Mandin, Wm	25	Blk	"	Lgt	5'	9"	VA	Richmond Cty	Barber
	273	McHorton, Robt	27	Brown		"	5'	8"	VA	"	"
	315	McHarris, W	30	Grey	Lt	"	5'	3"	VA	"	"
	317	Matthews, Henry	49	Blk	Dk	Dk	5'	11"	VA	"	Laborer
	318	Martin, Wm B.	22	Grey	Lt	Lt	5'	11"	VA	"	Barber
	339	Milkens, John	37	Dk	Blk	"	5'	7"	VA	"	Blk Smith
	401	Mann, Amias	18	"	"	Brown	5'	3"	VA	Chesterfield	Laborer
	402	Moore, Joseph	32	Grey	"	Lt	5'	5"	VA	Richmond	Depot Hand
	403	Martin, David	35	Dk	"	Brown	5'		VA	Waynesboro	Blk Smith
	440	Moore, James	47	Blk	Blk	Copper	5'	10"	VA	Montgomery Co.	
	456	Mason, John	26	Grey	Dk	Lt	5'	4"	VA	Richmond	Laborer
67	565	Mann, Wm	27	Blk	Blk	Blk	5'	8"	VA	Henry	
	566	Mays, Jas. E.	41	"	"	Brown	5'	6"	VA	Botetourt	
	581	Morgan, P G	47	Dk	Strait	Yellow	5'	10"	VA	Petersburg	
	582	McLain, Albert	45	Grey	Dk	Bright	5'	7 1/2"	VA	Do.	
	636	Moody, Jno	30			Blk	5'	7 1/2"	VA	Dinwiddie	
	637	Mason, Jno	24			Yellow	5'		VA	"	
	638	Mays, J	41						VA	Powhatan	
	639	Mayo, T	30						VA	"	
	640	Moseley, R	20						VA	"	Shoe Maker
	641	Mayo, Wm	34			Mult	5'	6"	VA	Cumberland	
	642	Mayo, Jos	34			Blk	5'	3 1/2"	VA	Do.	
	643	Mayo, Albert	49			Mult	5'	5"	VA	Do.	
	644	Mayo, Steve	41			"	5'	3"	VA	Do.	
	645	Mayo, Wilson	32			"	5'	6"	VA	Do.	
	646	Mayo, Robt	35			"	5'	10"	VA	Do.	
	647	Martin, I	23						VA	Powhatan	
	648	Mayo, Tom	48						VA	Do.	
	649	Mealey, A	24						VA	Do.	

Enlisted			Assigned		Remarks
When	Where	By Whom	When	Where	
				Navy Dept. til 1st May 1865	
				"	
				Detailed to Orville Jeffries til May 1865	
				Detailed to J(ames) R(iver) & K(anawha) Canal Co(mpany) till 1st May 1865	
				"	
May/64	Powhatan	Lt. Chafin		Detailed to J(ames) R(iver) & K(anawha) Canal Co(mpany) till 1st July 1865	
"	"	"			
				Detailed to C(onfederate) S(tates) Naval Works til 1st May/65	
				Detailed to Washington Heights til 1st May/65	
				Detailed to E Tyler til 1st May/65	
		Col. Withers		Eng(ineer) Dept.	
				Detailed to Maj. Randolph til 1st May1865	
				Eng(ineer) Dept.	
				Detailed to Capt. Wellford A.C.S. till 1st May 1865	
03-May	Petersburg	Lt. J E Heath		Eng(ineer) Dept.	
"	"	"		Do.	
"	"	"		Do.	
"	"	"		Eng(ineer) Dept.	
"	"	"		Do.	
"	"	"		Do.	
"	"	"		Do.	
"	"	R G Bosseau		Do.	
"	"	"		Do.	
"	"	"		Do.	
"	"	"		Do.	
"	"	"		Do.	
"	"	"		Do.	
01-May	Roanoke	Capt. Clement	April	T J Jenkins Q(uarter) M(aster)	
30-Apr	Washington Co.	W M Thompson			Unassigned
"	"	"			Do.
"	Greensville Co.	D J Godwin			
05-Apr	Richmond	Capt Coke		N(iter) & M(ining) Bureau	
"	"	"		Private Necessity	
07-Apr	"	"			Deserter
07-Apr	"	"			Deserter
					Disch(arged) Med(ical)
11-Apr	"	"		Exempt S Wm	Ex(amining) Board
14-Apr	"	"		Navy Dept.	
29-Apr	"	"	29-Apr	N(iter) & M(ining) Bureau	
29-Apr	"	"		VA Central R(ail) R(oad)	
29-Apr	"	"		Do.	
09-May	Montg Co.	Lt. Sydenstriker	09-May	Maj McMaken Q(uarter) M(aster) Dept.	
05-May	Richmond	Capt Coke			Deserter
	New Bern	Lt Poole		Q(uarter) M(aster) I H Lacy	
	"			"	
April	Petersburg	Lt. Heath		Eng(ineer) Dept.	
27-Jul	"	"		Do.	
22-Jul	Dinwiddie			Do.	
"	"			Do.	
12-Jun	Powhatan			Do.	
"	"			Detailed from this Office til 1st April 1865	
"	"			Do.	
30-Jun	Cumb			Do.	
06-Jul	"			Do.	
15-Jun	"			Q M Ag(en)t. for Cumb(erland)	
"	"			Do.	
"	"			Do.	
"	"			Do.	
06-Jun	Powhatan			Q M Ag(en)t.	Powhatan 1st May 1865
"	"			Do.	1st May 1865
"	"			Do.	1st May 1865

Page	No.	Name	Age	Eyes	Hair	Complex	Feet	In	State	Town or County	Occupation
	1122	Martin, Sam	53	Blk	Blk	Blk	5'	7"	VA	Albemarle	Carpenter
	1123	Martin, R	15	Br	"	Cho	5'	8"	VA	"	"
	1124	Middlebrook, L	30	Dk	Dk	Lt	6'	-	VA	"	Laborer
	1125	Martin, Sam	19	Bk	Bl	Lt	5'	8"	VA	"	Shoe Maker
	1126	Moon, William	20	"	"	"	6'	-	VA	"	Laborer
	1127	Mayo, Tom	37	"	"	Dk	5'	11"	VA	Nelson Co.	Blk Smith
	1128	Mayo, Ed	53	"	"	"	5'	7"	VA	"	Farmer
	1129	Mann, Saml	35	"	"	"	5'	8"	VA	"	Laborer
	1130	Mayo, Albert	49	"	"	Dk	5'	8"	VA	"	Farmer
	1131	Mason, G W	26	"	"	Lt	5'	10"	VA	Amhurst Co.	"
68	1132	Mukins, Len	23						VA	New Kent	
	1133	Mukins, Thos	24						VA	"	
	1134	Mukins, Ro	29						VA	"	
	1135	Madden, A	18	Dk	Dk	Lt	5'	-	VA	Rockinhgam	Lumber Man
	1136	McIntoch, Wm	41	Hz	"	Yellow	5'	11"	VA	Orange	Farmer
	1137	Miller, John	24	Blk	Blk	Bro	5'	10"	VA	Spottsylvania	"
	1138	Morlin, Stafford H	33	Hazel	"	Mulatto	5'	7"	VA	Caroline	"
	1139	Marlon, James	47	Blk	Blk	"	5'	10"	VA	"	Laborer
	1140	Mosby, John	17	Dk	Bro	Dk	5'	9"	VA	Louisa Co.	Barber
	1141	Morris, Jeff	28	"	Blk	Yellow	6'	2"	VA		Laborer
	1142	Madden, Abram	18	"	"	Blk	5'	5"	VA		"
	1143	Murry, George	24	"	Sand	Cop	5'	8"	VA	Bath	"
	1144	Moore, F	23	Blk	Blk	Blk	5'	10"	VA	Botetourt	
	1145	Miller, W	30	Dk	Dk	Dk	5'	8"	VA	Highland	Laborer
	1146	Miller, G	29	Dk	"	"	5'	10"	VA	"	
	1147	Mickens, Benjamin	24	Blk	Blk	Yellow	5'	11"	VA		
	1148	Mauzy, Madison	19	"	Dk	Cop	5'	9"	VA		
	1149	Morris, William	21	"	Blk	Dk	5'	8"	VA	Augusta	Laborer
	1150	Miller, Robert	46	"	"	Blk	5'	9"	VA	"	Tanner
	1151	Mayo, Wm	23	Dk	Dk	Dk	5'	6"	VA	Pittsylvania	Boatman
	1152	Mayo, C	20	"		Blk	5'	5"	VA	"	"
	1153	Mitchell, H	35	"	"	Brown	5'	8"	VA	"	"
	1154	Mayo, Jno A	24	Gray	"	"	5'	8 1/2"	VA	"	Blk Smith
	1155	Mason, Wm	27	Dk	Dk	Black	5'	8"	VA	"	Farm Hand
	1156	Morris, Tim	38		Blk	Dk	5'	8"	VA	Richmond	Bk Smith
	1157	Mills, Taylor	48	Blk	"	"	5'	5"	VA	"	Laborer
	1158	Makins, P	22	Bro	Dk	Lt	5'	6"	VA	"	"
	1159	Mann, W H	36	Blk	Blk	Bk	5'	10"	VA	Henry	Blk Smith
	1160	Murry, Anderson	18				5'		VA		
69	1161	Morgan, Jas.	29	Dk	Dk	Yellow	5'	6"	VA	Petersburg	Laborer
	1162	Mitchell, Henry	39	Blk	Blk	"	5'	10"	VA	"	Fireman
	1163	Myrick, Isaac	19	"	"	Bro	5'	9"	VA	"	Bk Smith
	1164	Malone, Soloman	27	"	"	Blk	5'	6"	VA	"	Laborer
	1165	Morgan, George	30	"	"	"	5'	6"	VA	"	"
	1166	Mumford, Joe	28	"	"	"	5'	11"	VA	"	"
	1167	Martin, Reubin	24	"	"	"	5'	7 1/2"	VA	Augusta	Farm Hand
	1168	Mann, George	20	"	"	"	5'	10"	VA	Henry	Farmer
	1169	Mann, James	24	"	"	"	5'	9"	VA	Stokes	Wagoner
	1170	Miles, Jas	26	"	"	M	5'	4"	VA	Dinwiddie	Laborer
	1171	Meredith, Jas H	20	"					VA	Richmond	
	1172	Moore, Luke	39	"	"	Blk	5'	7"	VA	Rockbridge	Teamster
	1173	Moore, James	30	Yell	Grey	"	5'	5"	VA	"	Cook
	1174	Mathews, Adam	42	"	Blk	"	5'	8"	VA	"	Depot Hand
	1175	Mason, Killer	38	"	"	"	5'	10"	VA	"	Laborer
	1176	McCoy, Chas L	19	"	"	Lt	5'	7"	VA	Appomatox	Farmer

Enlisted			Assigned		Remarks
When	Where	By Whom	When	Where	
25-Jun	Alber	Capt. Colston	26-Jun	Maj. Richard	
"	"	"	"	"	
26-Jun	"	"	28-Jun	"	
27-Jun	"	"	29-Jun	"	
28-Jun	"	"	01-Jun	"	
30-Jun	Nelson	Lt. Carpenter	01-Jul	"	
"	"	"	"	"	
"	"	"		"	
02-Jul	"	"	03-Jul	"	
04-Jul	-	Lt. Roane	06-Jul	"	
Oct		T Taylor	Oct	N(iter) & M(ining) B(ureau)	
"		"	"	"	
"		"	"	"	
"		Col C S Peyton	31-Jul	Gen. Ransom	
30-Jul	Orange	Lt. Lewis	04-Jul	Gordonsville	Maj. Richard
05-Jul	Fredburg	Lt. Williams		Unassigned	Petition for detail
04-Apr	Bowl Green	Lt. Hancock	19-Jul	Gen. Ewell	Richmond
19-Jul	"	"	"	"	"
"	Louisa CHo	Lt. Vaughan	10-Sep	N(iter) & M(ining) Bureau	
02-Sep				Col Shields detailed til 1st January '65	
				Eng(ineer) Dept.	
	Covington			N(iter) & M(ining) Bureau	
	"			"	
01-Jul	McDowell				Unaccounted
03-Sep	"				"
					Detailed til 1st
					Oct(ober)/64
					" 1st
					Jan(uary)/65
	Staunton			To M(edical) Dept.	
				"	
28-Apr		Lt. McClue		"	
"		"		"	
					Detailed til 1st
"		"			Nov(ember)/64
06-Jul		Lt. Williams		Armory	
"		"		Eng(ineering) Dept	
21-Apr		Capt. Coke		Detailed to Capt. G Corgain	
13-Jul		"		N(iter) & M(ining) B(ureau)	
19-Sep		"		"	
02-May		Capt. Bernard			Detailed by B(oard) of C
		Lt. Nowlin		gen To Gen. Mc Courtland Command	
20-Sep	Petersbg	Sgt. Winfree	20-Sep	To M(edical) Dept.	
22-Sep	"	"	22-Sep	"	
					15 days fur(lough) by
24-Sep	"	"			Ex(amining) B(oar)d
27-Sep	"	"	27-Sep	To M(edical) Dept.	
					Ex(empt) by M(edical)
"	"	"	"		B(oar)d
"	"	"	"	To M(edical) Dept.	
Oct				Eng(ineer) Dept.	
05-May	Henry CHo	Lt. Hawthorne	05-Jul	"	
"	"	"	"		Detailed 1st Jan(uar)y 65
					Detailed 1st Nov(ember)
19-Jul					64
13-Sep				N(iter) & M(ining) B(ureau)	
				To M(edical) Dept.	
				"	
					Unaccounted
				Eng(ineer) Dept.	
16-Sep		Capt. Anderson			

Page	No.	Name	Description						Where Born		Occupation
			Age	Eyes	Hair	Complex	Feet	In	State	Town or County	
	1469	Miles, William	34	Blk	"	Lt	5'	7"	VA	King William	"
	1470	Mann, Theo	32			Dk	5'	6"	VA		Laborer
	1471	Minnis, Jos									Fireman
	1472	Morris, Wm	44			Dk	5'	7 1/2"			Laborer
	1473	Mann, Woodson	29			"	5'	5 3/4"			"
	1474	Martin, Reubin									Messenger
	1475	Maxfield, Silas	52								
	1524	McNaughton, Robt	27								Barber
	1525	Meekins, Jas									Porter
	1526	Mose, Robt	32	Blk	Blk	Lt	5'	6"			Laborer
		Massie, James	28	Dk	Dk	Lt	5'	8"		Richmond	
		Moss, T	35	Blk	Blk	Lt	5'	4"		Do.	
		Macklin, Wm	20			Lt Brown	5'	9 1/2"		Do.	
70		Mayo, A								Richmond	Laborer
		Mayo, Jno	25	Dk	Dk	Brown	6'	-		Powahatan	Blk Smith
		Mickins, Jno	28	Blk	Blk	Mul	5'	8"		Richmond	Mechinist
		McKinney, John	25	"	"	Mul	6'	2 1/2"		Mecklenburg	Teamster
		Mann, Thos	29			Blk	5'	4"		Richmond	Striker
		Mayo, Robt	22			Lt	5'	6"		"	Carpenter
		Moss, Robt	30				5'	8"		Richmond	Fireman
		Moss, Wm	41	Blk	Blk	Lt	5'	8"		"	Blk Smith
		Moss, Herbert	34			Blk	5'	9"		Brunswick	Laborer
		Merwin, Jesse	37			Dk	5'	11"		Henrico	"
		Maiden, John								Richmond Co.	Farmer
		Morton, Jim	35	Blk	Blk	Blk	5'	10"		Essex Co.	Laborer
		Minter, Moe	24	Blue	"	Lt	5'	8"			"
		McGuigan, Saml	17							Northumberland Co.	
73											
	19	Norris, Jim	21	Dark		Yellow	5'	2"	VA	Petersburg	Barber
	20	Nichols, John	35	Blk	Blk	Dark	5'	7"	VA	"	Laborer
	123	Newsom, John	48	Dk	Dk	Dk	5'	6"	VA	Dinwiddie	"
	173	Newman, G. W.	35	Blk	Blk		6'	2"	VA	Roanoke	"
	174	Neice, Henry	36	"	"	Blk	5'	9 1/2"	VA	"	"
	237	Nash, Jacob	23	Blue	Blk	Yellow	5'	6"	VA	Washington Co.	
	309	Newton, William	45	Blk	Dk	Brown	5'	2"	VA	Richmond	Laborer
	410	Napolean		Dk	Blk	Bright	6'		LA	New Orleans	Gentleman
	573	Newman, Lewis							VA	Roanoke	Wagoner
	574	Newman, John							VA	"	"
	614	Norris, John	34	Blk	Blk	Blk	5'	6 1/2"	VA	Petersburg	Blk Smith
	1177	Norman, Tom	24	"	"	Bro	5'		VA		
	1178	Norman, James	33	"	"	Mulatto	5'	8"	VA	Caroline	Laborer
	1179	Newman, Mitten	23	"	"	Blk	5'	4 1/2"	VA		
	1180	Norris, William	29	"	"	Yellow	5'	9 3/4"	VA	Pittsylvania	Farmer
	1181	Nelson, Charles	20				5'		VA		
	1538	Nickens, George	19	Blk	Blk	Yellow	5'	10"	VA	Augusta	
		Nelson, Thomas	48	Blue	Blk	Mul	5'	8"	VA	Essex	Carpenter
		Newsom, F	21			Lt	5'	6 1/2"	VA	Henrico	Laborer
		Nelson, Carter	24	Blue	Blk	Lt	5'	5"	VA	Essex	"
		Nelson, Tom	49	"	"	"	5'	8"	VA	"	"
		Norris, Albert					5'		VA		
		Norris, Robt					5'		VA		
76	1182	Overton, Frank	45	Dk	Blk	Mu	5'	9"	VA	Augusta	Farmer
	1183	Otis, John	40	"	"	Yellow	5'	1"	VA	Pittsylvania	Boatman
	1184	Owen, Wm	23	"	Dk	Dk	5'	9"	VA	Augusta	Farm Hand
	1185	Owen, Preston	20	"	"	"	5'	5"	VA	"	"
		Osborn, George	40	"		Brown	5'	4"	VA	New Kent Co.	"
78	40	Parham, William	28	Blk	Blk	Blk	5'	10"	VA	Petersburg	Barber
	41	Pleasants, James	49	Little Red	"	"	5'	3"	VA	"	Shoemaker

Enlisted			Assigned		Remarks
When	Where	By Whom	When	Where	

When	Where	By Whom	When	Where	Remarks
19-Nov		Lt. Haw	20-Nov	Eng(ineer) Dept.	
Nov	Richmond	Lt. Blackford		R(ichmond) & D(anville) R(ail) R(oad)	Detailed to
"	"	"		"	"
"	"	"		"	"
"	"	"		"	"
"	"	"		"	"
				P H Wynne	
					Discharged by plage
				Detailed on grounds of private necessity	
				Detailed to W M Harris till 1st July	
				Appl(ication) for detail pending	
				Detailed to Navy til 1st May 1865	
				Detailed to C Bass Supt. Pent(inentiar)y to 1st May 1865	
				Detailed to O F Manson Med(ical) Dept till 1st May/65	
				Detailed to J(ames) R(iver) & K(anawha) Canal Co(mpany) till 1st May 1865	
	Powahatan	Lt. Chafin		Detailed to J(ames) R(iver) & K(anawha) Canal Co(mpany) till 1st May 1865	
	Richmond			Detailed to O S Naval Work till 1st May/65	
	Mecklbg			Detailed to Ord(nance) Shops Cl(ar)ksville till 1st May/65	
Jan 3/65		Lt. Blkford		Detailed to R. E. Blankenship	
"		"		Detailed to R. E. Blankenship	
Jan 6/65		"		Detailed E H Gill	
Jan 6/65		"		Detailed to Capt. Jas Dinwiddie	
Jan 12/65		"		Pending C(onfederate) S(tates) W(orks)	
				"	
		Lt. Dickinson		Detailed to Ann Marks 1st May 1865	
Dec 64		Lt. Bumpass		Detailed to B F Gresham till 1st June 1865	
"		"			
				till 1st April/65	
03-May	Petersburg	Lt. Heath		Eng(ineer) Dept.	
"	"	"		Do.	
"	"	R G Bosseau		Do.	
30-Apr	Roanoke	Capt. Clements	April	Engineer Corps	
"	"	"	"	Maj. McMahon Q(uarter) M(aster)	
"	Washington	W M Thompson			
07-Apr	Richmond	Capt. Coke			Deserter
29-Apr	"	"		Exempt under treaty 1803	Furloughed order Capt. C
18-Apr	Salem	Capt. Clements		Q(uarter) M(aster) T J Jenkins	
"	"	"		"	
25-Jul	Petsbg	Lt. Scott		Eng(ineer) Dept	
19-Jul	Bowl Green	Lt. Hancock	19-Jul	Gen. Ewell	Richmond Unaccounted
19-Apr		Lt. McCue			"
		Lt. Nowlin		N(iter) & M(ining) B(ureau)	
Dec		Capt. Matthews		Engineer Dept.	
				Exempt to 1st May 1865	
				Pending C.S.W.	
Dec /64		Lt. Bumpass		B. F. Gresham 1st June	
"		"		"	
				Detailed to Jos. R Anderson Co.	
				"	
15-Jul	Staunton			To M(edical) Dept	
26-Apr		Lt. McCue		"	
					Detailed till 1st Jan(uary)/65
01-Sep		Capt. Mathews			"
"		"			Detailed till May/65
03-May	Petersburg	Lt. Heath		Eng(ineer) Dept.	
"	"	"		Do.	

Page	No.	Name	Description						Where Born		Occupation
			Age	Eyes	Hair	Complex	Feet	In	State	Town or County	
	42	Penn, Algernon	32	Blue		Dark	6'		VA	"	Laborer
	43	Penn, David	42	"	"	Light	5'	8"	VA	"	"
	44	Parham, Wm	35	Blk	"	Dark	5'		VA	"	"
	45	Parham, Sam	39	"	"	"	5'	6"	VA	"	"
	46	Parham, Anthony	20	"	"	"	5'	4"	VA	"	"
	47	Parham, Thomas	37	"	"	"	5'	10"	VA	"	"
	124	Parham, Erick	32	"	"	Light	5'	8 1/2"	VA	Dinwiddie	"
	125	Pennngton, C	26	"	"	Dark	5'	3"			
	152	Paul, Robert	26				5'			Roanoke Co.	Shoemaker
	178	Powers, James	32	Dk	Blk	Yellow	5'	10"	VA	Washington Co.	
	179	Phillips, Marcellus	18	"	"	"	6'	1"	VA	"	
	180	Pool, Charles	33	Blue	Blk	"	5'	9"	VA	"	
	280	Penn, George	18	Blk	"	Lgt	5'	7"	VA	Richmond City	Barber
	321	Patterson, Dandy	49	Dk	Dk	Dk	5'	10"	VA	"	Blacksmith
	352	Pryor, Charles	22	"	Blk	"	5'	8"	VA	"	Laborer
	353	Patterson, Carter	48	Brown	"	Brown	5'	3"	VA	"	Blacksmith
	391	Peters, Samuel	20	Blk	"	Blk	5'	11"	VA	"	Laborer
	405	Patterson, Isaiah	19				5'	8"	VA	"	Finishing Shop
	406	Poindexter, D	44				5'	4"	VA	Charlottesville	Fireman
	443	Payne, Washington	40	Hazel	Blk	Blk	5'	9"	VA	Montgomery Co.	
	503	Parker, S	42		"		5'	9"	VA	Mecklenburg	Laborer
	504	Perkins, George	40				5'	8"	VA	Prince Edward	"
	567	Phillips, Governor	23	Blk	Blk	Yellow	5'	10"	VA	Patrick	
	624	Pennington, Wm	26			Blk	5'	5"	VA	Dinwiddie	Laborer
	625	Pritchett, Addison	20			Yellow	5'	7"	VA	"	"
	1186	Peters, Thomas	38	Blk	Blk	Lt	5'	6"	VA	Amherst	Farmer
	1187	Pin, Sam	34	"	"	"	5'	8"	VA	"	"
79	1188	Patterson, Dandridge	30							New Kent	Fireman
	1189	Page, Robert	18	Bro	Blk	Blk	5'	5"	VA	Spottsylvania	Barber
	1190	Pryor, Charles H.	17	Blk	"	Bro	5'	2"	VA	Caroline	Laborer
	1191	Parrit, Robert	25	"	"	Dk	5'	8"	VA		
	1192	Peters, James	22	"	"	Blk	5'	6 3/4"	VA	Harrisonburg	
	1193	Pointer, Samuel	21	Gray	Dk	M	5'	8 1/4"	VA		
	1194	Pleasants, P	29	Lt	Bk	Blk	5'	9"	VA	Richmond	Laborer
	1195	Pierce, Jno	30	Dk	Dk	Dk	6'	-	VA	Portsmouth	Cook
	1196	Peters, Thomas	24	"	"	"	6'	-	VA	Amherst	Laborer
	1197	Pearce, Sol	22	"	"	"	5'	8"	VA	Norfolk Co.	
	1198	Poindexter, J W	32	"	"	Lt	5'	9"	VA	Louisa	Blk Smith
	1199	Pearce, Jordan	25				5'		VA		
	1200	Parish, William	45	Bk	Bk	Yellow	5'	8"	VA	Petersburg	Laborer
	1201	Philips, William	39	"	"	Dk	5'	9"	VA	Augusta	Farm Hand
	1202	Pemberton, Peter	22			M	5'	8 1/2"	VA	Chesterfield	Bksmith
	1203	Puchman, M	30						VA	Richmond	
	1204	Poindexter, William	40	Bk	Bk	Bk	5'	8/12"	VA	Rockbridge	Teamster
	1476	Pittman, Dillard	32			Dk	5'	5 3/4"			En Cleaner
	1477	Pleasants, Sol	36			"	4'	10 1/4"			Laborer
	1478	Powell, Jos	43			Lt	5'	5 1/4"			"
	1479	Pittman, Gus	23			Dk	5'	7"			"
	1480	Pittman, Richard	23			Dk	5'	8 3/4"			Fireman
	1527	Pearman, Thos	38	Blk	Blk	"	5'	11"			
		Pleasants, Robt	36	Dk	Dk	Lt	5'	11"	VA	Henrico	
		Pearman, Joe	28	Blk	Blk	Yellow	5'	10"	VA	Do.	
		Patterson, Alexd	18	"	"	Lt	5'	8"		Richmond	Body Servant
		Pin, George								"	Laborer
		Pleasants, H								"	

Enlisted			Assigned		Remarks
When	Where	By Whom	When	Where	
"	"	"		Do.	
"	"	"		Do.	
"	"	"		Do.	
"	"	"		Do.	
"	"	"		Eng(ineer) Dept.	
"	"	"		Do.	
"		R G Bosseau		Do.	
				Do.	
01-May	Roanoke Co.	Capt. Clements	April	Maj. Green Q(uarter) M(aster)	
30-Apr	Washington Co.	W M Thompson	15-Jun	Q(uarter) M(aster) Dept.	
"	"	"	"	Do.	
"	"	"	"		Unassigned
06-Apr	Richmond	Capt. Coke	16-Apr	N(iter) & M(ining) Bureau	
12-Apr	"	"		Naval Ord(nance) Dept	
19-Apr	"	"		N(iter) & M(ining) B(ureau)	Deserter
19-Apr	"	"		Naval Ord(nance) Dept	
28-Apr	"	"			Deserter
29-Apr	"	"		Va Central R(ail) Road	
29-Apr	"	"		Do.	
					Detailed till Nov(ember)/64
31-May	Montgomery Co.	Lt. Sydenstriker			
01-Jul	Mecklenburg	W. Atkins	01-Jul	Ord(nance) Dept. Clarksville	
"	P Edward	Zimmerman	"	Eng(ineer) " High Bridge	
	New Bern	Lt. Poole		Q(uarter) M(aster) I H Lacy	
July				Eng(ineer) Dept.	
"				Do.	
04-Jul	Amherst	Lt. Roane	06-Jul	Maj. Richards	
08-Jul	"	"	11-Jul	Gen. Ransom	
Oct		T Taylor	Oct	N(iter) & M(ining) B(ureau)	
03-Apr	Fredericksburg	Lt. Williams		N(iter) & M(ining) B(ureau)	
18-Jul	Bowl Green	Lt. Hancock	19-Jul	Gen Ewell	Richmond Unaccounted 1st July 1865
				To M(edical) Dept.	Detailed 1st January 65 Unaccounted
04-Aug		Capt. Coke		N(iter) & M(ining) B(ureau)	
18-Aug		"			Deserter
07-Sep		"		N(iter) & M(ining) B(ureau)	
08-Sep		"		"	Unaccounted
26-Sep	Petersburg	Sgt. Winfree	26-Sep	To M(edical) Dept.	
Oct				Eng(ineer) Dept	Det(ailed) 1st Oct(ober) 64
20-Apr				N(iter) & M(ining) B(ureau)	
11-Sep				To M(edical) Dept.	
Nov	Richmond	Lt. Blackford		R(ichmond) & D(anville) R(ail) R(oad)	Detailed to
"	"	"		"	"
"	"	"		"	"
"	"	"		"	"
"	"	"		"	"
					Detailed to Mrs S. E. Pearman 1st May
					Detailed to 1st May Navy Dept.
					"
					Detailed to James K. Caskie to 1st May/65
					Detailed allowed till 1st May/65
					Detailed to J(ames) R(iver) & K(anawha) Canal Co(mpany)

Page	No.	Name	Description						Where Born		Occupation
			Age	Eyes	Hair	Complex	Feet	In	State	Town or County	
		Pearman, Thomas	45	Dk	Dk	Mult				New Kent	Blk Smith
80		Pritter, Sandy	29	Dk	Dk	Light	6'	-		Richmond	
		Parsons, Henry	48	Yellow	Blk	"	5'	11"		Buckingham	
		Pinn, James	20							Richmond	
		Pearman, Jones								New Kent	
84	1205	Quarles, Thompson	34	Gr	Blk	Copper	5'	7 1/2"	VA	Orange	Laborer
87	64	Robertson, William	40	Blk	Blk	Blk	5'	10"	VA	Petersburg	Laborer
	65	Ruff, Junius	21	Gray	"	Light	5'	6"	VA	"	"
	66	Randolph, George	34	Brown	Blk	Dark	5'	8"	VA	"	"
	67	Read, John	45	Blue	Blk	"	5'	8"	VA	"	
	77	Ruff, James	24	Blue	"	Brown	5'	6"	VA	"	Cooper
	78	Ricks, Jordan	39	"	"	Light	5'	8"	VA	"	Laborer
	131	Richardson, C	23	Dk	Dk	Dk	5'	3"	VA	Dinwiddie	"
	153	Raynolds, Pheling	19						VA	Roanoke Co.	Shoe Maker
	154	Rayford, Henry	26						VA	"	Wagoner
	297	Roberts, William	35	Blk	Dk	Lgt	5'	1"	VA	Richmond	Laborer
	298	Roots, John	28	"	Lt	"	5'	6"	VA	"	Carpenter
	337	Roberts, James	36	Dk	Blk	"	5'	5"	VA	"	Body Maker
	338	Robinson, B	35	Gray	"	"	5'	4"	VA	Henrico	Blk Smith
	359	Randolph, J H	22	Dk	Blk	Dk	5'	7"	VA	Richmond	Cooper
	383	Redcross, John	18	"	"	"	5'	5"	VA	"	Plasterer
	391	Roane, William	44	Gray	"	Lt	5'	5"	VA	"	Laborer
	408	Roy, John	22	Dk	"	Blk	5'	2"	VA	"	Wood House Hand
	420	Richards, James							VA	Essex	Shoe Maker
	444	Ruffin, Ezekeal	18	Dk	Blk	Dk	5'	7 1/2"	VA	Richmond	Laborer
	445	Rodgers, James	26	Gray	"	Lgt	5'	8"	VA	"	"
		Entered	18	Dk	"	Dk	5'	5"	VA	"	Plasterer
	449	Rodgerson, James	26	Gray	"	Lgt	5'	8"	VA	"	Laborer
	490	Rolfe, Young	36		"		5'	8"	VA	Appomatox	"
	491	Ransom, James	21		"		5'	7"	VA	Mecklenburg	"
	532	Rodgers, James	25	Blk	Blk	Blk	5'	10"	VA	Botetourt	"
	583	Roberts, Thomas	27	"	"	"	5'	8"		Petersburg	Blk Smith/Factory Hand
	584	Richardson, Geo	21	"	"	"	5'	8"			
	650	Reed, John	45			Brown	5'	9"		Dinwiddie	
	651	Russell, Dick	30			M	5'	10"		Cumberland	
88	1206	Ray, James	29	Bk	Bk	Yellow	5'	7"	VA	Dinwiddie	Farmer
	1207	Rawls, John	40	"	"	Dk	6'	-	VA	Orange	Laborer
	1208	Rawls, Harry	20	Dk	"	"	5'	11"	VA	"	"
	1209	Raves, James	23	Blk	Blk	Mulatto	5'	6"	VA	Caroline	"
	1210	Rich, Stafford	27	"	"	"	5'	8"	VA	"	"
	1211	Rich, Andrew	25	"	"	"	5'	10 1/2"	VA	"	"
	1212	Rawls, Henry	22	"	"	Blk	5'	10"	VA	Madison	"
	1213	Rolls, John	34	"	"	Mult	5'	10"	VA	"	"
	1214	Rawls, Andrew	18	"	"	Brit	5'	9"	VA	"	"
	1215	Rencher, William	43	"	"	"	5'	8"	VA	Washington	Barber
	1216	Robinson, Jack	43	"	"	Blk	5'	4"	VA	"	
	1217	Rogers, Sam	40	"	"	"	6'		VA	Botetourt	
	1218	Runningham, John	24	"	"	"	6'		VA	Fluvanna	
	1219	Reed, L	30	"	"	"	5'	9"	VA	Bath	
	1220	Rusk, D	45	"	"	"	6'	2"	VA	"	
	1221	Richardson, Jno	30	Hz	"	"	5'	8"	VA		
	1222	Robinson, Elias	45	Blk	"	"	5'	10 1/2"	VA		
	1223	Rawls, Jas A	25	"	"	"	5'	8 1/2"	VA		
	1224	Ralls, John	23	Gray	"	Yellow	5'	5 1/2"	VA		
	1225	Ross, William	35	Dk	Dk	Dk	5'	4"	VA	Pittsylvania	Coffin Maker

Enlisted			Assigned		Remarks
When	Where	By Whom	When	Where	
					Detailed to 1st May 1865
					Steamer J H Parker to 1st May/65
					James R(iver) & K(anawha) Canal Co(mpany) C. Q. Morris
					Do. Do.
					Maj. Harvie
					Private & P(ublic) Necessity to 1st May/65
25-Jun	Orange	Lt. Lewis	25-Jun	Gordonsville	Maj. Richards
03-May	Petersburg	Lt. Heath		Eng(ineer) Dept.	
"	"	"		Do.	
"	"	"		Do.	
"	"	"		Do.	
"	"	"		Do.	
"	Dinwiddie	R G Bosseau		Do.	
01-May	Roanoke Co.	Capt. Clements	April	Maj. Green Q(uarter) M(aster)	
01-May	"	"	"	T J Jenkins Q(uarter) M(aster)	
07-Apr	Richmond	Capt. Coke	18-Apr	N(iter) & M(ining) Bureau	
07-Apr	"	"	06-Apr	Navy Dept.	
14-Apr	"	"	"	Navy Dept. til 1st May 1865	
14-Apr	"	"	"	Eng(ineer) Dept.	
20-Apr	"	"	"	Detailed to Haxall & Crenshaw	
27-Apr	"	"	"	Nitre & M(ining) Bureau	Deserter
28-Apr	"	"	05-May	Capt. W W Baker	Not accounted for
29-Apr	"	"		VA Central R(ail) Road to 1st May 1865	
27-Apr				Sp(ecia)l applic(ation) to M. T. Hunter by Col. Shields	
06-May	Richmond	Capt. Coke	06-May	N(iter) & M(ining) Bureau	
05-May	"	"	05-May	"	
27-Apr	"	"		Entered Once	
05-May	"	"	"	N(iter) & M(ining) Bureau	
06-Jun	Appomatox	Lt. Fantross	08-Jun	Eng(ineer) Dept. Richmond	
01-Jul	Mecklenburg	W. Atkins	01-Jul	Ord(nance) Dept. Clarksville	
		E B Poole		Q(uarter) M(aster) Dept. I H Lacy	
02-Aug	Petersburg			" Road til Nov/64	
25-Jul	"			Eng(ineer) Dept.	
13-Jul	Dinwiddie			Do.	
13-Jun	Cumberland			Do.	
09-Aug	Dinwiddie	R G Bosseau	09-Aug	Eng(ineer) Dept.	
25-Jun	Orange	Lt. Lewis	25-Jun	Gordonsville	Maj. Richards
"	"	"	"	"	"
19-Jul	Bowl Green	Lt. Hancock	20-Jul	Gen. Ewell	Richmond
"	"	"	"	"	"
"	"	"	"	"	"
01-Jul	CHo	Lt. Adams	10-Jul	To M(edical) Dept. Gordonsville	
"	"	"	"	"	
"	"	"	"	"	
15-Jun	Abingdon	W M Thompson			Unaccounted
	Covington			N(iter) & M(ining) B(ureau)	
	"			"	
	"			"	
	"			"	
				Eng(ineer) Dept.	
					Detailed til 1st Jan/65
				Detailed to W Cook Private Nec(essity)	
19-Apr					

Page	No.	Name	Description						Where Born		Occupation
			Age	Eyes	Hair	Complex	Feet	In	State	Town or County	
	1226	Richardson, Wm	46	"	"	"	5'	8"	VA	"	Boatman
	1227	Reynolds, C	29	"	"	Yellow	5'	11"	VA	"	Farmer
	1228	Reynolds, Jno	25	Lt	Dk	Brt	5'	9"	VA	"	Laborer
	1229	Randolph, Wm	27	Blk	"	Lt	5'	5"	VA	Richmond	Shoe Maker
	1230	Roberts, John	24	"	"	Dk	5'	7"	VA	"	
	1231	Roberts, I	30	"	"	"	5'	3"	VA	"	
	1232	Redwood, Moses	30	"	"	"	5'	1"	VA	"	Laborer
	1233	Robertson, John	20	"	"	"	5'	8"	VA	"	"
	1234	Reed, Baker	40	Gr	"	Lt	5'	7"	VA	Dinwiddie	Farmer
89	1235	Rogers, Arthur	41								
	1236	Reynolds, Creed	49								
	1237	Rogers, Simmons	49								
	1238	Rogers, M I	38								
	1239	Rogers, Jerry	35								
	1240	Rix, Henry	45	Blk	Blk	Blk	5'	6"		Petersburg	Bricklayer
	1241	Rix, Jordan	39	"	"	Yellow	5'	8"		"	Laborer
	1242	Robertson, William	43	"	"	Blk	5'	11"		"	"
	1243	Rix, John	20	"	"	Yellow	5'	4"		"	"
	1244	Roach, N	33	"	"	"	5'	6"		Henry	Farmer
	1245	Rumley, Jas H	18	"	"	Blk	5'	10"		"	Laborer
	1246	Richardson, George	38	"	"	"	5'	11"		Chesterfield	"
	1247	Ross, James	30	"	"	"	5'	8"		Rockbridge	Blk Smith
	1248	Ross, Charles	28	"	"	"	5'	10"		"	"
	1249	Randolph, Saml V	25	Gray	Drk	Lt	6'	1"			Shoe Maker
	1481	Rainey, John	31			Dk	5'	4 1/2"			Fireman
	1482	Randall, Wilson	55			Lt	5'	4 1/2"			Laborer
	1483	Rendison, Alpheus	25			Dk	5'	5"			"
	1484	Rogers, Robert	30								
	1485	Richardson, Jacob				"	5'	4"			"
		Roberts, Charles	35	Dk	Dk	Yellow	5'	4 1/2"		York	
		Robertson, J								Richmond	
		Roberts, Ewd	27	Blk	Blk	Mul	5'	9"		Mecklenburg	
		Redcross, Paul E.	30	Brown	"	Brown	6'			Amherst	Wood Worker
		Robertson, Archer	28	Dk	Bright	Bright	6'	-		King & Queen	Farmer
		Rich, Henry								Richmond Co.	"
		Reames, Ned									"
		Rich, Thos	23			Dk	5'	6"		Richmond Co.	
		Richardson, A	25			"	5'	6"		Westemoreland	Farmer
		Richards, A	18			Lt	5'	9"		"	"
90		Rich, Jas	22			Lt	5'	8"	VA	Westmoreland Co.	Farmer
93		Banks, Henry									Messenger
		Brooks, Thos	28			Lt	5'	9"			Farmer
		Braxton, John	42			Blk	5'	7"			Laborer
		Brown, Henderson	43			Dk	5'	8"			"
		Bird, Ambrose	27			Lt	5'	10"			"
		Brooks, Moses	30								
		Bowser, Jim	31	Dk	Dk	Blk	5'	6"		York	
		Bradley, H								Richmond	
		Beasley, I								"	
		Banks, I								"	
		Bailey, Parke	36	Dk	Dk	Dk	5'	8"		New Kent Co.	Farmer
		Blake, Thomas	22	Lt	Dk	Lt	5'	10"		Bedford	Tobacconist
		Brown, Joe	19			"	5'	10"		Richmond	Baker
		Bassett, Johnson	35			Blk	5'	11"		"	Shearer
		Banks, John	17			"	5'	8"		"	Brakesman
		Butler, James	22	Blk	Blk	Lt	5'	8"		"	Blk Smith
		Beverly, Jas	34							"	Boatman
		Bracking, C	36			Lt	5'	8 1/2"		"	Laborer
		Belt, Frank	18	Dk	Dk	Mul	5'	7"		Augusta Co.	"

Enlisted			Assigned		Remarks
When	Where	By Whom	When	Where	
30-Apr		Lt. McCue			Unaccounted
23-Jun		"			"
16-Jun		Capt. Coke			Deserter
01-Jul		"		N(iter) & M(ining) B(ureau)	
07-Sep		"			Unaccounted
"		"		to Ambulance Committee til 1st July/65	
12-Sep		"		N(iter) & M(ining) B(ureau)	
14-Sep		"		"	
04-May		R G Bosseau			Unaccounted
		Lt. Nowlin		N(iter) & M(ining) B(ureau)	
		"		To M(edical) Dept.	
		"			Unaccounted
					"
					Detailed 1st Jan(uary) 65
21-Sep	Petersburg	Sgt. Winfree	21-Sep	To M(edical) Dept.	
23-Sep	"	"	23-Sep	"	
"	"	"	"	30 days furlough by Med(ical) Ex(amining) B(oar)d	
28-Sep	"	"	28-Sep	Q(uarter) M(aster) Dept	
05-May	Henry CHo	Lt. Hawthorne	05-Jul	Eng "	
"	"	"	"		
"		Lt. Spencer		Eng(ineer) Dept.	
				Detailed to 1st July/65	Unaccounted
					"
				To M(edical) Dept.	
Nov	Richmond	Lt. Blackford		R(ichmond) & D(anville) R(ail) R(oad)	Detailed to
"	"	"		"	"
"	"	"		"	"
					Exempt by Med(ical) B(oar)d
"	"	"		"	
				Navy till 1st May 1865	
				Detailed to J(ames) R(iver) & K(anawha) C(ompany) till 1st May 1865	
				Detailed to Ord(nance) Shops Clarksville till 1st May 1865	
				"	P(ublic) Necessity
				Detailed to 1st Jul/65	Dr. Bland
		Lt. Jenkins		Detailed to 1st May/65	Maj. Harvie
				Detailed to 1st May/65 Jos. R Anderson Co.	
		Lt. Jenkins		En(gineer) Dept.	
		"		"	
		"		"	
Jan/65	Westmoreland	Lt. J. P.Jenkins		En(gineer) Dept.	
Nov	Richmond	Lt. Blackford		R H Wynne	Detailed to
"	"	"		N(iter) & M(ining) B(ureau)	
"	"	"		"	
"	"	"		"	
"	"	"		"	
"	"	"			Exempt Med(ical) Board
				Navy	to 1st May 1865
				Detailed to J(ames) R(iver) & K(anawha) Canal Co(mpany) til 1st May 1865	
				"	
				"	
				Detailed to M Sherman 1st May 1865	
Jan 1/65				N(iter) & M(ining) B(ureau)	
Jan 3/65				Detailed to R C Blankenship	
Jan 3/65				"	
Jan 5/65				Detailed to E H Gill	
Jan 5/65				Detailed to Capt. Dinwiddie	
Jan 6/65				Detailed to J B Harvie	
Jan 12/65				Privacy C.S.W.	
Jan 6/65		Lt. Matthews		Genl Stevens Eng(ineer) Dept.	

Page	No.	Name	Description						Where Born		Occupation
			Age	Eyes	Hair	Complex	Feet	In	State	Town or County	
		Bluford, James	24	Blk	Dk	Mul	5'	8"		King & Queen Co.	"
		Ball, Peter								Westmoreland	Farmer
		Bluford, James	47	Blk	Dk	Dk	5'	10"		King & Queen Co.	"
		Burwell, Thos	45							"	"
		Burwell, Levy	30							Richmond Co.	"
		Brockenbrough, Moore	31	Blue	Blk	Dk	5'	6"		Essex Co.	Laborer
		Bush, John	21	Blk	Dk	Br	5'	10"		"	"
		Bush, Wm	24	Blk	"	"	5'	6"		"	"
		Bundy, Carter	20	Dk	Dk	Lt	5'	8"		"	"
		Bundy, Jim	24	"	"	"	5'	6"		"	"
		Bin, Jim	28	Dk	Dk	Bro	6'	1"		"	
94		Ball, Geo	28			Blk	5'	10"		Richmond Co.	Farmer
		Ball, Jno	22			Lt	5'	10"		"	"
		Barton, Anderson	25			Blk	5'	10"		"	"
		Ball, Armistead	27			"	5'	11"		Westmoreland Co.	"
96	24	Smith, Robert	20	Blk	Blk	Blk	4'	8"	VA	Petersburg	Driver
	25	Scott, Benjamin	19	"	"	Yellow	5'	9"	VA	"	Barber
	26	Stevens, Williams	21	"	"	Blk	5'	11"	VA	"	Shoe Maker
	27	Steves, Christopher	49	"	"	"	5'	9"	VA	"	Carpenter
	28	Scott, John	30	"	"	"	5'	3"	VA	"	Laborer
	29	Smith, David	43	"	"	"	5'	8"	VA	"	"
	30	Smith, William	36	"		Light	5'	7"	VA	"	
	31	Smith, Thomas	21	"	"		5'	7"	VA	"	Cook
	32	Stewart, James	21	"	Bushy	Ginger	5'	7"	VA	"	Laborer
	33	Stewart, Robert	23	"	Blk	Blk	5'	7"	VA	"	
	137	Smith, James	18	"	"	"	5'	5"	VA	Dinwiddie	"
	138	Stewart, Finton	35	"	"	Light	5'	10 1/2"	VA	"	Bricklayer
	139	Smith, Tom	35		"	Dk	5'	5"	VA	"	Laborer
	164	Scott, Anthony	43						VA	Roanoke	Cooper
	165	Sears, Wm. R.	20	Blk	Blk	Brown	5'	7"	VA	"	Laborer
	166	Sears, Andrew J.	18	Hazel	"	Dk	5'	7"	VA	"	"
	220	Singleton, Robert	27	Blk	Blk	Yellow	5'	8"	VA	Wythe	
	221	Smith, James	23	Blue	"	Brown	5'	9"	VA	Washington Co.	
	222	Smith, James	35	"	"	Yellow	5'	9"	VA	"	
	263	Smith, Edwin	45			Blk	5'	3"	VA	Greensville Co.	
	277	Smith, Charles	20	Blk	Blk	Lgt	5'	9"	VA	Prince Edward Co.	Blk Smith
	278	Scott, Daniel	21	"	"	Dk	5'	3 1/2"	VA	Richmond	"
	279	Smith, Beverly	20	"	"	"	5'	1 1/2"	VA	"	"
	286	Scott, John E.	37	"	"	"	5'	8"	VA	"	"
	287	Smith, George	40	"	"	"	5'	5"	VA	"	Shoe Maker
	288	Scott, Theodore	29	"	Dk	Lgt	5'	7 1/2"	VA	"	"
	299	Sykes, Henry	40	"	"	Dk	5'	4"	VA	"	Laborer
	310	Scott, Jas	41	"	"	Brown	5'	4 1/2"	VA	"	Barber
	311	Smith, Williams	40	"	"	"	5'	9"	VA	"	Carpenter
97	312	Scott, William	45	Dk	Dk	Dk	5'	6"	VA	Richmond	Laborer
	313	Scott, William	40	"	"	"	5'	2"	VA	"	Shoe Maker
	332	Spencer, Jeff	45	"	"	Lt	5'	5"	VA	Petersburg	Fireman
	333	Smith,Thomas	19	"	"	"	5'	11"	VA	Richmond	Body Maker
	348	Smith, Fredrick	34	Dk	Blk	Dk	6'	-	VA	"	Laborer
	349	Stewart, Peter	35	Grey	"	Lt	5'	6"	VA	"	Hackman
	358	Stevens, James	36	Dk	"	Dk	5'	6"	VA	"	Black Smith
	359	Smith, James	24	"	"	Lt	6'		VA	"	"
	393	Scott, Jos	35	Dk	Blk	Brown	5'	5 1/2"	VA	"	Laborer
	399	Scott, Robert	30	"	"	"	5'	6 1/2"	VA	Hanover Co.	Train Hand
	400	Scott, Thomas	34	Grey	"	Lt	5'	6 1/2"	VA	"	Emp R R
	425	Smith, Henderson	35			Blk	5'	6"	VA	Sussex Co.	
	437	Saunders, Noah	35	Brown	Blk	Lt	5'	10"	VA	Montgomery Co.	
	438	Saunders, John	49	Blk	"	Copper	5'	6"	VA	"	
	451	Stuart, Peter	19	Dk	"	Lgt	5'	1"	VA	Richmond	Laborer
	448	Stuart, Isaiah	23	"	"	"	5'	7"	VA	"	"
	459	Stuart, James	26						VA	Floyd Co.	
	467	Spencer, Abraham	30	Blk	Blk	Blk	5'	4 1/2"	VA	Rockingham	Laborer

Enlisted			Assigned		Remarks
When	Where	By Whom	When	Where	
Dec 3/65		Lt. Dickerson		John Y Bunton to 1st May 1865	
		J P Jenkins		Detailed to J. M. Harris 1st May 1865	
		Lt. Dickerson		Detailed to Dr. Bland 1st July 1865	
		J P Jenkins		Detailed to Mrs. Crabb 1 May/65	
		"		Detailed to Mrs. Smith 1 May/65	
Dec/64		Lt. Bumpass		Detailed to Major Robertson 1st May/65	
Dec/64		"		Detailed B. F. Gresham till 1st June	
"		"		"	
"		"		"	
"		"		"	
"		"		"	
Jan/65	Richmond Co.	Lt. J P Jenkins		En(gineer) Dept.	
"	"	"		"	
"	"	"		"	
"	"	"		"	
03-May	Petersburg	Lt. Heath		Eng(ineer) Dept.	
"	"	"		Do.	
"	"	"		Do.	
"	"	"		Do.	
"	"	"		Do.	
"	"	"		Do.	
"	"	"		Do.	
"	"	"		Do.	
"	"	"		Do.	
"	"	"		Do.	
"	Dinwiddie	R G Bosseau		Do.	
"	"	"		Do.	
"	"	"		Do.	
01-May	Roanoke	Capt. Clements		Extended till 1st July detailed to 1st Jan(uar)y/65 as cooper maker	
"	"	"	April	Capt. Morton N(iter) & M(ining) B(ureau)	
"	"	"	"	Do.	
30-Apr	Washington	W M Thompson	15-Jun	Q(uarter) M(aster) Dept.	
"	Washington Co.	W M Thompson			Unassigned
"	"	"			Do.
"	Greensville Co.	D J Godwin			
06-Apr	Prince Edward Co.	Capt. Coke	16-Apr	Col. Carter C	
06-Apr	Richmond	"	16-Apr	N(iter) & M(ining) Bureau	
06-Apr	"	"			Deserter
06-Apr	"	"	16-Apr	N(iter) & M(ining) Bureau	
06-Apr	"	"	15-Apr	Do.	
06-Apr	"	"	April "	Do.	
07-Apr	"	"	07-Apr	Navy Dept.	
07-Apr	"	"		Major Peyton	Also Major Peyton
07-Apr	"	"			Deserter
09-Apr	Richmond	Capt. Coke	22-Apr	N(iter) & M(ining) Bureau	
"	"	"		Detailed Navy May 1st 1865	Deserter
13-Apr	"	"		Detailed to E H Gill	Not accounted for
14-Apr	"	"		Navy Dept.	
18-Apr	"	"			Deserter
19-Apr	"	"		WW Crump, Asst. Secty. Treasy (Assistant Secretary of the Treasury)	
20-Apr	"	"		Detailed A F Harvie	
20-Apr	"	"			Not accounted for
28-Apr	"	"	09-May	N(iter) & M(ining) Bureau	
29-Apr	"	"		VA Central R(ail) Road til 1st May/65	
05-May				"	
05-May	Sussex Co.	D J Godwin			
06-May	Montgomery Co.	Lt. Sydenstriker			Employ Capt. Shields
31-May	"	"		N(iter) & M(ining) Bureau	
05-May	Richmond	Capt. Coke	05-May	N(iter) & M(ining) Bureau	
"	"	"	05-May	N(iter) & M(ining) Bureau	
June	Floyd Co.	Lt. Farrar			
May & June	Rockingham	Col. Peyton			

Page	No.	Name	Age	Eyes	Hair	Complex	Feet	In	State	Town or County	Occupation
	468	Strother, Archer	25	"	"	"	5'	1 1/2"	VA	"	Blasting Hand
	469	Spangler, Jacob	27	"	"	"	5'	9"	VA	"	Cook
	470	Solomon, John	25	"	"	"	5'	9"	VA	"	Laborer
	471	Spencer, Wm	22	"	"	"	5'	5 1/2"	VA	"	"
	472	Spencer, George	25	Grey	"	Yellow	5'	7 3/4"	VA	"	"
	473	Spangler, John	39	Dk	Dk	Dk	5'	7 1/2"	VA	"	Blk Smith
	474	Strother, Wm	22	Blk	Blk	"	5'	3"	VA	"	Laborer
	475	Smith, James	30	"	"	Yellow	5'	6"	VA	"	"
	516	Stewart, John	33		"		5'	6"	VA	Mecklenburg	Blk Smith
	517	Salley, R	28		"		5'	9"	VA	Do.	"
	518	Salyard, R	48		"		6'	1"	VA	"	Laborer
	519	Sutherlin, John	30				5'	11"	VA	Halifax	Tanner
98	528	Smith, James	46		Dk		5'	10"	VA	Micklenburg	Farmer
	533	Steward, Henry	23	Blk	Blk	Blk	5'	5"	VA	Henry	
	534	Spencer, Frank	29				5'	9"	VA	"	
	535	Stewart, Granville	21				5'	4"	VA	Patrick	
	536	Shevely, Moses								Roanoke	Wagoner
	537	Shepard, William	44	Hzel	Blk	Copper	5'	4"	VA	Botetourt	Chopper
	585	Slaughter, Robert	30	Blk	Strt	Yellow	5'	8"	VA	Petersburg	Barber
	586	Scott, William	38	Brwn	Blk	Blk	5'	10"	VA	"	Carpenter
	587	Scott, Benjamin	19	Blue	Blk	Lght	5'	8"	VA	"	Laborer
	588	Scott, William	18	Blk	Blk	Brown	5'	9"	VA	"	"
	589	Smith, Benjamin	44	Blk	Blk	Blk	5'	7"	VA	"	"
	1250	Smith, Sam	22	Blk	Blk	Dk	5'	-	VA	Dinwiddie	Farmer
	1251	Shelton, E	17	Blk	Blk	Cho	5'	5"	VA	Albermarle	"
	1252	Sullivan, J	16	Blk	Blk	Lt	5'	6"	VA	"	Blk Smith
	1253	Shears, William	23	Blk	Blk	Lt	5'	8"	VA	"	Laborer
	1254	Sprouse, A	30	Blk	Blk	Dk	6'	-	VA	"	"
	1255	Scott, Thomas	27	Blk	Blk	Lt	5'	8"	VA	"	Shoe Maker
	1256	Stauntton, JT	32	Blk	Blk	Mu	5'	9"	VA	Buckingham	Farmer
	1257	Stauntton, John	26	Blk	Blk	Mu	5'	10"	VA	"	"
	1258	Simpson, Peter	33	Blk	Blk	Blk	6'	1 1/2"	VA	Culpeper	Laborer
	1259	Satterwhite, James	18	Blk	Lt	Mul	5'	10"	VA	Caroline	"
	1260	Smith, William	17	Blk	Blk	Mul	5'	9"	VA	"	"
	1261	Scrannage, Robert	38	Blk	Blk	Bro	6'	-	VA	"	"
	1262	Stuart, Trigg	38	Blk	Blk	Blk	5'	7"	VA	Wythe	Farmer
	1263	Stewart, George	46	Blk	Blk	Blk	5'	6"	VA	Grayson	"
	1264	Smith, Leander	23	Grn	Blk	Yellow	5'	8"	VA	Russell	Laborer
	1265	Strother, William	20	Brn	Blk	Cop	5'	9"	VA		
	1266	Scott, Norman	29	Brn	Blk	Blk	5'	8"	VA	Albermarle	
	1267	Strother, James	27								Laborer
99	1268	Shorter, Aaron	35	Blk	Blk	Blk	6'	2"	VA	Augusta	Shoe Maker
	1269	Strother, James	27	"	"	"	5'	6"	VA	"	Farmer
	1270	Strother, Samual	36	Dk	Dk	M	5'	7"	VA	"	"
	1271	Smith, Edwin	24	"	"	Blk	5'	11"	VA	Greensville	Laborer
	1272	Scott, S J	38	"	"	Yellow	5'	3"	VA	Pittsylvania	Coffin Maker
	1273	Sawyers, J T	49	"	"	Brown	5'	6 1/2"	VA	"	Boatman
	1274	Squire, Henry	30	"	"	Blk	5'	5"	VA	"	Blk Smith
	1275	Scott, Pickett	32	"	"	Yellow	5'	6"	VA	"	Barber
	1276	Starr, David	18	"	"	Blk	5'	6"	VA	"	Farm Hand
	1277	Selden, William	38	"	"	Dk	5'	11"	VA	"	"
	1278	Stephens. George	34	"	"	Blk	5'	8"	VA	"	"
	1278	Shafer, Thos	20	"	"	Brown	5'	6"	VA	"	Boatman
	1279	Stephens, Scott	44	"	"	Blk	5'	11"	VA	"	"
	1280	Stephens, Jordan	30	"	"	"	6'	-	VA	"	Striker
	1281	Smith, Barry	47	"	"	"	5'	9 1/2"	VA	"	Carpenter
	1282	Starr, James	26	"	"	"	5'	9"	VA	"	Farm Hand
	1283	Smith, Ben	34	Dk	Bl	Dk	6'	-	VA	Richmond	Laborer
	1284	Smith, William	45	"	"	"	5'	7"	VA	"	"
	1285	Scott, E	29	Blk	"	Lt	5'	11"	VA	Henrico	Fisherman

Enlisted			Assigned		Remarks
When	Where	By Whom	When	Where	
"	"	"		Q(uarter) M(aster) Dept.	Capt. Bell
"	"	"		"	"
"	"	"			Detailed til 1st Jan/65
"	"	"			"
"	"	"			"
"	"	"			
"	"	"			Detailed til 1st
"	"	"			Jan(uary)/65
"	Mecklenburg	W. Atkins	July	Ord(nance) Dept. Clarksville til 1st May/65	
"	"	"	"	"	
"	Halifax	Lt. Edwards			
01-Aug	Micklenburg	W. T. Atkins			Detailed 1st January/'65
	Newbern	E.B. Poole		I. H. Lacey Q(uarter) M(aster) Dept.	
	Newbern	"		Do.	
	Newbern	"		Do.	
	Salem	Capt. Clements		Capt. Morton Do.	
	Fincastle	Lt. Nowlin	26-Aug	J. R. Anderson and Co.	N(iter) & M(ining)
		Lt. Scott		Eng(ineer) Dept.	
		Lt. Scott		M(edical) Dept. to Nov(ember)/64	
		Lt. Scott		Eng(ineer) Dept.	
		Lt. Scott		Do.	
		Lt. Scott		Do.	
04-May	Dinwiddie	R G Bosseau	21-Jun	Do.	
25-Jun		Capt. Colston	25-Jun	Capt. Richards	
27-Jun		"	28-Jun	"	
"		"	28-Jun	"	
28-Jun		"	29-Jun	"	
"		"	29-Jun	"	
10-Jun		A. T. Moseley	13-Jun	Col. Scott	High Bridge
"		"	13-Jun	"	High Bridge
22-Aug	Culpeper	Lt. Graves			
19-Jul	BGreen*	Lt. Hancock	19-Jul	Gen Ewell	Richmond
"	BGreen*	"	19-Jul	"	Richmond
"	BGreen*	"	19-Jul	"	Richmond
26-Aug	Abingdon	W. M. Thompson	25-Aug	To M(edical) Dept.	Capt. T. H. Gibbony
02-Jun		Lt. Hammer		Term Ex(empt) by Med(ical) Ex(amining) Board	
"		Lt. Sawyer			Unaccounted
				T. M(edical) Dept.	Capt. Bell
				N(iter) & M(ining) B(ureau)*	
				T. M(edical) Dept.	Capt. Bell
19-Jul					Unaccounted
24-Aug				To M(edical) Dept.	
"				"	
					Unaccounted
					Exempt by Med(ical)
19-Apr		Lt. McCue			Ex(amining) B(oar)d
"		"			Unaccounted
"		"			"
"		"			"
23-Apr		"			"
"		"			Detailed 1 Jan(uary)/65
"		"			Unaccounted
28-Apr		"		To M(edical) Dept.	
"		"		"	
06-Jun		Lt. Williams		Danville Arsenal	
06-Jul		"		Eng(ineer) Dept.	
06-Oct		"		"	
18-Apr		Lt. Coke			Unaccounted
18-May		"		Navy Dept. 1 May 1865	
06-Jun		"		"	

Page	No.	Name	Description						Where Born		Occupation
			Age	Eyes	Hair	Complex	Feet	In	State	Town or County	
	1286	Smith, William	44	Bro	"	Dk	5'	7 1/2"	VA	Richmond	Laborer
	1287	Smith, Ed	35	Lg	"	"	5'	11"	VA	"	"
	1288	Stephens, Jas	36	Dk	"	Blk	5'	6"	VA	"	Bk Smith
	1289	Scott, Jno	24	Blk	"	Lt	5'	5"	VA	"	Barber
	1290	Smith, Robert	39	"	"	Blk	5'	7"	VA	"	Shoemaker
	1291	Scott, Ben	25	"	Dk	Dk	5'	8"	VA	"	Laborer
	1292	Staples, A	50	"	"	"	5'	7"	VA	"	"
	1293	Sutherland, Sam	21	"	"	Lt	6'	-	VA	"	Barber
	1294	Spurlock, Jno	26	"	Blk	"	5'	8"	VA	Hanover	Farmer
	1295	Scott, Taz	27								
100	1296	Simms, William	22								
	1297	Sorrell, Ed	30								
	1298	Small, William	20	Blk	Blk	Blk	5'	-		Petersburg	Laborer
	1299	Sibourne, "	35	"	"	Yellow	5'	5"		"	"
	1300	Smith, James	25	"	"	Blk	5'	6 1/2"		"	Butcher
	1301	Stephens, John	23	"	"	"	5'	5"		"	Laborer
	1302	Seward, William	29	"	"	"	6'	-		"	"
	1303	Scott, Daniel	47	"	"	Dk	5'	7 1/2"		"	Farmer
	1304	Scott, J S	49	"	"	Blk	5'	6"		"	Laborer
	1305	Smith, Robert	19	"	"	Brown	5'	1"		"	"
	1306	Scott, Tom	48	"	"	Yellow	5'	11"		"	Carpenter
	1307	Shelton, Jos	35							Henrico	Boatman
	1308	Strother, Saml	38	Blk	Blk	M	5'	6"		Augusta	Farm Hand
	1309	Strange, R	28	"	"	"	5'	7 3/4"		Frederick	Shoe Maker
	1310	Smith, Geo	35							Richmond	
	1311	Spriggs, Alexander	36	Yell	Bk	Bk	5'	9"		Rockbridge	Carpenter
	1312	Sorrell, Samual	48	"	"	"	6'	-		"	Farmer
	1313	Sampson, James	38	Bk	"	"	6'	-		"	Laborer
	1314	Scott, H	31	"	Dk	Lt	6'	-		Lynchburg	R R Hand
	1315	Starr, Wm	19	"	Bk	Bk	5'	10"		Campbell	Farm Hand
	1316	Saunders, John	49	"	"	"	5'	8"			Tob Factory
	1486	Smith, Grandison	25			Lt	5'	10 1/2"			Laborer
	1487	Smith, James	43			Dk	5'	8 3/4"			En Cleaner
	1488	Smith, Augustus	31			"	5'	7 1/4"			"
	1489	Smith, Jno	20			Lt	5'	6"			"
	1490	Smith, Jas	21			"	5'	5 1/2"			"
	1528	Staves, Jas									
	1529	Scott, Jos									
101	1533	Scott, John	40	Blk	Blk	Dk	6'	0"	VA	Richmond	Messenger
	1534	Shavers, Henry	25	Dk	Blk	Blk	5'	8 1/2"	VA	"	Laborer
	1535	Smither, J. R.	20	Blk	Blk	Lt	5'	6"	VA	"	Messenger
	1536	Strother, Geo W.	19	Blk	Blk	Lt	5'	7 1/2"	VA	Augusta	
		Scott, Harrison	37	Blk	Blk	Dk	5'	4"	VA	Richmond	
		Scott, Archer	38	Blk	Blk	Yell	5'	8"	VA	Henrico	
		Scott, Miles	17						VA	Do.	
		Sampson, Henry	28	Blk	Blk	Lt	6'	0"	VA	Richmond	
		Swan, John	21	Blk	Blk	Lt	5'	4"	VA	"	
		Staunton, B.							VA	"	
		Sparrow, B.							VA	"	
		Sparrow, John	19						VA	"	
		Staunton, Decker	30	Blk	Blk	Lt	5'	6"	VA	"	
		Stewart, George	27	Blk	Blk	Mu	5'	8 1/2"	VA	Mecklenburg	Blacksmith
		Southgate, James	48	Dk	Dk	Bright	5'	7"	VA	King & Queen	Farmer
		Staunton, Daniel	20	Blk	Blk	Bright	5'	5"	VA	Buckingham	
		Spencer, Emmett	17			Dk	5'	4"	VA	Petersburg	Train Hand
		Smith, Jacob	20			Dk	5'	6"	VA	Richmond	Train Hand
		Sparrow, Jas	29						VA	"	Boatman
		Slaughter, Albert	47						VA	"	Boatman
		Smith, J.T.	37						VA	"	Boatman
		Starr, Isaac	44						VA	Pittsylvania	Laborer
		Staterwhite, C.	35	Blk	Blk	Lt	5'	6"	VA	Essex	Laborer

Enlisted			Assigned		Remarks
When	Where	By Whom	When	Where	
"		"		N(iter) & M(ining) B(ureau)	
16-Jun		"			Unaccounted
20-Apr		"			"
29-Jul		"		Light Duty	Detailed to Maj. Turner
29-Aug		"		To M(edical) Dept.	
09-Sep		"		N(iter) & M(ining) B(ureau)	
12-Sep		"		Dis(charged) by Med(ical) B(oar)d	
15-Sep		"		N(iter) & M(ining) B(ureau)	
03-Sep		"		"	
		Lt. Noland		"	
		Lt. Nowlan		N(iter) & M(ining) B(ureau)	
		"			Deserter
19-Sep	Petersburg	Sgt. Winfree	20-Sep	To M(edical) Dept.	
19-Sep	"	"	"	"	
					Exempt by Med(ical)
22-Sep	"	"	23-Sep	"	Ex(aminig) B(oar)d
22-Sep	"	"	"	30 days furlough	"
22-Sep	"	"	"		"
26-Sep	"	"	27-Sep	To M(edical) Dept.	
28-Sep	"	"	29-Sep	"	
					Exempt by Med(ical)
28-Sep	"	"	"		Ex(aminig) B(oar)d
28-Sep	"	"	"		
Oct				N(iter) & M(ining) B(ureau)	
"				Eng(ineer) Dept.	
					Capt(ure)d by Enemy
					Exempt
					Deserter
					Unaccounted
				Eng(ineer) Dept.	
01-Aug		Capt. Anderson			
09-Aug		"			
26-Jun				Eng(ineer) Dept.	
Nov	Richmond	Lt. Blackford		R(ichmond) & D(anville) R(ail) R(oad)	Detailed to
"	"	"		"	"
"	"	"		"	"
"	"	"		"	"
"	"	"		"	"
				Detailed to A J. Rahm 1st Mar(ch)	
				Detailed to Capt. Fry 1st July	
19-Dec	Richmond	Lt. Bok	19-Dec	Capt. Blackford	
30-Nov	Richmond	Lt. Bok	30-Nov	N(iter) & M(ining) B(ureau)	
04-Dec	Richmond	Lt. Bok	04-Dec	Capt. Coke	
		Cpl. Matthews		Engineer(ing) Dept.	
				Detailed Navy till 1st May '65	
				Do.	
				Do.	
				Detailed to C Bass Supt. Pent(inentiar)y to 1st May 1865	
				Do.	
				Detailed to J(ames) R(iver) & K(anawha) Co(mpany) till 1st May '65	
				Do.	
				Do.	
				Do.	
				Detailed to 1st May '65 Cl(ar)ksville Ord(nance) shops	
		Lt. Dickerson		Detailed to 1st May '65 to W. F. Bland	
				Detailed to J(ames) R(iver) & K(anawha) (Canal) Co(mpany) till 1st May '65	
		Lt. Blackford		Detailed to E. H. Gill	
		Lt. Blackford		Do.	
				Detailed to Maj. J. B. Harvie	
				Do.	
				Do.	
				Detailed to Col. Withers	Eng(ineer) Dept.
		Lt. Bumpass		B.F. Gresham	till 1st June

Page	No.	Name	Description						Where Born		Occupation
			Age	Eyes	Hair	Complex	Feet	In	State	Town or County	
104	93	Turner, Benjamin	26	Blk	Blk	Dark	5'	8"	VA	Petersburg	Butcher
	149	Tyler, William	25						VA	Roanoke Co.	Shoemaker
	150	Thomas, William	32						VA	"	
	151	Tanner, John	22						VA	"	Laborer
	195	Thompson, Charles	25	Blk	Dk	Blk	5'	9"	VA	Mecklenburg	"
	196	Trent, James	39	Blue	Blk	Yellow	5'	8"	VA	Washington Co.	Blksmith
	197	Trent, Claiborne	40	"	"	"	5'	8"	VA	"	Farmer
	198	Thomas, Wm	17	"	"	"	5'	10"	VA	"	"
	199	Turner, James	48				5'	5"	VA	Scott Co.	Tanner
	264	Thrut, Jerry							VA	Greensville Co.	
	265	Thrut, John	28			Blk	5'	4"	VA	"	
	305	Turner, Martin	49	Blk	Dk	Brown	5'	8"	VA	Richmond	Cooper
	306	Thurston, Charles	27	"	"	"	5'	6"	VA	"	Blacksmith
	307	Tinsely, John L.	29	"	"	Lgt	5'	8"	VA	"	Carpenter
	325	Thompson, B	48	"	"	"	5'	6"	VA	"	"
	351	Taylor, Robert	32	Dk	Blk	"	5'	10"	VA	"	Laborer
	390	Thacker, Joseph	31	Grey	"	"	5'	7"	VA	"	Hackman
	411	Tyree, Robert	32	"	"	"	5'	9"	VA	Louisa	Train Hand
	442	Trisler, Isaac	44	Haz	"	Blk	5'	11"	VA	Montgomery Co.	
	455	Thomas, Richard	39	Dk	"	Lt	5'	7"	VA	Henrico Co.	Bricklayer
	476	Tams, Morgan	25	Blk	Blk	Yellow	5'	8"	VA	Rockingham	Hand
	477	Toatee, James	33	"	"	Blk	5'	4"	VA	"	Miller
	492	Toney, Field	36		"		6'		VA	Appomatox	Laborer
	493	Thomhill, W	36		"		5'	10"	VA	"	"
	494	Thomas, Wm	33				5'	9"	VA	Prince Edward	"
	495	Thomas, W H	30				5'	10"	VA	Mecklenburg	Shoemaker
	575	Tyree, Jack	24	Blk	Blk	Mulatto	5'	11"	VA	Botetourt	Miner
	576	Turpin, James							VA	"	Cooper
	619	Tynes, John	25	Blk	Blk	Blk	5'	5 1/2"	VA	Petersburg	Laborer
105	663	Tyler, Geo	25			Blk	5'	9"	VA	Powhatan	Laborer
	664	Tyler, I	23							"	Farmer
	665	Tyler, G Sr.	34							"	"
	666	Tyler, G Jr.	28							"	"
	667	Tyler, W	33							"	"
	1317	Tyree, Luther	17	Blk	Blk	Lt	6'	-		Albemarle	"
	1318	Tyree, Brazil	35	"	"	"	6'	1"		"	"
	1319	Tylor, Phil	36	"	"	Dk	5'	8"		"	Shoe Maker
	1320	Terry, Oliver	23	"	"	Lt	5'	9"		Amherst	Farmer
	1321	Terry, Mar	19	"	"	"	5'	11"		"	"
	1322	Terry, Adison	35	"	"	"	5'	8"		"	"
	1323	Taylor, William	33	Hz	"	Bright	5'	10 1/2"		Culpeper	Laborer
	1324	Taylor, Henry Clay	18	Blk	"	Copper	5'	11"		Caroline	"
	1325	Tyree, Quintin	26	Dk	"	Mu	5'	2"		Augusta	Teamster
	1326	Taylor, John	27	Blk	Blk	Mu	5'	9"		"	Laborer
	1327	Todd, Adison	39	Dk	Dk	Dk	5'	7"		"	Farmer
	1328	Turner, George	49	"	"	Yellow	6'	1"		Pittsylvania	Waggoner
	1329	Thompson, Danl	20	"	"	"	6'	4 1/2"		"	Farmer
	1330	Tuppence, Lewellyn	22	Lt	"	Blk	5'	6"		Richmond	Braker
	1331	Thomas, Rich	39	"	Blk	Dk	5'	7"		Henrico	Laborer
	1332	Timple, Henry	38	Dk	Dk	Dk	5'	5"		King & Queen	"
	1333	Tarns, Isham	28	Bk	Bk	Bk	5'	5"		Augusta	Farm Hand
	1334	Tyree, Q	26	"	"	M	5'	7"		"	Teamster
	1335	Turner, James	36				5'			Chestefield	Laborer
	1336	Thomas, John	37				5'			Richmond	
	1491	Twopence, Bill	21	Bk	Bk	Drk	5'	6"		King William	Laborer
	1492	Thompson, Chas	52			Dk	5'	4 1/2"			En Cleaner
	1493	Turner, Wm	19			"	5'	4 1/2"			Laborer

Enlisted			Assigned		Remarks
When	Where	By Whom	When	Where	
03-May	Petersburg	Lt. J E Heath		Eng(ineer) Dept.	
01-May	Roanoke Co.	Capt. A. Clement	April	Capt. Morton N(iter) & M(ining) B(ureau)	
"	"	Do.			Deserter
"	"	Do.		Maj McMahon Q(uarter) M(aster)	
30-Apr		I M Smith	15-Jun	Q(uarter) M(aster) Dept.	13th D(istrict)
"		W. M. Thompson	"	Do.	
"		"	"	Do.	
"		"			Unassigned
"					Do.
"	Greensville Co.	D J Godwin			
"	"				
07-Apr	Richmond	Capt. Coke		Commissary Dept.	
"	"	"		Med(ical) Dept.	
"		"	18-Apr	N(iter) & M(ining) Bureau	
12-Apr	"	"			
18-Apr	"	"	05-May	Eng(ineer) Bureau	
28-Apr	"	"	07-May	N(iter) & M(ining) Bureau	
29-Apr	"	"		Va Central R(ail) R(oad)	
31-May	Montg Co.	Lt. Sydenstriker	31-May	Maj McMakin Q(uarter) M(aster)	
04-May	Richmond	Capt. Coke			Detailed 1st Jan(uary)/65
May & June	Rockingham	Col. Peyton		Q(uarter) M(aster) Dept.	Detailed to Capt. Baker
"	"	"			Detailed till Jan(uary)/65
01-Jul	Appomatox	Lt. Fantross	02-Jul	Eng(ineer) Dept. High Bridge	
"	"	"	"	"	
14-Jun	Prince Edward	Zimmerman	15-Jun	"	
31-Jul	Mecklenburg	Atkins	1-Aug		
26-Jul	Fincastle	Lt. Nowlin	27-Jul	N(iter) & M(ining) J(ames) R(iver) & Kanawha Canal Co(mpany)	
28-Jun	"	"		Detailed from this office 1 July/65	
26-Jul	Petersburg	Lt. Scott	27-Jul	Eng(ineer) Dept.	
15-Jul	Powhatan			Eng(ineer) Dept.	
12-Jun	"			Do.	
"	"			Do.	
"	"			Do.	
"	"			Do.	
26-Jun		Capt. Colston	28-Jun	Maj Richards	
"		"	"	"	
28-Jun		"	30-Jun	"	
08-Jul	Amherst	Lt. Roane	11-Jul	Gen. Ransom	
"	"	"	"	"	
"	"	"	"	"	
19-Sep	Culpeper	Lt. Graves			
19-Jul	B Green	Lt. Hancock	20-Jul	Gen. Ewell	Richmond
26-Aug	Staunton			So Ex Co.	
	"			To M(edical) Dept.	
				Per Exempt by Med(ical) Ex(aming) B(oar)d	
19-Apr		Lt. McCue			Not Accounted
06-Jul		Lt. Williams		Eng(ineer) Dept.	
06-Apr		Capt. Coke			Not Accounted
04-May		"			Deserter
13-Sep		"		N(iter) & M(ining) B(ureau)	
Oct				Eng(ineer) Dept.	
"				"	
15-Sep			15-Sep	Eng(ineer) "	
12-Sep					Exempted
19-Nov			20-Nov	Eng(ineering) Dept	
Nov	Richmond	Lt. Haw		R(ichmond) & D(anville) R(ail) R(oad)	Detailed to
"	"	Lt. Blackford		"	"

Page	No.	Name	Description						Where Born		Occupation
			Age	Eyes	Hair	Complex	Feet	In	State	Town or County	
106	1494	Tate, Wm	23			Brown	5'	2"			Laborer
	1495	Tyler, Robt									Messenger
		Taylor, Zebedee	27	Hazel	Blk	Tawny	5'	4"			
		Taylor, Isaiah	29	Blk	Blk	Dr	5'	4"			
		Tucker, Wm	21				5'	8"		Dinwiddie	Blk Smith
		Turner, Wm	20	Blk	Blk	Blk	5'	7"		Richmond	"
		Thompson, Chas	18	"	"	Mul	5'	6"		Mecklenburg	"
		Turner, John	23			Lt	5'	4"		Richmond	Striker
		Thomas, C	33			Dk	5'	5 1/2"		Henrico	Laborer
		Thompson, Robt	18							King & Queen	Farmer
		Tate, Wm								Richmond Co.	"
		Turnsily, John								Henrico	
		Taylor, Jim								"	
		Thompson, Henry	18			Blk	5'	6"		Richmond Co.	"
		Thompson, Ladwell	25			Dk	5'	7"		"	"
		Tate, Campbell	48			"	6'	-		Westmoreland	"
		Tate, Bushrod	25			"	6'	1"		"	"
112	1337	Ustall, Nat	29	Bl	Blk	Blk	5'	5"	VA	Greensville	Laborer
114	52	Valentine, Frank	28	Blk	Blk	Blk	5'	4"	VA	Petersburg	Laborer
	113	Valentine, Archer	42	Dk	Dk	Dk	5'	8"	VA	Dinwiddie	"
	114	Valentine, Robt	22	"	"	"	5'	3"	VA	"	"
	115	Valentine, Jesse	35	"	"	"	5'	1 1/2"	VA	"	"
	116	Valentine, Peter	22	"	"	"	5'	9 1/2"	VA	"	"
	169	Valentine, John	19						VA	Roanoke	"
	190	Valentine, James	30	Blk	Blk	Yellow	5'	10"	VA	Mecklenburg	"
	191	Valentine, O	20	"	"	"	5'		VA	"	
	346	Vanwright, John	28	"	"	Dk	5'		VA	Manchester	
	529	Valentine, James	47	"	"	"	6'	-	VA	Mecklenburg	Engineer
	1338	Vaughn, W	24	"	"	"	5'	6"	VA	Nelson	Farmer
	1339	Valentine, Thomas	42						VA	Cumberland	"
	1340	Valentine, Robert	19						VA	"	Cooper
	1341	Vaughan, William	22	Blk	Blk	Dk	5'	10"	VA	Augusta	-
	1342	Verny, Yancey	45	"	"	Blk	5'	8"	VA	"	Blk Smith
	1343	Verny, Jno Ed	26	"	"	"	6'	1"	VA	"	
	1344	Vaughn, Thomas	35	"	"	M	5'	8"	VA	"	
	1345	Valentine, William	38	Dk	Dk	Blk	5'	6"	VA	Pittsylanvia	Blk Smith
	1346	Valentine, Peter	26	"	"	"	5'	9"	VA		
	1347	Valentine, John	30	"	"	Gin	5'	10"	VA	Chesterfield	Laborer
	1348	Valentine, W H	24	Hz	Bk	Mu	5'	6"	VA	"	"
	1349	Valentine, Robert	20	"	Dk	"	5'	8"	VA	"	"
	1350	Valentine, Thomas	42	"	Blk	"	5'	8"	VA	"	Cooper
	1496	Vainwright, Jno	26			Dk	5'	10 1/2"	VA		Farmer
		Vaughn, Thomas	45							Richmond	Fireman
		Venie, Jerry								Westmoreland	Boatman
		Vessels, Ben	19	Bk	Dk	Bro	5'	6"		Essex	Farmer
		Vessels, Pedro	19	"	"	"	5'	8"		"	Laborer
		Venie, Geo	22			Blk	5'	5"		Richmond Co.	"
		Venie, Henry	26			Dk	5'	6"		"	Farmer
115		Venie, Travis	30			Dk	5'	7"	VA	Richmond	Farmer
		Venie, James	40			Lt	5'	10"	VA	"	"

Enlisted			Assigned		Remarks
When	Where	By Whom	When	Where	
Nov	Richmond	Lt. Blackford		R(ichmond) & D(anville) R(ail) R(oad)	Detailed to
"	"	"		Surg. C D Rice	"
				Navy til 1st May 1865	
				"	
	Richmond			VA Central Railroad to 1st May/65	
				C.S.W. Works to 1st May/65	
	Mecklenburg			Detailed to 1st May/65 Cl(ar)ksville Ord(nance) Shops	
Jan 2/65				Detailed to R G Blankenship	
" 12				Pending C.S.W.	
				Detailed to Wm Crabb 1st May 1865	
				Detailed to Jane Hungerford "	
				Jos R. Anderson and Co.	
				"	
	Richmond Co.	Lt. Jenkins		En(gineer) Dept.	
	"	"		"	
	Westmoreland	"		"	
	"			"	
				Unaccounted	
3-May	Petersburg	Lt. Heath		Eng(ineer) Dept.	
"	Dinwiddie	R G Bosseau		Do.	
"	"	"		Do.	
"	"	"		Do.	
"	"	"		Do.	
01-May	Roanoke	Capt. Clement	April	Capt. Morton N(iter) & M(ining) B(ureau)	
30-Apr	Mecklenburg	T M Smith	15-Jun	Q(uarter) M(aster) Dept.	13th D(istrict)
"	"	"	"	Do.	"
18-Apr	Manchester	Capt. Coke			
01-Aug	Mecklenburg	W F Atkins			Detailed 1st Jan(uar)y 65
02-Jul	Nelson	Lt. Carpenter	03-Jul	Maj Richards	
19-Jul				Col. J Scott	
"				"	
31-Aug					Detailed 1st Jan(uar)y 65
					"
					"
					"
					" 1st
					Dec(ember) 64
23-Apr					
22-Sep	Petrbg	Sgt. Winfree	22-Sep	To M(edical) Dept	
20-Apr		Lt. Spencer			Det 1 Jan(uar)y 65
"		"		Eng(ineer) Dept.	
"		"		"	
18-Jul		"		"	
Nov		Lt. Blackford		R(ichmond) & D(anville) R(ail) R(oad)	Detailed to
					J(ames) R(iver) &
					K(anawha) Canal
Jany 6/65		"		Maj. Harvie	Co(mpany)
		Jas P. Jenkins		Detailed to J.W. Harris	1st May 1865
Dec/64		Lt. Bumpass		W. B. F. Gresham	1st June
"		"		"	"
Jan /65		Lt. J P Jenkins		En(gineer) Dept	
				"	
Jan /65	Richmond	Lt. J P Jenkins		En(gineer) Dept.	
"	"	"		"	

203

Page	No.	Name	Age	Eyes	Hair	Complex	Feet	In	State	Town or County	Occupation
			Age	Eyes	Hair	Complex	Feet	In	State	Town or County	
117	68	Walker, Charles	23	Blk	Blk	Blk	5'	8"	VA	Petersburg	Laborer
	69	Walker, William	38	"	"	Brown	5'	5"	VA	"	"
	70	Williams, John	35	Blue	"	Lgt	5'		VA	"	"
	96	Whitfield, Lod	32	Dark	"	Dk	5'	10"	VA	Dinwiddie	"
	97	Whitfield, Lernon	29	"	"	"	5'	6 1/2"	VA	"	"
	98	Walker, Pompey	40	"	"	"	5'	7 1/2"	VA	"	"
	99	Walker, Theodore	30	"	"	Light	5'	6"	VA	"	"
	100	Wynn, Robert	40	"	"	Dk	5'	7"	VA	"	"
	170	Wilson, Charles	37	Blk	Blk	Dk	5'	9"	VA	Roanoke	"
	171	Wilson, John	28	"	"	B M	5'	10"	VA	"	"
	172	Wright, Robert	22	"	"	Dk	5'	11"	VA	"	"
	212	Wright, Elijah	19	Blk	Blk	Blk	5'	1"	VA	Smythe	Laborer
	213	Wright, Thomas	44	Blue	"	Yellow	5'	8"	VA	Russell	Laborer
	214	Wright, Charles	23	Blk	"	Blk	5'	10"	VA	"	"
	215	Wright, Henry	27	"	"	"	5'	10"	VA	"	
	216	Wright, Oliver	28	"	"	"	5'	10"	VA	"	
	217	Watson, Dave	25	Blue	"	Yellow	5'	11"	VA	Washington Co.	
	218	Wright, Charles	50	"	"	"	5'	6"	VA	"	
	219	Willoughby, John	32				5'	5"	VA	"	
	266	Woodley, Daniel	35			Blk	5'	10"	VA	Greensville Co.	
	272	Wingfield, O A	37	Brown	Blk	Lght	5'	10 1/2"	VA	Richmond Cty	Braker
	293	White, William	24	Blk	Blk	Brown	6'		VA	"	Blk Smith
	340	Woodson, James	48	Dk	Lt	Dk	5'	7 1/2"	VA	Henrico	Body Maker
	360	Wart, Michael	49	"	Blk	Lt	5'	7 1/2"	VA	Richmond	Blk Smith
	361	Whitlock, John	22	"	"	Dk	5'	1"	VA	"	"
	373	Whitlock, Robt	24	"	"	"	5'	8"	VA	"	Laborer
	374	Wilkerson, W H	21	Grey	"	Lt	5'	8 1/2"	VA	Louisa	"
	375	Williams, James	18	"	"	"	5'	6"	VA	Richmond	Deck Hand
	384	Wright, Robt	18	Dk	"	Dk	5'	3"	VA		Laborer
118	385	Wilder, John	27	Blue	Blk	Lgt	5'	6"	VA	Richmond	Barber
	429	White, Thomas	28			Brown	6'	1"	VA	Sussex Co.	
	430	Wilborn, Madison	40			Yellow	5'	8"	VA	"	
	522	Wilkes, George	26		Dk		5'	4"	VA	Lunenburg	Laborer
	539	Wingfield, Jo T	26	Blk	Blk	Yellow	6'		VA	Montgomery	"
	592	Williams, Joseph	19	"	"	Light	5'	4"	VA	Petersburg	"
	623	Whitfield, Wm	47	"	"	Blk	5'	6"	VA	"	"
	1351	Wood, Jim	20	"	"	Dk	5'	8"	VA	Nelson	"
	1352	Womick, James	40	"	"	"	5'	5"	VA	"	Fireman
	1353	Winn, William	20						VA	New Kent	Trader
	1354	Wright, --	28	Blk	Blk	Yellow	5'	7"	VA	Spottsylvania	Blk Smith
	1355	Williams, Calvin	35	"	"	"	5'	6 1/2"	VA	"	Shoe Maker
	1356	Walker, James E	16	"	"	Bro	5'	2"	VA	Caroline	
	1357	Wilkinson, Williams	30	Dk	"	Dk	5'	9"	VA	Louisa	
	1358	Wilkinson, Edward	20	Dk	Dk	Dk	5'	7"	VA	"	
	1359	White, Monroe	42	"	"	Blk	5'	10 1/2"	VA	Cumberland	
	1360	Wauser, George	40	Blk	"	Yellow	5'	6"	VA		
	1361	Wist, John	23	"	Bk	Bk	5'	10 3/4"	VA		
	1362	Williams, John	32	Blue	"	Lt	5'	5"	VA	Augusta	Cooper
	1363	Williams, Joe	32	Blk	Dk	Blk	5'	11"	VA	"	Farmer
	1364	Wallace, William	21	Dk	"	Yellow	5'	8"	VA	Pittsylvania	"
	1365	Watkins, John	35	"	"	Brown	5'	8"	VA	"	Boatman
	1366	White, Wm G W	19	"	"	Dk	5'	7"	VA	"	Train Hand
	1367	Wissley, Jno	20	"	Blk	Brown			VA	Richmond	House Servant

Enlisted			Assigned		Remarks
When	Where	By Whom	When	Where	
03-May	Petersburg	Lt. J E Heath		Eng(ineer) Dept.	
"	"	"		Do.	
"	"	"		Do.	
30-Apr	Dinwiddie	R G Bosseau		Do.	
"	"	"		Do.	
"	"	"		Do.	
"	"	"		Do.	
"	"	"		Do.	
"	Roanoke	Capt. Clements	April	T J Jenkins Q(uarter) M(aster)	
"	"	"			No information of
"	"	"	May	Maj. McMahon	
"	Washington	W M Thompson	15-Jun	Q(uarter) M(aster) Dept.	
"	"	"	"	Do.	
"	"	"	"	Do.	
"	"	"	"	Do.	
"	"	"	"	Do.	
"	Washington Co.	W M Thompson	"	Do.	
"	"	"		-	Over Age
"	"	"	15-Jun	Q(uarter) M(aster) Dept.	
"	Greensville Co.	D J Godwin			No Account of
05-Apr	Richmond	Capt. Coke	14-Apr	N(iter) & M(ining) Bureau	
06-Apr	"	"	Do.	"	
14-Apr	"	"		Navy Dept til 1st May/65	
20-Apr	"	VA Central Railroad till 1st May/65			Detailed A F Harvie
23-Apr	"	"	23-Apr	N(iter) & M(ining) Bureau	
25-Apr	"	"	25-Apr	N(iter) & M(ining) Bureau	
25-Apr	"	"	April	Eng(ineer) Dept.	
27-Apr	"	"	"	Detailed to I H Dill	
27-Apr	"	"	"	Detailed to I H Dill	
27-Apr	Richmond	Capt. Coke			Deserter
05-May	Sussex Co.	D J Godwin			
"	"	"			
05-Jul	Lunenburg	S Lester	07-Jul	P. M. Richmond	
	New Bern	Lt. Poole		Q(uarter) M(aster) Dublin	
23-Apr	Petersburg	Lt. Scott		Eng(ineer) Dept.	
27-Jul	"	"		Do.	
30-Jun	Nelson	Lt. Carpenter	01-Jul	Maj. Richards	
08-Jul	"	Lt. Roane	11-Jul	Gen. Ransom	
Oct		T Taylor	Oct	N(iter) & M(ining) B(ureau)	
04-Apr	Fredksbg	Lt. Williams		Unassigned	
"	"	"			Petition for detail
19-Jul	Bowl Green	Lt. Hancock	20-Jul	Gen. Ewell	Richmond
01-Sep	Louisa CHo	Lt. Vaughan	04-Sep	N(iter) & M(ining) B(ureau)	
04-Sep	"	"	"	"	
15-Jun				Col. J Scott	
					Detailed 1st January 65
					" "
				To M(edical) Dept.	
13-Aug				"	
23-Apr		Lt. McCue			Detailed 1st Octo(ber)/64
28-Apr		"		To M(edical) Dept.	
20-Sep		Lt. Williams		Eng(ineer) Dept.	
29-Jun		Capt. Coke		"	

Page	No.	Name	Description						Where Born		Occupation
			Age	Eyes	Hair	Complex	Feet	In	State	Town or County	
	1368	Walker, Henry	34	"	"	"			VA	Manchester	Brakesman
	1369	Wright, Williams	22	"	Dk	Dk	5'	6"	VA	Richmond	Laborer
	1370	White, Geo. W.	22	"	"	"	5'	8"	VA	Henrico	"
	1371	Washington, Geo	48	"	"	"			VA	New Kent	
	1372	Winston, Ed	29	"	"	"	5'	8"	VA	Hanover	Laborer
119	1373	Whitehead, L	23	Dk	Dk	Lt	5'	10 1/2"	VA	Richmond	Laborer
	1374	Winston, Carter	19	"	"	Dk	5'	6"	VA	"	"
	1375	Williams, George	33	Blk	Bk	Mu	5'	4"	VA	Franklin	Farmer
	1376	Wilson, Cary	37						VA		
	1377	Wood, Griffin	41						VA		
	1378	Williams, Wm	35	Dk	Dk	Mu	6'	-	VA	Augusta	Laborer
	1379	Woodley, Henry	18	Blk	Blk	Bro	5'	6"	VA	Petersburg	"
	1380	Wright, William	48	"	"	"	5'	7"	VA	"	
	1381	Whitehead, Joseph	45	"	"	"	5'	11"	VA	"	
	1382	Winston, L							VA		
	1383	Winston, Jno							VA		
	1384	Winston, Isaac							VA		
	1385	Wilkinson, Henry	23	Bk	Bk	Bk	5'	7"	VA	Augusta	Farm Hand
	1386	Williams, John		"	"	M	5'	7"	VA	"	Cooper
	1387	Williams, John	35	"	"	Blk	5'	10"	VA	Henry	Tobacco Hand
	1388	Waller, Henry	20	"	"	M	5'	10"	VA	Chesterfield	
	1389	Winston, Ed	29						VA	Richmond	
	1390	Wood, John	36	Yel	Gray	Blk	5'	10"	VA	Rockbridge	Teamster
	1391	Williams, Calvin	39	Blk	Bk	"	5'	9"	VA	"	Farmer
	1392	Watton, John	35		"	"	5'	10"	VA		Mason
	1497	Williams, John	43			Lt	5'	6"	VA	Richmond	En Cleaner
	1498	Walden, Jas	36			Dk	5'	5 3/4"	VA	"	Laborer
	1499	Wingo, Geo	35			"	5'	4 1/2"	VA	"	"
	1500	Wallace, BEn	36			Blk	5'	7"	VA	"	Cook
	1501	Wilder, John	27			Lt	5'	7"	VA	"	Barber
	1502	Williams, Major	27			"	5'	10"	VA	"	Huckster
	1530	Wilder, John	24	Lt	Blk	Lt	5'	7"	VA	"	Barber
	1531	Wilkes, Geo	18	Lt	Gray	Lt	5'	5"	VA		Laborer
	1532	Wright, Sully	49	Blk	Blk	Dk	5'	6"	VA		House Servant
120		Wilson, Joel								Wythe County	
		Winters, John	30	Gray	Blk	Dk	5'	7"		Amherst "	Farmer
		Wood, Charles	28			Mul	5'	10"		New Kent	Miller
		Wash, John	23	Blk	Blk	Yellow	5'	10 3/4"			
		Wood, Chas								Lancaster Co.	
		Weldon, Thos	18			Dk	5'	5"		Richmond Co.	
		Weldon, Geo	21			Blk	5'	7"		" "	
124	148	Young, Humphrey	27	Brown	Blk	Yellow	5'	11"	VA	Spottsylvania	Farmer
	436	Young, Andrew	28	Blk	"	Copper	5'	8"	VA	Montgomery Co.	"
	497	Young, G. E.	33		"		5'	6"	VA	Lunenburg	"
	1393	Young, Atwell	22	Bro	Blk	Yellow	6'	3"	VA	Spottsylvania	"
	1394	Young, Henry	30	Blk	"	Bro	5'	11"	VA	Caroline	Laborer
		Young, Thomas	30	Dk	Dk	Dk			VA	Lunenburg	
		Young, Clem	28							Richmond	Boatman
		1829 names									

Enlisted			Assigned		Remarks
When	Where	By Whom	When	Where	
"		"		Det(ailed) S E Harvie to 1st May/65	
19-Aug		"			Deserter
24-Aug		"		" " "	
06-Sep		"		To M(edical) Dept.	Unaccounted
09-Sep		"		N(iter) & M(ining) B(ureau)	
					Disch(arged) by President Davis
14-Sep		Capt. Coke			
15-Sep		"		N(iter) & M(ining) B(ureau)	
02-May		Capt. Bernard			Unaccounted
		Lt. Nowlin		N(iter) & M(ining) B(ureau)	
		"		Detailed till 1st Jan(uar)y/65	
01-Sep		Capt. Mathews		"	
19-Sep	Petersburg	Sgt. Winfree	29-Sep	To M(edical) Dept.	
22-Sep	"	"	22-Sep	" " "	
26-Sep	"	"	26-Sep	" " "	
Oct				Eng(ineer) Dept.	
"				" "	
"				" "	
"				" "	
"				" "	
05-May	Henry CHo	Lt. Hawthorne	05-Jul		Det 1st Jany 65
26-Apr		Lt. Spencer			Deserter
09-Sep				N(iter) & M(ining) B(ureau)	
					Unaccounted
				Eng(ineer) Dept.	
Nov	Richmond	Lt. Blackford		R(ichmond) & D(anville) R(ail) R(oad)	Detailed to
"	"	"		"	"
"	"	"		"	"
"	"	"		N(iter) & M(ining) Bureau	
"	"	"			Detail applied for
				"	
Dec	"	"			Public Necessity
"	"	"		N(iter) & M(ining) B(ureau)	
				Detailed to Lt. Roberts 1st July/65	
				Detailed to Mrs Genl Terry 12 Jany 1865	
		Lt. Roane		Detailed till 1st July 1865	
				Detailed to R T Boone till 1st July 1865	
				Detailed as Miller till 1st July/65	
Januy/65	Richmond	Lt. Jenkins		En(gineer) Dept.	
"	"	"		"	
01-May	Spottsylvania	Lt. Williams			
02-May	Montgomery Co.	Lt. Sydenstriker		Q(uarter) M(aster) Dept.	Woodson
05-Jul	Lunenburg	S. Lester	06-Jul	Navy Dept. to 1st May 1865	
04-Apr	Fredbg	Lt. Lewis			Petition for detail
19-Jul	Bowl Green	Lt. Hancock	20-Jul	Gen. Ewell	Richmond
				Detailed Navy Dept. to 1st May/65	
				Detailed to Maj J. B. Harvie	

Bibliography

Official Records

Confederate Correspondence, Etc. Serial 128. Series IV. Vol. 2 Broadfoot Publishing Company (1995).

Confederate Records, Manuscript Rolls, No. 5912 64. National Archives and Records Administration, Washington, D.C.

Index to Bills and Resolutions of the Confederate Congress; Departmental Reports; etc. National Archives and Records Administration, Washington, D.C: 1861-1865.

Journal of the Congress of the Confederate States of America, 1861-1865, Volumes I-VII. Washington, D.C: Government Printing Office, 1905.

"Legislative and Executive Papers" Congressional Bills and Resolutions. National Archives and Records Administration, Washington, D.C: 1861-1865.

Register of Free Negroes Enrolled and Detailed. May 1864 – January 1865, Chapter 1, Volume 241, Bureau of Conscription, VA. War Department Collection of Confederate Records, Group 109. National Archives and Records Administration, Washington, D.C.

The War of the Rebellion: A Compilation of the Official Records of the Union and Confederate Armies, Serial IV, 128 vols. Washington, D.C: War Department, 1880-1901.

Books

Bacon, Donald C., Roger H. Davidson and Morton Keller. eds. Volume 1. *The Encyclopedia of the United States Congress.* New York: Simon & Schuster, 1995.

Barrow, Charles Kelly, J. H. Segars and R.B. Rosenburg. *Forgotten Confederates: An Anthology about Black Southerners.* Atlanta, Ga.: Southern Heritage Press, 1995.

Battaile, Andrew Chandler, Arthur W. Bergeron, Jr., Thomas Y. Cartwright, Ervin L. Jordan, Jr., Richard Rollins and Rudolph Young. *Black Southerners in Gray.* Rank and File Publications, Redondo Beach, Calif.: 1994.

Berlin, Ira, Joseph P. Reidy and Leslie S. Rowland. eds. *Freedom's soldiers: the Black military experience in the Civil War.* Cambridge, U.K., New York: Cambridge University Press, 1998.

Berlin, Ira and Leslie S. Rowland. eds. *Families and Freedom: A documentary history of African American kinship in the Civil War era.* New York: New York Press, 1997.

Berlin, Ira. *Slaves without Masters: the free Negro in the antebellum South.* New York: New Press, 1992.

Blackerby, H.C. *Blacks in Blue and Gray: Afro-American Service in the Civil War.* Tuscaloosa, Ala.: Portals, 1979.

Brewer, James H. *The Confederate Negro Virginia's Craftsmen and Military Laborers, 1861-1865.* Durham, N.C: Duke University Press, 1969.

Franklin, John Hope. *From Slavery to Freedom: A History of Negro Americans.* 4th ed. New York: Knopf, 1974.

Frassanito, William A., *Grant and Lee: The Virginia Campaigns 1864-1865.* New York: Charles Scribner's Sons, 1983.

Guild, June Purcell. *Black Laws of Virginia: A Summary of Legislative Acts of Virginia Concerning Negroes From Earliest Times to the Present.* 1936, Leesburg, Va.: Willow Bend Books, reprint 1996.

Jackson, Luther Porter. *Negro Office-Holders in Virginia, 1865-1895.* Norfolk, Va.: Guide Quality Press, 1945.

Jordan, Jr., Ervin L. *Black Confederates and Afro-Yankees in Civil War Virginia.* Charlottesville, Va.: The University Press of Virginia, 1995.

Moebs, Thomas Truxton. *Black Soldiers – Black Sailors – Black ink: research guide on African - Americans in U.S. Military history, 1526-1900.* Chesapeake Bay, Va.: Moebs Publishing Company, 1994

Quarles, Benjamin. *The Negro in the Civil War.* New York: Da Capo Press, Inc., 1953.

Waitt, Jr., Robert W. *Confederate Military Hospitals in Richmond.* Official Publication #22, Richmond, Va.: Richmond Civil War Centennial Committee, 1964.

White, Charles W. *The Hidden and the Forgotten: Contributions of Buckingham Blacks to American History.* Marceline, Mo.: Walsworth Press, 1985.

Wiley, Bell I. *Southern Negroes, 1861-1865.* Baton Rouge, La.: Louisiana State University Press, 1974, 1938.

Wilson, Joseph T. *The Black Phalanx: African American Soldiers in the War of Independence, The War of 1812, and the Civil War.* New York: De Capo Press, Inc., 1994.

Magazines

Johns, Frank S. and Anne Page. "Chimborazo Hospital and J. B. McCaw, Surgeon and Chief." *Virginia Magazine of History and Biography,* Vol. LXII. 1954.

Nelson, Bernard H. "Confederate Slave Impressment Legislation 1861-1865."
Journal of Negro History, No. 31 (October, 1946).

Spraggins, Tinsley Lee. "Mobilization of Negro Labor for the Department of Virginia and North
Carolina, 1861-1865. *North Carolina Historical Review,* XXIV, No. 2 (April, 1947).

Wesley, Charles H. "The Employment of Negroes as Soldiers in the Confederate Army." *Journal of
Negro History,* Vol. IV, No. 3 (July, 1919).

Wesley, Charles H. "The Collapse of the Confederacy." *Journal of Negro History,* No. 2
(May, 1922).

Newspapers

Daily Richmond Examiner, Richmond, Va. 22 December, 1862.
                                       25 December, 1862.
                                       1 August, 1863.
                                       3 August, 1863.
                                       7 August, 1863.

Richmond Daily Examiner, Richmond, Va. 7 November, 1864.

D

Dabney
  Ben, 160
  Henry, 160
Dailey
  William, 162
Daily Richmond Examiner,
    119, 120, 121
Dalton, 25, 30
  (Assistant Clerk of House
    of Representatives), 84,
    96, 105
Dandridge
  Byrd, 160
Dangerfield
  David, 160
Dangerford
  Joseph, 160
Daniel
  Henry, 160
  John, 160
Danville Arsenal, 161, 197
Darby
  John, 160
Darden
  (Tex.), 67, 69, 71, 72, 73,
    75, 76, 77, 79, 92, 103
Dargan
  (Ala.), 20, 21, 24
Davenport
  Emual, 160
  John, 160
Davis
  Charles, 160
  Daniel, 160
  George, 160
  Isaac, 160
  James, 160
  Jefferson, 43, 46, 100,
    113, 207, vi
  Moses, 160
  Nelson, 160
  President, 207
  R., 160
  Samuel, 160
  W., 162

William, 160
Day
  Abner, 160
  Bryant, 160
  Caleb, 160
  David, 158
  Edward, 160
  Henry, 158, 160
  Lebulone P., 158
  Lemuel, 158
  Robert, 158
  Samuel, 160
  Wesley, 160
  William, 160
De Jarnette
  (Va.), 68, 69, 70, 71, 76,
    79, 91, 92, 93, 103,
    107, 108
Deane
  Julius, 160
  W., 160
  William, 160
Dear
  Henry, 160
Deer
  William, 160
Dennis
  Fertian, 160
  Lang, 160
Denson
  William, 162
Derris
  John, 160
Desmal
  John, 162
Desmul
  S., 160
Dickerson
  Lt., 142, 195, 199
  Nathaniel, 158
Dickinson
  (Ala.), 66, 67, 68, 69, 70,
    71, 72, 73, 75, 76, 78,
    79, 83, 91, 92, 93, 103,
    107, 108
  Lt., 149, 179, 187

W. T., 147
Diggins
  Charles, 158
  Robert, 158
Diggs
  George, 158
  Robert, 160
  William, 160
Dill
  I. H., 205
Dimock
  N., 158
Dinkin
  Septimous, 158
Dinnock
  Capt., 161
Dinwiddie
  Capt., 187, 193
  Jackson, 160
Dinwiddie Co., 145, 148,
    150, 152, 154, 158,
    160, 164, 166, 168,
    174, 176, 182, 184,
    186, 188, 190, 192,
    194, 196, 202, 204
Dixon
  B., 162
  Bob, 160
  George, 160
  James, 158
Dobbins
  Floyd, 158
  W., 160
Dodson
  Amos, 160
  John, 160
  Manuel, 158
Dom
  Charles, 158
Donning
  James, 160
Dooley
  Dennis, 160
Doors, 160
  James, 160

Wash, 140
Washington, 182
William, 180
London
John, 180
Olm, 180
Long
Atwell, 178
Henry, 180
Lookadoo
William, 180
Louisa Co., 119, 162, 170, 174, 178, 184, 188, 200, 204
Lovely
Griffin, 178
Lowndes
Tom, 182
Lowry
Archer, 180
Lucas
Arnold, 182
John, 180
Lucus
Phil, 180
William, 180
Lundige
Greenberry, 180
William, 180
Lunenberg Co., 162, 178, 204, 206
Lunenburg Co., 38
Lynch
George, 180
Madison, 180
Robert, 182
Washington, 182
William, 180
Lynchburg, 119, 152, 168, 172, 198
Lyon
(Ala.), 66, 67, 68, 70, 71, 72, 73, 75, 76, 78, 79, 83, 92, 93, 103
Lyons
W. B., 178

Lysy
Peter, iii

M

Mabry
Henry, 182
Machen
(Ky.), 20, 66, 69, 71, 72, 73, 75, 76, 77, 79, 80, 83, 91, 92, 93, 98, 103
Macklin
William, 186
MacMurdo
Capt., 145, 147, 159, 163, 169, 177
Madden
A., 184
Abram, 184
Madison Co., 2, 145, 156, 160, 164, 190
Mahon
Maj., 161
Maiden
John, 186
Majors
J., 153
Makins
P., 184
Malone
Andrew, 182
Soloman, 184
Malory
Daniel, 182
Manchester, 134, 152, 158, 202, 206
Mandin
William, 182
Mann
Amias, 182
George, 184
James, 184
Samuel, 184
Theo, 186
Thomas, 186
W. H., 184
William, 182

Woodson, 186
Manson, 147
O. F., 147, 187
Surg., 145
Map
Benjamin, 182
Benjamin Tom, 182
Maple
Joe, 182
Marks
Ann, 187
Marlon
James, 184
Marshall
(Ky.), 67, 68, 69, 70, 71, 72, 73, 75, 104, 107, 108
(La.), 103
Martin
David, 182
Frank, 182
I., 182
R., 184
Reubin, 184, 186
Sam, 184
William, 182
Mason
G. W., 184
John, 182
Killer, 184
Thomas, 182
William, 184
Massie
James, 186
Mathews
Adam, 184
Capt., 173, 177, 187, 207
Matthews
Capt., 187
Cpl., 142, 199
Henry, 182
Lt., 149, 193
Mauzy
Madison, 184
Maxfield
Silas, 186